Hiking Trails of Mainland Nova Scotia, 9th edition

Also by Michael Haynes

Hiking Trails of Cape Breton

Trails of Halifax Regional Municipality

Hiking Trails of Ottawa, the National Capital Region and Beyond

Hiking Trails of Nova Scotia

MICHAEL HAYNES

Hiking Trails of Mainland
NOVA SCOTIA

9th edition

GOOSE LANE

Edited by Charles Stuart.
Cover and interior photographs by Michael Haynes
(unless otherwise noted).
Maps prepared by Digital Projections.
Cover and page design by Julie Scriver.
Printed in Canada.

10 9 8 7 6 5 4 3 2

Library and Archives Canada Cataloguing in Publication

Haynes, Michael, 1955-
  Hiking trails of mainland Nova Scotia / Michael Haynes. —
9th ed.

Previous ed. published under title: Hiking trails of Nova Scotia.
Includes bibliographical references and index.
ISBN 978-0-86492-685-2

  1. Trails — Nova Scotia — Guidebooks.
  2. Hiking — Nova Scotia — Guidebooks.
  3. Nova Scotia — Guidebooks.
  I. Haynes, Michael, 1955- . Hiking trails of Nova Scotia.
  II. Title.

GV199.44.C2H393 2012   796.5109716   C2012-905158-6

Goose Lane Editions acknowledges the generous support of
the Canada Council for the Arts, the Government of Canada
through the Canada Book Fund (CBF), and the Government
of New Brunswick through the Department of Tourism,
Heritage and Culture.

Goose Lane Editions
500 Beaverbrook Court, Suite 330
Fredericton, New Brunswick
CANADA E3B 5X4
www.gooselane.com

Contents

Foreword

Writing a book about Nova Scotia's trails is no easy task because so many diverse and informal trails exist. Picking an appropriate sampling of these trails is where Michael Haynes excels. His experience as Executive Director of the Nova Scotia Trails Federation from 1993 to 2003, plus twenty-five years of hiking — exploring, inventorying, assessing, and writing about trails old and new — give this book a real leading edge as one of the best Nova Scotia trail guides.

Michael hiked, biked, and walked around 3,000 km (1,875 mi) of trails for the ninth edition of *Hiking Trails of Nova Scotia*. In this book, *Hiking Trails of Mainland Nova Scotia*, he offers solid advice to both the novice and seasoned hiker. Readers who are new to hiking will be gratified to learn that even the most challenging trails can be conquered as one's fitness level increases. And with sixty trails to choose from in this volume, there should certainly be a trail for everyone who consults it. We hope that this book succeeds in its ultimate aim to inspire you to explore Nova Scotia's landscape of woods, wetlands, rugged coastline, mountains, waterfalls, and everything else that is Nova Scotia.

Michael has a particular sensibility in guiding folks on an exploration. In CBC Radio interviews in Halifax, Sydney, and Ottawa, Michael shares his acquired knowledge with a sense of humour. Making the trail experience come alive over the airwaves is no easy task; however, Michael has inspired many people to hike Nova Scotia's trails through his talks (more than 350); through many presentations; and through eight books that profile more than 410 trails, with additional tidbits on hiking in general. He has earned much respect from many regions of the province and throughout the world, as he promotes trails and hiking in his home province of Nova Scotia, throughout Canada, and abroad.

We often refer to Michael affectionately as one of Nova Scotia's leading "hiking gurus." Our association, Hike Nova Scotia, presented him with the "HIKE NS Honorary Life Award" for his outstanding leadership and commitment to the promotion and development of hiking in Nova Scotia.

The purpose of Hike NS is to create a dynamic and unified voice for the Nova Scotia hiking community, and to create a culture of walking, hiking, and snowshoeing, one step at a time. Hike NS also wishes to ensure that a diversity of hiking adventures exists in Nova Scotia through advocacy, promotion, and support for hiking opportunities. The organization wants to ensure that world-class coastal and inland hiking opportunities exist, and that adequate resources are allocated to the various provincial agencies, municipalities, and volunteer organizations to make that happen.

Hike NS is about creating opportunities for guided hikes, encouraging dynamic discussions, and exciting people about hiking. After all, it is just plain fun to experience the outdoors by foot, through the forests and fields, highlands and lowlands, wetlands and coastline.

The many trails described in this book constitute important Nova Scotia infrastructure and need to be supported. Please look kindly upon the agencies and organizations that build them, and give your feedback and support. We hope you will join us and learn more about us at www.hikenovascotia.ca.

The key is to hike your own hike and explore the trails on your own, with a friend, or with your family. Now that you have this book in your hands, just make a plan and go.

One final note: you can follow the Hiking Trails of Nova Scotia blog at hikingnovascotia.blogspot.ca, also written by Michael. This is the author's way of keeping information up to date and sharing it with readers.

Happy Hiking!

Debra Ryan
President
Hike Nova Scotia

Preface

For the first time in its history, *Hiking Trails of Nova Scotia* has been published as more than one volume. What was once covered in the pages of one book is now, in 2012, contained in three separate and distinct manuscripts. *Trails of the Halifax Regional Municipality* features thirty routes in the HRM, none of which is more than 10 km (0.6 mi) long, and it is designed for casual and novice walkers. *Hiking Trails of Cape Breton* profiles forty paths in the four counties of Cape Breton Island, while *Hiking Trails of Mainland Nova Scotia* highlights sixty walking routes in the fourteen counties south of the Canso Causeway.

These three volumes combined outline detailed descriptions and maps for 130 different hiking routes, almost 1,500 km (940 mi) of trails in total, by far the greatest amount of Nova Scotia walking paths profiled in published hiking guides. And each is accompanied by a map, photographs, and the trailhead GPS coordinates.

In order to write this book, I hiked or biked every route profiled in *Hiking Trails of Mainland Nova Scotia*, and many others that ultimately were not included as part of this collection. Wherever possible, I have tried to profile managed trails, selecting them over unmanaged trails. I have written the descriptions found in the book based upon what I viewed at the moment I walked each path.

There have been many changes to the trails in the province in the ten years since the eighth edition was published. The development of hundreds of kilometres/miles of abandoned rail line as recreational trails has more than doubled the distance of managed trails in Nova Scotia over the past decade. Although some might not find these routes to be the best walking experience, in some areas of the province — in particular the South Shore, and Yarmouth and Digby counties — rail trails have been almost the only new development.

Fortunately, in addition to new rail trails, there has also been an explosion of wilderness hiking paths, particularly in the Halifax Regional Municipality and along the route of the proposed Cape to Cape Trail in Antigonish, Pictou, Colchester, and

Cumberland counties. There are now some truly challenging long-distance managed footpaths available in the province, and I have attempted to include a fair number of these.

In order to provide some balance, and not have the book be nothing but routes for experienced hikers, I have added some of the more interesting municipal park trails, such as Victoria Park in Truro and Trenton Steeltown Centennial Park. Even so, this book contains more intermediate and advanced routes than the previous edition.

The ninth edition also sees the return of Kejimkujik National Park as a separate region with ten trail listings. This is partly because new trail construction has meant that I can now find at least ten useable routes in each of the Annapolis Valley (Evangeline) and South Shore (Lighthouse) regions without using something in Kejimkujik, and also because we have expanded this book from fifty to sixty trails.

One final important note: in a number of cases, if I felt there was a substitute route nearby, I replaced a listing from the eighth edition with the new trail. For example, I did not relist the Beechville–Lakeside Timberlea (BLT) Trail, instead profiling the new Chain of Lakes Trail. However, the listing for the BLT Trail in the eighth edition is still usable.

Please check the "Updates" section for at least fifteen trail listings from the eighth edition that you can still use.

I hope you find this new edition of *Hiking Trails of Mainland Nova Scotia* useful. I especially hope it encourages you to explore Nova Scotia's truly magnificent outdoors in the way it can best be experienced: on foot.

Michael Haynes
June 2012

Introduction

Nova Scotia is known as Canada's Ocean Playground, and it has always been defined by its intimate embrace by the Atlantic Ocean. The province escapes being an island only by the most tenuous of land connections, and its corrugated coastline, dotted with countless small islands and indented by hundreds of hidden bays, boasts an astonishing length of at least 7,000 km (4,375 mi). Wherever you travel in Nova Scotia, you are never more than 60 km (37.5 mi) from the ocean. Yet this also makes the province a fabulous place to hike because of its exceptional coastal scenery.

The economic realities of the modern world have affected the pattern of human settlement in the province. A large percentage of its population of fewer than 1 million, nearly 40%, lives in the provincial capital of Halifax, and as the countryside has depopulated so has the forest reclaimed the ground that had once been cleared for family farms and pasture. In 1900, nearly 75% of the land area of Nova Scotia was cleared land and 25% forested. By 2000, the figures were almost exactly reversed.

As a result of this demographic shift, the province is filled with the remains of abandoned communities and criss-crossed with former settlement or logging roads. Walking through a seemingly mature forest, you may come across a moss-covered stone wall or flowering apple trees in a field rapidly growing over. Many of the newest trails in Nova Scotia, such as the rail trails, have been developed on properties that have been abandoned for their original purpose. These are hikes through human, and not only natural, history.

Hiking Trails of Mainland Nova Scotia profiles sixty walking routes spread across the length of the entire province, excepting Cape Breton, which is covered in a separate book. For the purpose of selecting which trails to include, and to attempt to ensure representation by at least one track in every county, I divided mainland Nova Scotia into six geographic districts, five roughly based upon the provincial tourism regions, and the sixth in Kejimkujik National Park.

In each of these districts ten hiking

paths have been profiled. The selections have been made to ensure that each region contains a variety of challenges. Of the ten routes in each district, some are easy — designed for casual walkers, some moderately challenging — requiring at least two to three hours and some effort to complete, and at least one or two are more demanding — exceeding 15 km (9.4 mi) in distance and/or of above average difficulty.

Regrettably, the choice to provide a representative sample of the trails available, rather than a comprehensive listing, means that I have left out some very good routes — some of the Cape to Cape paths in Colchester and Pictou counties, for example, or McNabs Island — but doing so means that I have been able to profile each route listing in far greater detail. *Hiking Trails of Mainland Nova Scotia* is intended to be the start of your explorations, not their end.

The selection of the routes in *Hiking Trails of Mainland Nova Scotia* was mine alone. If I left out your favourite trail, please let me know.

The six regions are as follows:
1. Halifax–Marine Drive: composed of the Halifax Regional Municipality and Guysborough County.
2. Evangeline Scenic Travelway: made up of Hants County

(West), Kings, Annapolis, and Digby counties. (There is one exception: Uniacke Estate.)
3. Glooscap Scenic Travelway: encompassing the portions of Cumberland and Colchester counties that border on the Bay of Fundy and the Minas Basin, and Hants County (East).
4. Lighthouse Route Scenic Travelway: composed of Lunenburg, Queens, Shelburne, and Yarmouth counties.
5. Sunrise Scenic Travelway: includes the portions of Cumberland and Colchester counties facing the Northumberland Strait, and all of Pictou and Antigonish counties.
6. Kejimkujik National Park, including the Seaside Adjunct.

HOW TO USE THIS BOOK

You should begin with the Trails at a Glance table (pp. 22-25). This lists all the routes found in the book, showing their length and degree of difficulty, indicating the uses permitted, and providing an estimated time required to complete the walk profiled. It also indicates on what page you will find the full route description.

The Trails at a Glance table uses a number of abbreviations and notations used of which you should be aware:

Permitted Uses (no snow): These are the uses either formally permitted, or likely possible, anywhere on the route being profiled during those times of the year when the trail is not covered by snow. Typically, that means spring, summer, and fall — but not always.

Any use marked with a "*" means that it occurs, and might be encountered, along some sections of the profiled route, but not throughout the entire distance. For example, The Bluff Wilderness Hiking Trail–Bluff Loop (pg. 29) permits walking only. However, the first 550 m/yd from the closest parking area to the formal trailhead of The Bluff Wilderness Hiking Trail follows the BLT Trail, which permits bicycling, horseback riding and ATVs. In the permitted uses, these are shown: W, B*, H*, A*

W = walking/hiking
B = bicycling, either touring or mountain biking
I = inline skating, skateboarding
H = equestrian/horseback use
A = ATV and other off-highway vehicles

Permitted Uses (snow): These are the uses either formally permitted, or likely possible, anywhere on the route being profiled during those times of the year when the trail is covered by snow. Typically, that means the late fall, winter, and early spring.

S = snowshoeing
X = cross-country/Nordic skiing
Sm = snowmobiles and other motorized winter vehicles

Dog Use: Disagreements between dog owners and non-dog owners are among the greatest source of conflict on managed trails. Many of the trails profiled in this book have strict regulations about dog use, particularly those within national and provincial park properties. Please respect non-dog owners and observe these guidelines — and always "poop & scoop"!

L = dogs permitted on leash
O = dogs permitted off leash

If the regulations change along the route profiled (e.g., Guysborough Shoreline Trail), then the most restricted use will be listed, but with an asterix: "L*."

Once you have selected the trail you wish to hike from the Trails at a Glance, turn to the page indicated. At the start of each profile you will find a capsule synopsis; every full trail description follows the same basic format:

Name of Trail: Official name if maintained pathway, start/finish for portions of longer trails.

◄- - -►: Indicates return-trip distance in kilometres and miles, rounded up to the nearest half kilometre (and tenth or quarter mile).

🕐: Indicates time of hike, based on an average walker's rate of 4 km (2.5 mi) per hour. This may not accurately reflect the time that you will require to complete any particular hike. Each person sets his or her own pace, which will vary according to weather conditions, length of the trail, and fitness level.

Rating: A designation from 1 to 5, with 1 indicating suitability for all fitness and experience levels and 5 suitability only for experienced and very fit outdoor people. These ratings are based on considerations of length, elevation change, condition of treadway, and signage.

Novices should choose level 1 and 2 hikes initially, and work up with experience. Level 4 and 5 hikes include an indication of what qualifies them for a their higher rating.

Type of Trail: Indicates the footing that will be encountered.

Uses: Mentions possible types of recreational use, including hiking, biking, cross-country skiing, horseback riding, snowmobiling, and ATVing.

Cautionary Notes ⚠: Hunting season, cliffs, high winds, road crossings, or anything I believe you should be especially cautious about on this route will be mentioned here. A complete list may be found later in this section under "Hazards."

Cellphone Coverage 📱: How well a cellular phone will work on this trail, including locations of dead spots (based on my use of a Bell/Virgin Mobile smartphone).

Facilities: Services such as washrooms or water that will be found either at the trailhead or along the trail.

Gov't Topo Map: The National Topographic System 1:50,000-scale map showing the terrain covered by the trail.

Trailhead GPS Reference: The latitude and longitude of the start/finish of the hike. This data was collected using a GARMIN GPS 12XL receiver and verified with Google Earth.

The detailed trail outline is divided into the following sections:

Access: How to drive to the trail's starting point from a convenient landmark:

The directions to trails in the Halifax–Marine Drive region begin either from the closest exit of Highway 103, 104, or 107. In some cases they are listed in reference to Highway 7. Metro Transit directions are given to Chain of Lakes, in Halifax, and also for the Bluff Loop.

For routes in the Evangeline Scenic Travelway, directions usually begin from the nearest exit from Highway 101.

Directions to trails in the Glooscap Scenic Travelway begin from the closest exit on Highway 104 or 102.

Directions to trails in the Lighthouse Route Scenic Travelway begin from the closest exit on Highway 103.

The directions to trails in the Sunrise Scenic Travelway begin from the closest exit on Highway 104.

The directions to trails in Kejimkujik National Park begin from the park entrance road where it connects to Highway 8.

Introduction: Background about the trail, possibly including historical, natural, or geographical information, as well as my personal observations or recommendations.

Route Description: A walk-through of the hike, relating what I found when I last travelled this route. In every case

I describe junctions and landmarks from the perspective of someone following the trail in the direction I have indicated. If travelling in the opposite direction, remember to reverse my bearings.

SIDEBAR NOTES

Scattered throughout the book are forty-five brief capsule descriptions of some of the plants, animals, geological features, and human institutions that you might encounter on the various trails. These are intended to be brief samples to whet your curiosity about the world through which you are hiking, and to encourage you to learn more. An index of Sidebars and User Tips can be found on page 347.

🏃 USER TIPS

Unless you are an experienced hiker, you might not know how much water to carry on your hike, or why wearing blue jeans is not the best idea. An assortment of helpful hints is sprinkled among the trail descriptions. An index of Sidebars and User Tips can be found on page 347.

GETTING STARTED

New or occasional walkers should begin by selecting routes with a difficulty rating of 1 or 2. These are likely to be completed within one or two hours by people of almost any fitness level. With experience, trails with a higher difficulty level can be attempted. Level 1 routes should be comfortable for most children; level 2 routes, which can be as long as 10 km (6.25 mi), should only be considered with children once you are familiar with their capabilities.

Clothing and footwear are extremely important. For shorter walks in comfortable weather, there is little need for specialized gear. However, as distance and time walked increase, comfort and safety will be substantially improved by wearing hiking shoes and outfits specially designed for outdoor activity. There is a bewildering array of products available, more than enough for a book on its own, and choosing the right gear is also dependent upon individual preferences. I, for example, like to hike in sandals, while friends often wear heavy boots. Once you have decided that hiking is a regular part of your lifestyle, you can visit the outdoor stores and find what works for you.

However, there are a few items that should always be carried, even if you are only going for a short hike. Doing so may help make every hiking experience an enjoyable and safe one.

Water: Nothing is more important than water. You can survive up to two weeks without food; you may die in as few as three days without water. I carry one litre per person on a hike up to 10 km (6 mi), more if the distance is greater, if the day is particularly hot or humid, or if I am taking children with me. Dehydration occurs rapidly while hiking, and the accompanying headache or dizziness diminishes the pleasure of the experience. Drink small sips of water often and do not wait until you are thirsty to do so. Portable water filtration systems are available in any outdoor store and are worth carrying, especially on hot summer treks.

Map: I consider a map crucial. With a map, I have a context of the terrain through which I will be hiking. Is it swampy? Are there hills? If I get confused, what direction do I follow to find people? In parks a special map of the trail is often available. Otherwise, I carry the National Topographic System of Canada 1:50,000-scale map of the area. I have included maps for every route profiled in this book, but these are for general information, and I recommend obtaining specialized trail maps if they are available.

Food: Though not essential on a day hike, I always carry something to snack on while I walk, and who does not enjoy a picnic? Apples, trail mix, bagels: anything like this is good.

Chocolate bars, chips, and other junk food are not the best choice, and should be avoided.

Whistle: If you are lost and want to attract attention, a whistle will be heard far better than your voice, and is less likely to wear out from continuous use. Test it: take one outside the house and give a couple of blasts. See how much attention you attract. (Feel free to blame me if you get any complaints.)

First Aid Kit: When in the woods, even little problems can become very important. A small first aid kit with bandages, gauze, tape, moleskin, etc., permits you to deal with blisters and bruises that require attention.

Garbage Bag: You should always carry your trash out: food wrappers, juice bottles, and even apple cores should go into the bag. If you are hiking on a well-used trail, you will probably find litter left behind by others. Take a moment to put as much as you can into your own garbage bag. If you don't do it, it probably will not get done.

Protective Clothing: Weather is highly changeable, especially in spring and fall and along the coastline. Cold rains and high winds can create uncomfortable, possibly life-threatening, conditions. No matter how good the weather seems to be, always carry some protective clothing.

Backpack: You need something to carry everything, so I recommend that you invest in a quality day pack. It should have adjustable shoulder straps, a waist strap, a large inner pouch, and roomy outer pockets. The equipment listed earlier will fit easily inside a good pack and will sit comfortably on your back. After one or two trips, wearing it will become just another part of your walking routine. In fact, I never hike without my pack.

Optional (but Recommended) Equipment: Sunscreen, hat, bug repellent, camera, bandana, binoculars, field guides, extra socks, and toilet paper.

Other Possible Equipment: Tarp, rope, eating utensils, flashlight, towel, bathing suit, small stove, fuel, toothbrush, toothpaste, soap, writing paper and pen, and sleeping bag.

HAZARDS

Even well-used trails may contain potential hazards. At the start of each route description are cautionary notes, provided in one- or two-word descriptions. Following is a more detailed explanation of what each one means:

Animals: This means there is a reasonable possibility of encountering one of any number of wild beasts, including, but not limited to, moose, coyote, bear, bobcat, fox, or lynx. However, you are more likely to see squirrel, deer, and porcupine.

Cliffs/cliff edge: Although a number of trails take you next to cliffs, few have guardrails. Watch where you are walking. (Take special care at Cape Split.)

Exposed coastline: Similar to "High waves," but indicates that there is very little shelter from high winds.

Extreme weather common on open hilltops: Hilltops such as Cape Split have no shelter. They are also at high elevation and close to the ocean. They can enjoy the best, but also the very worst, of weather conditions.

High waves: The coastal walks are among my favourites, but during storms, the North Atlantic Ocean can generate waves of awesome height and power. Too often some unwary visitor strays too close to the water's edge and gets swept away. Be aware.

High winds and waves: Indicates that these are common on this route.

Hunting is permitted, in season, in many of the areas covered in this book. Usually starting in early October, hunting season varies from year to year for different types of game and in different areas within the region. Consult the Department of Natural Resources Web site (www.gov.ns.ca/natr/hunt) for detailed information before going into the woods in the fall.

Motorized vehicles in some sections/Motorized vehicles/farm equipment: Sometimes motorized vehicles such as ATVs and snowmobiles share the trail with walkers. Hikers should yield to farm equipment.

No signage/poor signage: At least six of the routes profiled in *Hiking Trails of Mainland Nova Scotia* are not managed or are informal footpaths. For all of these, and even some of the managed routes, there is no signage of any type — except sometimes at the trailhead — to indicate the route to be followed. That is why a very detailed description of each route, and a map, are provided.

Poison ivy: This plant is not very common, although it is becoming more so. It is often found along the edges of many trails and fields. Managed trails will usually post warning signs, but as the plant is spreading due to climate change, it could be almost anywhere. The best way to avoid it: stay on the path.

Remote location: Several of the routes in *Hiking Trails of Mainland Nova Scotia*, such as Crowbar Lake, Kenomee, or Queensport Road, take you into areas where few travel. You would be wise to advise someone of your route and expected time of return for any hike, but for these routes, it is especially important.

Road crossing: If your route must cross a public road, I will list this to remind you to watch for traffic when you must cross.

Rugged terrain: Some of the paths profiled in this book are wide, level, and surfaced in crushed stone. Others, however, wander over the landscape regardless of hills, rocks, rivers, or any other obstacle. When I think that the ground is of a more than average challenge, I mention it.

Seasonal flooding: Several routes follow rivers, and during the spring runoff many streams overflow their banks and flood the neighbouring trail, making it impassable. In some cases flooding may also occur during or shortly after heavy rainstorms, especially during the fall hurricane season.

Steepness/steep climb: There is a considerable difference between walking on an abandoned rail line, with its 1% grade, and the ski hill on the High Head Trail. If a trail has a section I think will be unusually challenging to the weekend walker, I will mention it.

Variable weather conditions: Weather along the Atlantic coastline can change rapidly, especially in the spring and fall. Even in seemingly good weather, you should be prepared for wet and cold conditions.

Weather conditions are often extreme: A variation of several of the above.

* * *

Congratulations! You have read the entire preamble, and you are now ready to begin your discovery of mainland Nova Scotia's hiking trails. I hope you enjoy your explorations as much as I did.

Share your pictures of your hikes on the Hiking Trails of Nova Scotia Facebook page at www.facebook.com/HikingTrailsOfNovaScotia, or visit the blog at http://hikingnovascotia.blogspot.ca/ for updates and details of other trails.

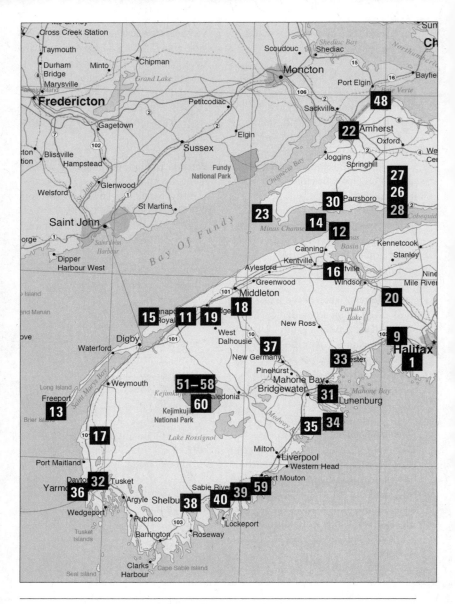

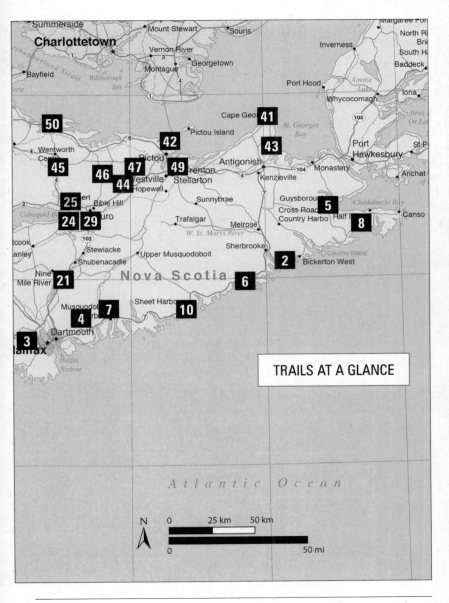

TRAILS AT A GLANCE

TRAILS AT A GLANCE

Trail Name	Difficulty level 1-5	Length km (mi)	Time to complete (hours)	Permitted Uses (no snow)	Permitted Uses (snow)	Dog Use	Page
				Features			

Uses (no snow): W = Walk, B = Bike, I = Inline Skating/Skateboarding, H = Horseback Riding, A = ATV
Uses (snow): S = Snowshoe/Walk, X = Cross-Country Ski, Sm = Snowmobile
Uses (dog): L = Dogs permitted on leash, O = Dogs permitted off leash
Items marked with an asterisk (*) indicate that use is permitted on some sections of the route but not on all

Trail Name	Difficulty level 1-5	Length km (mi)	Time to complete (hours)	Permitted Uses (no snow)	Permitted Uses (snow)	Dog Use	Page
HALIFAX–MARINE DRIVE							
1. The Bluff Wilderness Hiking Trail–Bluff Loop	5	26 (16.25)	7+	W, B*, H*, A*,	S, X*, Sm*	L	29
2. Cape St. Marys	4	14 (8.75)	4+	W, A	S	O	35
3. Chain of Lakes	3	14.5 (9.1)	4+	W, B, I	S, X	L	39
4. Crowbar Lake	5	18 (11.25)	6+	W	S	L	43
5. Guysborough Shoreline Trail	3	15 (9.4)	4+	W, B, H*, A*	S, X, Sm*	L*	47
6. Liscomb River	3	8 (5)	3+	W, B*	S, X*	O	53
7. North Granite Ridge Trail	4	17.5 (10.9)	5+	W, B*	S, X*	L	57
8. Queensport Road	5	18 (11.25)	5+	W, B*, H*, A*	S, Sm*	O	61
9. St. Margarets Bay Rails to Trails	2	10 (6.25)	2+	W, B, H, A	S, X, Sm	O	67
10. Taylor Head Provincial Park–Bull Beach/Bobs Bluff	3	11.5 (7.2)	3+	W	S	L	71
EVANGELINE SCENIC TRAVELWAY							
11. Belleisle Marsh	1	4.5 (2.8)	1+	W, B	S, X	O	77
12. Blomidon Provincial Park	4	12.5 (7.8)	4+	W	S	L	81
13. Brier Island	5	20 (12.5)	5+	W, B*, H*, A*	S, X*, Sm*	O	87

Trail Name	Difficulty level 1-5	Length km (mi)	Time to complete (hours)	Permitted Uses (no snow)	Permitted Uses (snow)	Dog Use	Page
14. Cape Split	4	16 (10)	4+	W, B, A*	S	O	93
15. Delaps Cove	2	9.5 (5.9)	2+	W, B*, A*	S, X*, Sm*	O	105
16. Gaspereau River	3	9 (4.5)	2+	W	S	O	111
17. Hectanooga	2	10 (6.25)	2+	W, B, H, A	S, X, Sm	O	115
18. Nictaux Station	4	21 (13)	5+	W, B, H, A	S, X, Sm	O	119
19. Roxbury	5	18 (11.25)	5+	W, B, H, A	S, X, Sm	O	123
20. Uniacke Estate	3	12 (7.5)	3+	W	S, X*	L	127
GLOOSCAP SCENIC TRAVELWAY							
21. 9 Mile River	3	10 (6.25)	2+	W, B	S, X	L	135
22. Amherst Point Migratory Bird Sanctuary	2	6 (3.75)	1+	W	S, X	O	139
23. Cape Chignecto Provincial Park	5	51 (31.9)	3 days	W	S	O	143
24. Cobequid Trail	3	14 (8.75)	3+	W, B	S, X	L	149
25. Debert Mi'kmawey	1	4.5 (2.8)	1+	W, B, A*	S, X	O	155
26. Devil's Bend	4	13 (8.1)	4+	W	S	O	159
27. Kenomee Canyon	5	21 (13.1)	6+	W	S	O	163
28. Thomas Cove	2	7 (4.4)	2+	W	S	L	167
29. Victoria Park	1	5.5 (3.4)	1+	W, B	S, X	L	171
30. Wards Falls	2	7 (4.4)	2+	W, B	S, X	O	175
LIGHTHOUSE ROUTE SCENIC TRAVELWAY							
31. Bay to Bay Trail	4	21.5 (13.4)	5+	W, B, H*, A*	S, X, Sm*	L*	181

Trail Name	Difficulty level 1-5	Length km (mi)	Time to complete (hours)	Permitted Uses (no snow)	Permitted Uses (snow)	Dog Use	Page
32. Chebogue Meadows Wildlife Interpretive Trail	1	5.5 (3.4)	1+	W	S	0	185
33. Chester Connector	5	23 (14.4)	6+	W, B, H, A,	S, X, Sm	L*	189
34. Gaff Point	2	6.5 (4.1)	2+	W	S	L	195
35. Green Bay – Broad Cove	4	12 (7.5)	4+	W	S	0	199
36. Hebron – Yarmouth	3	12 (7.5)	3+	W, B, H, A	S, X, Sm	L*	211
37. New Germany	3	11 (6.9)	2+	W, B, H, A	S, X, Sm	0	217
38. Shelburne Trail	2	8.5 (5.3)	2+	W, B	S, X	L	221
39. Thomas Raddall Provincial Park	3	8 (5)	2+	W, B*	S, X	L	225
40. Tom Tigney Trail	5	23 (14.4)	6+	W, B, H*, A*	S, X, Sm*	L*	231
SUNRISE SCENIC TRAVELWAY							
41. Cape George	4	18.5 (11.6)	5+	W	S	0	239
42. Caribou – Munroes Island Provincial Park	2	10 (6.25)	2+	W	S	L	243
43. Fairmont Ridge	4	12 (7.5)	3+	W	S, X	0	247
44. Gully Lake	4	17.5 (10.9)	5+	W	S, X	0	251
45. High Head	4	12 (7.5)	4+	W, B, A*	X	0	257
46. Rogart Mountain	2	6.5 (4.1)	2+	W	S	L	261
47. Six Mile Brook	4	10 (6.25)	3+	W, A*	S, X*	0	265
48. Tidnish Dock	2	8 (5)	2+	W, B, A*	S, X	L*	269
49. Trenton Park	1	4.5 (2.8)	1+	W, B	S, X	L	273
50. Wallace Bay National Wildlife Area	1	4 (2.5)	1+	W	S	L	277

Trail Name	Difficulty level 1-5	Length km (mi)	Time to complete (hours)	Permitted Uses (no snow)	Permitted Uses (snow)	Dog Use	Page
KEJIMKUJIK NATIONAL PARK							
51. Channel Lake	5	24 (15)	7+	W	S, X	L	283
52. Gold Mines	1	3 (1.9)	1+	W	S, X	L	287
53. Hemlock and Hardwoods	1	5 (3.1)	1+	W	S, X	L	291
54. Liberty Lake	5	61 (38.1) one way	3 days	W, B*	S, X*	L	295
55. Mason's Cabin	4	37 (23.1)	2 days	W, B	S, X	L	313
56. Mersey River	2	9 (5.6)	2+	W, B	S, X	L	317
57. Mill Falls	1	5 (3.1)	1+	W	S	L	321
58. Peter Point–Snake Lake	2	6 (3.75)	2+	W, B*	S, X	L	325
59. Seaside Adjunct	2	10.5 (6.6)	2+	W	S	L	329
60. West River	5	14 (8.75)	4+	W	S, X	L	333

Etiquette

Many trails are open to more than one use: walkers and cyclists, skiers and snowshoers. Here are a few simple rules that make "sharing the trail" easier:

- Be friendly and courteous.
- Ride, walk, or run on the right, pass on the left.
- Stay on the trail. Creating your own trail or cutting switchbacks creates erosion, damages habitat, and causes new trails that can't be maintained.
- Bicyclists yield to equestrians, runners, and hikers. Keep your bike under control and at a safe speed.
- Runners and hikers yield to equestrians.
- Downhill traffic should yield to uphill traffic. When in doubt, give the other user the right of way.
- Pack out your litter.
- Dogs should be kept on leashes and under control.
- Respect private property.

4. Crowbar Lake

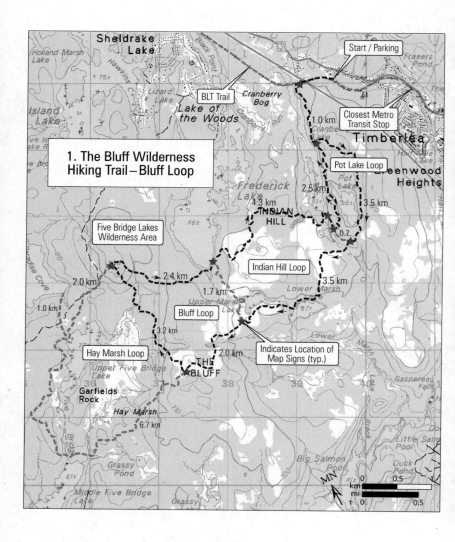

1. The Bluff Wilderness Hiking Trail — Bluff Loop

Sheldrake Lake

Start / Parking

BLT Trail

Closest Metro Transit Stop

Pot Lake Loop

Five Bridge Lakes Wilderness Area

Indian Hill Loop

Bluff Loop

Hay Marsh Loop

Indicates Location of Map Signs (typ.)

THE BLUFF

Garfields Rock

Hay Marsh

1.0 km
2.5 km
4.3 km
INDIAN HILL
3.5 km
0.7
3.5 km
1.7 km
2.4 km
2.0 km
1.0 km
3.2 km
2.0 km
6.7 km

1. The Bluff Wilderness Hiking Trail – Bluff Loop

◄- - -► 26 km (16.25 mi) return

🕐 : 7+hrs

🏃 : 5 [distance]

Type of Trail: crushed stone, natural surface, rocks

Uses: walking, biking*, horseback riding*, ATVing*, snowshoeing, cross-country skiing*, snowmobiling*

⚠ : Animals. Hunting is permitted in season. Isolated. Rugged terrain. Motorized vehicles (on the BLT Trail).

📱 : Good throughout.

Facilities: bike racks, garbage cans

Gov't Topo Map: 11D12 (Halifax)

Trailhead GPS: N 44° 39' 55.4" W 63° 45' 47.1"

Access: From Exit 4 on Highway 103, turn onto Highway 3 and continue for 2 km (1.25 mi) back in the direction of Halifax. The trailhead is on the right, marked by a road sign, at 2890 Highway 3.

Route 21, Metro Transit, stops at the intersection of Forestglen Drive and Fraser Road, on the Beechville–Lakeside Timberlea (BLT) Trail. Walk 1.5 km (0.9 mi) away from Halifax to reach The Bluff Wilderness Hiking trailhead.

Introduction: Concerned by the rapid growth of the Halifax urban area, several conservation groups undertook efforts to preserve the unpopulated centre of the Chebucto peninsula. This culminated in the designation, in October 2011, of 8,600 ha (21,250 ac) as the new Five Bridge Lakes Wilderness Area.

Few expect to find such a large, isolated area so close to downtown Halifax, where small populations of bear and even the rare mainland moose survive. However, the challenging terrain, mostly barrens supporting dense brush unsuitable for either harvesting wood or for agriculture, has meant that few other than hunters and fishers ever venture into the area.

For walkers, The Bluff Wilderness Hiking Trail is a gem, comprising a system of four stacked loops providing well over 30 km (18.75 mi) of dedicated footpaths. You might need to share the trail with bikes and even ATVs on the short approach walk on the BLT Trail, but once on The Bluff Wilderness Hiking Trail it is foot traffic only. For this book I have profiled the namesake route, the Bluff Loop.

Route Description: Leaving the parking lot, you turn right to enter the wide, crushed-stone-surfaced multi-use BLT Trail. For the first 550 m/yd to the official entrance to The Bluff Wilderness Hiking Trail system, cyclists and ATVs are common, so be cautious. You will notice a speed limit sign of 20 kph (12.5 mph) as well as the BLT's 7 km (4.2 mi) marker.

About 50 m/yd beyond two impressively massive culverts beneath Highway 103, you reach the Bluff Loop trailhead, on your left. A bike rack and garbage can sit next to a large sign, which includes a map. The sign warns that this is an unsupervised route suitable for experienced hikers: walking only.

The first kilometre (0.6 mi) provides an indication of the terrain you will encounter. A slender footpath, the trail meanders through dense vegetation and crosses several boardwalks over substantial wet areas. Watch closely for the yellow metal route markers and for painted arrows on the rocks where the route crosses extensive areas of barrens. Providing excellent views of Cranberry Lake to the right, the trail drops swiftly to water level to the junction with the Pot Lake Loop, 1.6 km (1 mi) from the parking lot.

The junction signs stand out prominently, each one featuring a large, excellent topographical map. And the paths are usually well marked, with coloured metal tags — a different colour for each loop — on trees and rocks, and cairns of stones or painted arrows in areas where there are no trees.

Turn left, away from the lake. The path climbs steeply, then wanders between thick forest and open rock, continuously climbing and descending and working its way around the many wet areas. You are almost 2 km (1.25 mi) from the junction before you actually reach the shore of Pot Lake, briefly, reaching water level only once, before the path turns away into the forest to skirt another large swampy area.

Your twisting path eventually brings you out into areas of open rocks, and it is here that you find the junction with the Indian Hill Loop.

You have walked 5 km (3.1 mi). Turn left, following the blue metal markers and the very distinct footpath for the next 3.5 km (2.2 mi), passing close to small Upper and Lower Marsh lakes, to the junction with the Bluff Loop. This section is much easier walking, and more scenic, especially on the sections of open rock.

The next 2 km (1.25 mi), signed with red markers, passes quickly, with the highlight being the view from The Bluff, which is strewn with glacial erratics. You will also sight Upper Five Bridge Lake. Turning right at the junction with the Hay Marsh Loop, remaining on the Bluff Loop, the next 3.2 km (2 mi) takes you downhill into a very wet area of thick vegetation before climbing up another rocky hill, which is fairly challenging.

At the next junction, also with the Hay Marsh Loop — you have walked nearly 14 km (8.75 mi) to this point — you turn sharply right again, dropping quickly and steeply. Then the route levels, which usually means wet feet, before meandering through lovely hardwoods to connect with the Indian Hill Loop, 2.4 km (1.5 mi) later.

This junction is located adjacent to Frederick Lake and is a canoe access point. Continuing left, or straight, you face the longest individual segment, 4.3 km (2.7 mi), signed with blue markers. You start with a fairly

steady climb, with the trail making more than one 90°+ turn. This section also features extensive stretches of bare rock, especially on Indian Hill, and care must be taken to keep to the trail. The trail wiggles all over the landscape to navigate the rugged, broken terrain. When the path reaches Cranberry Lake, another canoe access point, where there is another map, only 400 m/yd remains in this section. But it is all a rocky scramble up a hillside, at the top of which is the next junction, with the Pot Lake Loop.

Turn left, now following yellow markers. The path worms through narrow defiles between rocky ridges, and works around scattered boulders, dropping onto the slender corridor of land separating Cranberry and Pot lakes, to cross the little stream between the two lakes — without benefit of a bridge. From here, the trail parallels Cranberry Lake, working its way up the slope and into an area of huge glacial boulders. This is difficult walking, and when you descend back to the water level it is sudden and steep, crossing a short boardwalk before you arrive back at the first junction and complete your loop.

Continue straight, retracing your route back to the BLT Trail and the trailhead.

Moose

Moose (*Alces alces americana*) are native to eastern North America. However, their population in Nova Scotia is estimated at no more than one thousand, or possibly less, and is largely restricted to the Tobeatic Region, Chebucto Peninsula, Cobequid Mountains, Pictou-Antigonish highlands, and the interior of the eastern shore area from Tangier Grand Lake through Guysborough.

Although large and physically intimidating, moose are herbivores, consuming twigs and leaves from such trees as sugar maple, red maple, yellow birch, and balsam fir. In the summer moose also eat aquatic vegetation such as pond weed and water lily. When the food supply is low, usually in late winter, moose will strip and eat the bark of some trees.

Krummholz

The effects of high winds and salt spray can be seen in the trees that grow near the ocean, especially those at the edge of barrens. Few species, particularly hardwoods, can survive the massive amounts of salt that are deposited on them by the fogs that roll in from offshore. Almost all the trees found by the ocean edge are the very hardy white spruce.

Fierce Atlantic gales produce a most dramatic visual effect. They stunt and shape the white spruce, causing dense branching that grows in the opposite direction from the prevailing winds. Several trees will cluster together in thick stands, forming a dense curtain of branches that insulates the lee side and protects the walker on a blustery day.

This phenomenon of stunted trees is called "krummholz," from the German word meaning "crooked wood."

2. Cape St. Marys

Cooper Brook Bridge

Wine Harbour

Wine

Harbour

To Sherbrooke

St. Marys River

Hirschfields Island

Lucys Pond

Freshwa Pond

The Gravel Bar

Road Begins

Wine Harbour

The Bar

Horse Shoal

Anika's Place

90

Walter Isle

Bay

Start / Parking

Shag Reef

Wharf Rock

Cape Lake

Black Head Shoal

Slate Rock

CAPE

Black Head

Mills Pond

ST MARYS

89

Jumping Jack Bank

Old Well

Tom Pyes Bank

88

Atlantic Ocean

APE

GEGOGAN

MN

km

mi

0   0.5   1

0   0.5

2. Cape St. Marys

◄━ ━ ━► 14 km (8.75 mi) return

⏱: 4+hrs

🏃: 4 [rugged terrain, navigation]

Type of Trail: compacted earth, natural surface

Uses: walking, ATVing, snowshoeing

⚠: Animals. Motorized vehicles. Rugged terrain. Exposed coastline. Hunting is permitted in season. Variable weather conditions. No signage.

: Good throughout, except dead zone between km 2.5 (mi 1.6) and km 4.5 (mi 2.8).

Facilities: none

Gov't Topo Map: 11F04 (Country Harbour)

Trailhead GPS: N 45° 03′ 26.1″ W 61° 53′ 39.8″

Access: From the end of Highway 107 at Musquodoboit Harbour, continue on Highway 7 for 155 km (97 mi) to Sherbrooke. Turn right onto Sonora Road, and follow for 12.5 km (7.8 mi), turning right onto Sonora South Road. Drive 150 m/yd; park near the entrance to Wharf Rocks Road.

Introduction: The coastline of Guysborough County is some of the most unspoiled on mainland Nova Scotia. Unfortunately, there are few managed trails to enable you to experience it on foot, and none of any length.

I found Cape St. Marys on a list of hiking routes posted on the Guysborough Regional Development Authority Web site, where they recommend the area because it "consists of Pleistocene raised beaches and glacial till containing fossils of marine shells. As IBP Proposed Ecological Site 55, this cape has a salt marsh and sand dune system." It was everything I hoped for and expected from the Guysborough coastline: rugged, raw, and rough.

Route Description: Walk down the gravelled Wharf Rocks Road 200 m/yd to the final house, #27. The road continues past the house, although it seems as if the track has become part of the yard. You quickly move into forest, where the road drops downhill, crossing a creek then arriving at a junction at about 250 m/yd. Turn right; you will notice that the surface appears to be covered in clamshell fragments. This unique layer continues for 350 m/yd.

You reach the ocean 200 m/yd later, and for a short distance the track is on rocky cobble providing fine views of the mouth of the

Barachois Ponds

Apparently we like to make up our own words for things here in Atlantic Canada, so when we encountered all these small ponds, partly fresh and partly salt, that were separated from the ocean by a sandy or rocky beach, we made up a name for them: barachois.

Some say the origin is French, some say Basque, but whatever its derivation barachois ponds are common along much of our coastline — which is probably why we thought we needed a new word to describe it!

St. Marys River and Cape Gegogan opposite. A little more than 900 m/yd into the walk, you reach another junction; keep straight/right. To your left is a grassy hillside on which is perched a trailer. Painted on a rock is the notice "Anika's Place."

Continue along the old road. It returns to water level about 450 m/yd beyond Anika's, at which point you are looking at McDiarmid Cove and Wharf Rock, then climbs into a large grassy field. As you climb into it, the trail splits into three tracks. In fact, there are distinct ATV tracks all over the hillside.

Take the centre path. This leads you, in about 150 m/yd, to the top of the hill where there is an old well. The views from here are superb. Turn left at the well, and in another 100 m/yd you return to the woods following a continuation of the old road.

The next 650 m/yd are difficult, the trail wet and often partially blocked by fallen trees — the majority of spruce through here are dead. So when you emerge onto another, smaller field, it is with some relief. The trail splits again. I followed the most distinct, or left. It led me over the field, which looked as if it was once cleared for farming. The trail — now a footpath — works its way down to the shore of the ocean, about 2.4 km (1.5 mi) from the start.

You emerge onto the coastline with small Mills Pond to your left. Your route is now the wide, rocky cobble beach. A faint, but distinct, ATV track continues in the stones. For the next 2 km (1.25 mi) you trek along the small, flat stones, or on the occasional grassy strip, towards the tip of Cape St. Marys. On your left, the cape looms above you, and ATV tracks keep heading onto it. On the right, several kilometres away, tiny Wedge Island sits alone in the Atlantic. You should have an excellent view of the light station at Barachois Point on Cape Gegogan.

No trees protect you from the Atlantic gales, as you turn sharply left at the point. The rocks are larger here, and loose, so the walking is more difficult. For the next 1.5 km (0.9 mi) you face the most challenging conditions, working over the big rocks along the shoreline, although there are one or two grass-covered drumlins where you may obtain some relief.

Dune Systems

Dunes are sand deposits on beaches that develop into a series of one or more ridges through wind and wave action and become stabilized by the growth of American beach grass. New dune ridges develop on the seaward side depending upon the sediment supply, the pace of erosion, and the rate of sea level rise.

All sand beaches have some measure of dune systems, although beaches on the Atlantic coast of the mainland tend to be retreating landward too rapidly for full successional series development.

The fragile grasses that populate the dunes are essential to their survival. Many provincial beaches and other protected sites have extensive boardwalks to prevent human passage that can quickly kill the plants, causing more rapid sand erosion. Please stay on these boardwalks at all times.

When you have passed the largest pond yet, you have reached Jumping Jack Bank. Directly ahead, across the bay, you can see the houses of Wine Harbour. The track here turns left again, but this time into the thick spruce, and slightly higher than water level.

This is no longer a very distinct path, and whenever it meanders to the edge of the coastal cliff you see that this is very actively eroding. You continue in the thick vegetation

Bandana

One of the more useful small items you can carry, bandanas make great headbands and neck protection. They can even substitute for a hat to provide shade from the sun. During hot weather, soaking your bandana and wetting your hair and face is almost as refreshing as a cool drink, and I regularly use mine to wipe acrid perspiration from my eyes. They take no space and weigh nothing: carry two!

Blisters

Even the most careful hiker will get blisters. Left untreated, they can turn the shortest walk into a painful nightmare. Treat a blister like an open wound: clean it with soap and water and dress it with Second Skin or an adhesive bandage. If your feet are dirty or sweaty, clean them with an alcohol-saturated wipe to help adhesive tape adhere.

for 500 m/yd, before coming back into the open, then 150 m/yd later returning to cobble beach.

Unlike the Sonora side of Cape St. Marys, facing Wine Harbour the trees grow right to the edge of the rocks, leaving a narrower and more sloping beach. There is much more evidence of erosion on this coast, and there are large eroding drumlins on the facing shore.

After another 500 m/yd of difficult shoreline walking, there is a brief, 100 m/yd respite of ATV path through the forest, but then you return to the rocky beach. You next reach the largest pond so far, crossing the high barrier beach restraining it — although you will need to cross the unbridged outflow. At the far end of this beach, you connect to a road, about 7.7 km (4.8 mi) from the start.

Less than 100 m/yd later you reach a junction. To the right, it heads onto an area called The Gravel Bar, which, with large Hirschfields Island, separates Wine Harbour from Wine Harbour Bay. The road follows along the shoreline of Wine Harbour, except for 400 m/yd when it goes behind a point, for 2.4 km (1.5 mi) until you reach the bridge crossing Cooper Brook.

Turn left onto the rough-looking forest road climbing the hillside. You have turned away from the ocean, and for the next 2.4 km (1.5 mi) you will follow this former road up over Cape St. Marys and back down to Sonora. Ignore the many side trails, accept philosophically the many — many — wet areas, and you will soon arrive back at the first junction with the clamshells.

Continue straight to return to your car in 450 m/yd.

3. Chain of Lakes

◄ - - - ► 14.5 km (9.1 mi) return

🕐 : 4+hrs

🏃 : 3

Type of Trail: asphalt, crushed stone

Uses: walking, biking, inline skating, snowshoeing, cross-country skiing

⚠ : Road crossings.

👜 : Adequate throughout.

Facilities: bench, garbage cans, picnic tables

Gov't Topo Map: 11D12 (Halifax)

Trailhead GPS: N 44° 05′ 34.6″ W 66° 01′ 43.1″

Access: Metro Transit routes: 2, 3, 4, 17, 52, 80, and 81 stop at the entrance to the Atlantic Superstore at 3601 Joseph Howe Drive. Cross at the street lights; the trail is on the opposite side of the road from the store.

Introduction: In 1993, the Canadian National Railway track between Bridgewater and Halifax was abandoned, with the exception of the section from the Lakeside Industrial Park back to the peninsula. Plans were soon underway to develop the derelict sections as a recreational trail, and these have been successful, but everyone dreamed of the day that this final segment, like the last piece of a jigsaw puzzle, would be available.

When CN abandoned the final few kilometres of what was known as the "Chester Spur," the Halifax Regional Municipality was ready, acquiring the land in 2009 and opening the new Chain of Lakes Trail in 2010. With its development, it is now possible to begin walking from the urban core of Halifax and continue on a developed rail trail as far as Bridgewater, more than 100 km (62.5 mi) away.

Chain of Lakes is a very family-friendly walk, and on a sunny day it is extremely busy with walkers, runners, and bikers. I have profiled the route from near its start to where it connects to the Beechville–Lakeside Timberlea (BLT) Trail, but you may turn around at any point if you wish a shorter stroll.

Route Description: You start on a wide asphalt surface. From the street lights, turn left in the direction of Bayers Road. You are in the middle of the city, the trail running parallel to and only 10 m/yd from Joseph Howe Drive. The trail crosses the driveway entrances to several businesses — last chance to obtain some refreshments — then the busy intersection of Joseph Howe and Bayers/Dutch Village roads 500 m/yd from the start.

An even more dangerous road crossing, the entrance/exit ramp to Highway 102, must be negotiated 200 m/yd later. Then you pass under that highway, cross the entrance to Ashburn Golf Club, and finally, 850 m/yd from your start, begin to move away from busy Joseph Howe.

The next 450 m/yd, to the crossing of Springvale Avenue, makes for a lovely walk. On your left are houses, including the large Nova Scotia Teachers Union building. To your right are the grounds of the Ashburn Golf Course. Just before you reach Springvale, as the trail begins a turn to the left, you cross high above a pond, which in the spring at dusk provides a chorus of peeping frogs. Wooden rail fences have been placed at embankments and on curves.

The road crossings are well signed and include crosswalks. Garbage cans and plastic bags for dog waste are usually also located at road crossings. The next 700 m/yd, to Brook Street, are also pleasant. Although there are houses on both sides of the trail, the land on the right is quite a bit higher, and there is a solid fringe of vegetation as a buffer. The houses on the left are lower, and closer, but many trees have been planted to thicken their leafy shield.

Once across Brook Street, about 2 km (1.25 mi) from the start, you pass through a set of metal gates. The trail runs parallel and close to quiet Crown Drive for the next 500 m/yd. The hill on the right is much higher here, and the new housing above probably cannot even be seen. You might catch glimpses of Chocolate Lake, to your left.

The trail curves to the right as you leave Crown Drive and most of the housing behind. To your left, and lower, the terrain is more wooded and rocky, and you might be able to spot a small stream. There is a perceptible, though gentle, climb.

Looming overhead is the massive concrete overpass of Northwest Drive, which you reach at almost exactly 3 km (1.9 mi) from your start. Just before going underneath the overpass, the asphalt ends, being replaced by crushed stone. To your left are First Chain Lake and the dam at its base.

The next 1.6 km (1 mi) is the most remote section of the trail, as it works through the wooded watershed properties past First and Second Chain lakes. It continues to climb, but is very wide and extremely easy walking. When you sight another massive road overpass ahead, this time Highway 103, you have almost

3. Chain of Lakes

Start / Parking
Busy Road Crossings
BLT Trail
Geizer Hill
Bayers Lake Business Park
Ashburn Golf Club
Black Duck Ponds
Fairmount
Clayton Park
Fairview
Bayers Lake
Lovett Lake
First Chain Lake
Second Chain Lake
Beechville
Armdale
Chain of Lakes Trail Ends
Highway 103
Northwest Arm Drive
Ragged Lake
Cranberry Lake

reached the end of this moderately secluded section.

About 200 m/yd after passing beneath Highway 103, you reach wide and busy Chain Lake Drive, where an asphalt surface resumes. I found this the most challenging road crossing of all, as it is four lanes wide, traffic moves quite quickly, and there is no crosswalk. However, with due caution it is safely negotiated. There are metal gates on the trail on both sides of the road.

For the next 1.2 km (0.75 mi), you proceed through the middle of the busy Bayers Lake Business Park, the drone of cars very prominent. Yet you pass through a pleasingly attractive pocket of forest, particularly as the route curls tightly around Bayers' Lake.

At about 6 km (3.75 mi), another four-lane street, Horseshoe Lake Drive, must be crossed, and on the far side the asphalt ends again. A 700 m/yd straightaway follows, reaching a junction with a former rail siding that curves off to the right. On your left is small Lovett Lake, and on your right one of the Black Duck Ponds.

Little more than 500 m/yd remains. The trail passes between large industrial buildings, ending at Lakeside Park Drive, 7.25 km (4.5 mi) from your start. Across the road is the trailhead of the BLT Trail, inviting further exploration.

Retrace your steps back to the start, or walk 300 m/yd left along Lakeside Park Drive to the St. Margarets Bay Road, where Metro Transit routes 21 and 23 stop.

4. Crowbar Lake

◄---► 18 km (11.25 mi) return

⊘: 6+hrs

🏃: 5 [distance, rugged terrain]

Type of Trail: natural surface

Uses: walking, snowshoeing

⚠: Animals. Remote location. Rugged terrain.

🐾: None at trailhead or in most low-lying areas. Good on all hilltops.

Facilities: benches

Gov't Topo Map: 11D14 (Musquodoboit Harbour)

Trailhead GPS: N 44° 47′ 44.6″ W 63° 22′ 37.8″

Access: Take Exit 19 off Highway 107. Turn left onto West Porters Lake Road; continue 1.4 km (0.9 mi) to Highway 7. Turn left and continue for 200 m/ yd, then turn right onto Myra Road. Follow for 8.3 km (5.2 mi); the trailhead parking lot is on the left.

Introduction: The Crowbar Lake Hiking Trail is located in the Waverley–Salmon River Long Lake Wilderness Area, a rugged pocket of pristine lakes, high granite ridges, and diverse vegetation, including old-growth pine and hemlock, found surprisingly close to the urban centre of the Halifax Regional Municipality. This footpath system was developed and is maintained by volunteers of the Porters Lake and Myra Road Wilderness Area Association.

Anyone planning to hike this route should be aware that it will require a high level of fitness to complete, and will take you into remote, rugged terrain where cellphones will not necessarily work. Adequate preparation, including packing food, water, and extra clothing, is essential. I also strongly advise notifying people where you are heading, and when you expect to return.

Of course, I also recommend that this is a wilderness hike you definitely should undertake!

Route Description: Starting from the parking area, you will realize how challenging this walk will be; the rugged, rocky landscape requires careful foot placement, and the steep hillside quickly causes your heart rate to elevate. You will also notice many fallen trees, a legacy of the damage caused by Hurricane Juan in 2003 and other powerful storms since. Various regulatory signs dot the first few hundred

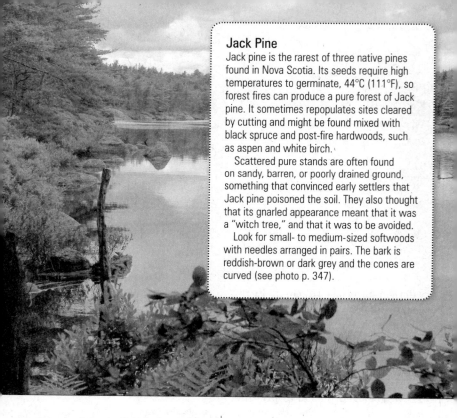

Jack Pine

Jack pine is the rarest of three native pines found in Nova Scotia. Its seeds require high temperatures to germinate, 44°C (111°F), so forest fires can produce a pure forest of Jack pine. It sometimes repopulates sites cleared by cutting and might be found mixed with black spruce and post-fire hardwoods, such as aspen and white birch.

Scattered pure stands are often found on sandy, barren, or poorly drained ground, something that convinced early settlers that Jack pine poisoned the soil. They also thought that its gnarled appearance meant that it was a "witch tree," and that it was to be avoided.

Look for small- to medium-sized softwoods with needles arranged in pairs. The bark is reddish-brown or dark grey and the cones are curved (see photo p. 347).

metres, and the trail is indicated by red metal markers on trees.

Within 400 m/yd the path levels off, and you find yourself on a boardwalk next to a tiny, tranquil pond. There is even a rough-hewn log bench. At 500 m/yd you reach the first junction; keep right, where you begin a very challenging climb up a steep hillside to the next junction, 600 m/yd later, where you will find another system map. (There is one at every junction.)

Keep right, where after a brief additional climb the narrow, but distinct, footpath gradually descends, meandering through thick vegetation, with few views available, for the 1.8 km (1.1 mi) to Spriggs Brook. On the far bank, the trail climbs, turning left to parallel the stream. Within 500 m/yd, the path drops back to water level

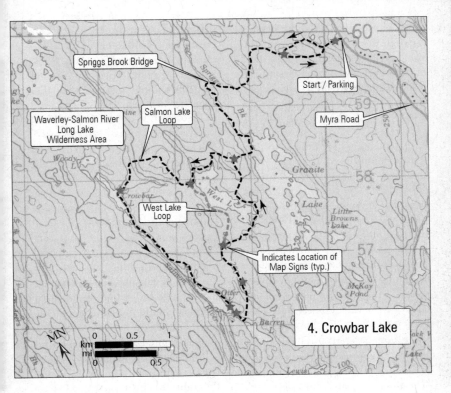

Spriggs Brook Bridge

Start / Parking

Myra Road

Salmon Lake
Loop

Waverley-Salmon River
Long Lake
Wilderness Area

West Lake
Loop

Indicates Location of
Map Signs (typ.)

4. Crowbar Lake

MN

km 0   0.5   1

mi 0   0.5

briefly before climbing to a beautiful pine-covered ridge. When it drops back to water level, you have reached to the shore of Granite Lake, about 4 km (2.5 mi) from the trailhead.

The trail traces Granite Lake for another few hundred metres/yards, then turns away from the water and begins to climb the next ridge, where 300 m/yd uphill you will reach the junction with the West Lake Loop. Turn right, climbing briefly before

dropping very steeply down walls of granite to the shore of West Lake. The path stays reasonably close to the water, crossing two small unbridged brooks, reaching the junction with the Salmon River Loop nearly 6 km (3.75 mi) from the start.

Once again, you turn right, climbing to the highest point on the trail, 110 m/yd above sea level, a rounded granite knoll populated by Jack pine about 500 m/yd past the junction.

From here, the path drops down through thick vegetation, and considerable storm damage, to the bank of Crowbar Lake, which is long and thin, nestled between parallel ridges. This isn't a trail junction, but there is a map. You are 7.7 km (4.8 mi) into your hike.

The next 2.5 km (1.6 mi), following the shoreline of Crowbar Lake, then the Salmon River, and finally Otter Lake, I enjoyed very much, but then, I like water, except for a wet path, which this quite often is in the first 500 m/yd. The river is tea coloured, as are so many of Nova Scotia's watercourses, and shallow in the summer. There are many exposed rocks through here, and occasionally some granite ridges on the left; along the shoreline of Otter Lake these become moss-covered cliffs, and require some climbing along their sides.

When you reach the next junction, keep straight, heading towards Barren Lake. About 100 m/yd later there is another map, because an informal trail connects outside the trail system. Keep left here, paralleling the creek between Otter Lake and small Barren Lake, which is surrounded by granite knolls. As soon as it touches Barren Lake, the trail begins to climb, then swings almost 180° up the steepest slope yet, including another massive granite rock face.

The vista from the top is excellent,

following a granite ridge along its crest for a considerable distance, including past the next junction. (Keep straight, or right.) There are views of the surrounding ridges, some smaller lakes in the nearby terrain, and even in the direction of Lake Echo. When the trail turns away from the ridge, it is only about 300 m/yd to the next intersection, where you turn right again.

This next 1.9 km (1.2 mi) section provides some of the best waterside walking of the entire route. The trail passes over some large granite outcroppings that are almost free of trees and sit right beside West Lake. The final 500 m/yd climbs up another 100 m/yd+ high hill, where you pass by a remarkably large erratic about 150 m/yd before you reach the junction above Granite Lake.

Retrace the 3.6 km (2.25 mi) to the junction 1.1 km (0.7 mi) from the trailhead. Turn right; this 800 m/yd descent provides views of Porters Lake, and takes you through an area of remarkable, and oddly impressive, storm damage. (The massive felled trees bring to mind dinosaur skeletons.) This path reconnects to the main trail in the fern-covered ground just before the small pond. Turn right; 500 m/yd remains to the trailhead.

5. Guysborough Shoreline Trail

◄- - -► 15 km (9.4 mi) return

⏱: 4+hrs

🏃: 3

Type of Trail: compacted earth, crushed stone

Uses: walking, biking, horseback riding*, ATVing*, snowshoeing, cross-country skiing, snowmobiling*

⚠: Animals. Road crossings. Motorized vehicles.

☂: Adequate throughout.

Facilities: benches, garbage cans, interpretive panels, outhouses, picnic tables,

Gov't Topo Map: 11F05 (Guysborough), 11F06 (Chedabucto Bay)

Trailhead GPS: N 45° 23' 19.8" W 61° 29' 44.2"

Access: Turn off Highway 104 at Exit 37, driving towards Canso. Drive on Highway 4 for 1.2 km (0.75 mi), then turn at Highway 16. Continue for 31.1 km (19.4 mi) to the village of Guysborough. Continue straight on Main Street, when Highway 16 turns right. Continue about 200 m/yd, past Green Street and the last house, #11, and park here.

Introduction: The proposed Guysborough railway extended nearly 100 km (62.5 mi) from Guysborough to the village of Ferrona Junction near New Glasgow. Between 1929 and 1931 considerable work was undertaken before the project was cancelled, but the rails were never laid and bridges not built even though the concrete abutments were poured, some of them quite massive.

The people of Guysborough never forgot their promised rail line. When the concept of the Trans Canada Trail was introduced, they were among the first to see that it could turn their rail line into a transportation corridor of another kind. The Guysborough Rail Trail was the first section of the Trans Canada Trail built in Nova Scotia and officially opened on June 1, 1996.

This route is a combination of the Guysborough Shoreline Trail and a section of the Trans Canada Trail. Dogs must be leashed on the Shoreline Trail, but may be off leash on the rail trail.

Route Description: Your route begins where the road ends. In fact, this was once an extension of Main Street. You continue straight to the water, less than 100 m/yd, where the path swings right and works its way around Guysborough Harbour. This

is an exceptionally scenic area, with the slender finger of Hadley Beach extending into Chedabucto Bay from McCaul Island, across the water. In the 250 m/yd on a crushed-stone surface before you cross an old concrete bridge and turn left, you will pass new interpretive panels, a picnic table, and garbage cans.

After touching onto a street, briefly, the trail continues along the water for another 650 m/yd, passing more panels and benches, before reaching a gate and a dirt road. A sign indicates that you continue along this road, Lower Water Street. You do so for another 1 km (0.6 mi) until you reach Highway 16. (Did you see the Guysborough Trail Association's caboose by the water on your left?)

Cross Highway 16, and follow the dirt road for only 50 m/yd. To your left, you sight a trail and bridge over a small creek. Follow this uphill, about 200 m/yd, where you reach the rail trail. Turn left again, and in 300 m/yd you reach the Old Mill Pond.

At the Old Mill Pond, site of a former sawmill, there are two interpretive panels, one outlining the human history, and the other, a Trans Canada Trail panel, about the black-fly. A bench here overlooks the small pond.

The trail parallels Highway 16, although in woods thick enough that you hear traffic but do not see it. With

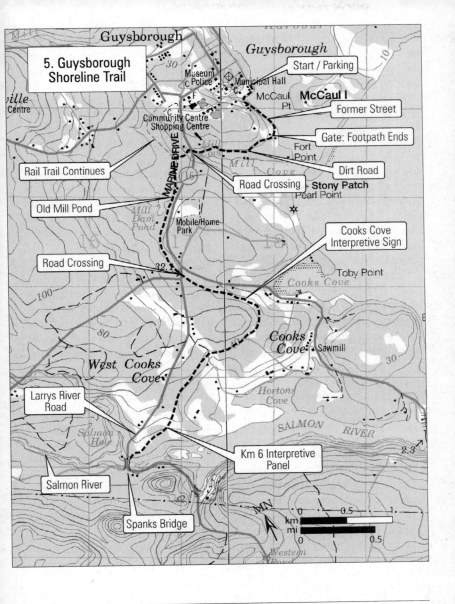

5. Guysborough Shoreline Trail

Start / Parking

Former Street

Gate: Footpath Ends

Dirt Road

Road Crossing

Rail Trail Continues

Old Mill Pond

Road Crossing

Cooks Cove Interpretive Sign

Larrys River Road

Km 6 Interpretive Panel

Salmon River

Spanks Bridge

the exception of a driveway 300 m/yd past Mill Pond, you see nothing until you reach, and cross, the Larrys River Road, at 3.5 km (2.2 mi).

On the far side, there is an interpretive panel and a Trans Canada Trail marker; the path is wide and in good condition. Less than 300 m/yd later you pass a sign warning that you are on private property and 150 m/yd after that you emerge into an open area where a house is situated right next to the trail. A fence has been built on the left, but there are structures on both sides. The trail through here is entirely grass covered.

Returning to the woods, the path climbs slightly before emerging onto a large grassy field that slopes downhill to your left. Highway 16 is visible at the bottom of the hill, and the ocean beyond that. An interpretive sign, which you reach 850 m/yd after Larrys River Road, tells you that this is Cooks Cove. At the far end of the field, picnic tables sit on the grass overlooking the water a good place to rest. There is another interpretive panel — Chedabucto Bay — which has a green "KM 4" (mi 2.5) marker attached underneath. Just past here, also on your left, is an outhouse.

Back in the thick forest, the track twists more than you might expect for a rail bed; you see why just 100 m/yd later, when you find a pond, on your right, in the rail-line route. To avoid

this flooded section, the path sits on the bank above, and continues so for 350 m/yd, just after you reach an area of clear-cut.

The trail is easy to follow, and you pass the "KM 5" (mi 3.1) marker about 500 m/yd later. At the Hortons Cove interpretive panel, reached 150 m/yd farther, there is no longer any view, and the picnic tables have been destroyed. Over the next 1 km (0.6 mi), you cross several wood roads, but keep straight. At the "KM 6" (mi 3.75) marker there is also an interpretive panel: Dickie Brook Power Station.

The final 750 m/yd mostly descend through an area of recent clear-cut where no buffer has been left, and it is clear that the trail was used as a road. At least this provides good views of the landscape, and the concrete bridge abutments, on your left. The trail reaches the Larrys River Road just before it crosses the Salmon River at Spanks Bridge, about 7.5 km (4.7 mi) from your start in the village.

Walk onto the bridge. To your left you can gain excellent views of the massive concrete bridge abutments that were erected in anticipation of finishing the rail line. They have stood here as silent sentinels since the 1930s.

Retrace your route to return to the trailhead.

Natural Guysborough County

Guysborough County contains seven of the thirty-one Wilderness Protected Areas in Nova Scotia, covering more than 31,630 ha (78,126 ac) of its land area. When the system plan was developed, it was intended to protect representative examples of all the different natural landscape types within the province. This turned out not to be possible, because there are so many (seventy-seven), and some of them are geographically quite small. Since the province restricted its efforts to trying to protect Crown land only, that meant that many of these ecosystems were not in their possession, but in private ownership. However, much of Guysborough County is owned by the Crown, so several excellent protected places could be designated.

Almost within sight of Black Duck Cove is the Canso Coastal Barrens protected area: 8,501 ha (20,997 ac) of excellent granite barrens. It contains several species of rare plants, old coastal coniferous forest, distinct fault lines, and an abundance of relatively undisturbed coastal habitats. There is an outstanding opportunity here for both long-distance coastal hiking and canoeing/kayaking around its many islands, coves, and headlands.

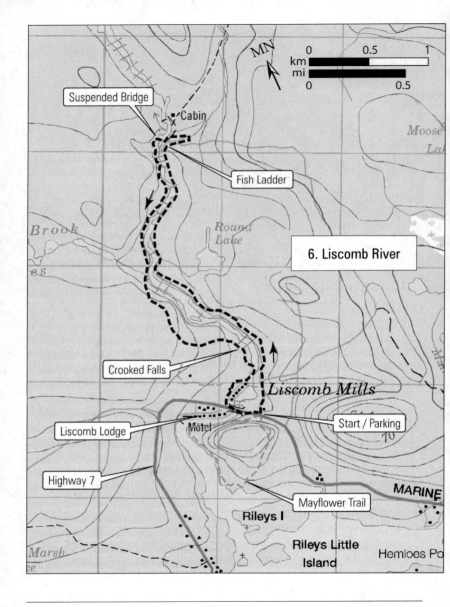

Suspended Bridge

Cabin

Fish Ladder

MN

km
mi

0   0.5   1

0   0.5

Moose Lake

Brook

Round Lake

6. Liscomb River

Crooked Falls

Liscomb Mills

Liscomb Lodge

Motel

Start / Parking

Highway 7

Mayflower Trail

MARINE

Rileys I

Rileys Little Island

Hemloes Po

Marsh

6. Liscomb River

◄ - - - ► 8 km (5 mi) return
🕐 : 3+hrs
🏃 : 3
Type of Trail: natural surface, compacted earth, crushed stone
Uses: walking, biking*, snowshoeing, cross-country skiing*

⚠ : Animals. Cliffs. Road crossing. Hunting is permitted in season.
📵 : None except near the lookoff.
Facilities: interpretive panels
Gov't Topo Map: 11E01 (Liscomb)

Trailhead GPS: N 45° 00′ 44.5″ W 62° 05′ 43.2″

Access: From Halifax, drive on Highway 7 about 111 km (70 mi) to Sheet Harbour. Liscomb Lodge is a further 54 km (34 mi) east on Highway 7. The trailhead is found at the roadside after crossing the bridge over the Liscomb River.

Introduction: Although this trail was probably originally created by generations of eager salmon fishers following the banks of this well-known stream, the lodge has made an effort to improve the signage and make the route much more accessible to walkers. However, this is a fairly rugged trail, with many rocks and outcroppings, and frequent small hills. There are also many small creeks, bridged either with simple logs across the stream or nothing at all.

I also found the distance to be considerably shorter than that indicated on all the maps, and the trail on the east bank, below Long Lakes Brook, was completely different from the route shown on all the maps.

This is not a walk for beginners. Instead, there are a number of other, shorter walks available. The most enjoyable of these is the Mayflower Trail, starting at the same trailhead as the river path, which heads to the mouth of the Liscomb River opposite Rileys Island, then traces the riverbank opposite the Lodge, about 2.5 km (1.5 mi).

Route Description: The Liscomb River Trail begins at a fairly large parking lot on Highway 7 on the opposite side of the Liscomb River from the Lodge, where there is a large interpretive sign that includes a map (although somewhat out of date). The path actually starts about 100 m/yd on the opposite side of the road from the parking lot. You head down a gravel road past a lone house. Several blue "Trail" signs direct you onto a grassy path, where 350 m/yd from the start you find a large gate with the trail name overhead, next to an interpretive panel. The river is visible to your left.

Within 50 m/yd the path changes markedly, from a wide grassy track to a narrow, rock-strewn footpath with vegetation crowding in from either side. (I hiked this on August 1.) About 175 m/yd from the gate the trail meanders down to the edge of the river; it looks like a good place to swim.

Signage is varied. Sometimes you will see red flashes or yellow rectangles or orange diamonds (sometimes with arrows underneath) or even something else. It is all helpful, because it does not look as if the brush is cleared very often. Fortunately, the route follows the river, so if in doubt just keep to the left.

Having said that, however, I noticed that the trail had been rerouted up higher on the ridge for several hundred metres/yards. It returns to its original route at the 1 km (0.6 mi) mark. Most of the spruce through this section has died, and the path has been moved to avoid the deadfall. The regenerating woods are mostly young spruce, so views of the river are often limited unless you are right on it.

The Liscomb River is often fairly narrow and fast running. At several places, the rapids are almost mini-waterfalls. But at frequent intervals the river widens, forming ponds where the water flows slowly. Salmon tarry in these pools, taking the opportunity to rest on their upstream trip. These pools are well-known to fishers, and they all have names, which are found on the trail map signs: Water Gauge, Grassy Island, Long Lake, Hemlock, and Powerhouse.

After about 3 km (1.9 mi), after increasingly challenging footing, you reach a little sandy spot beside the water, where the river is narrower and livelier. The river appears to split, and you can see a suspended bridge ahead of you, but the trail curves right, exiting into a field overgrowing with alders and beech.

A road connects at this point, from the right. You might notice, almost hidden by the leaves, signs that say "Fish Ladder" and "Liscomb River Trail East Side." In order to permit the salmon access to the waters above the dam, a fish climb of fifteen small (0.6 m [2 ft]) steps has been constructed. You might need to fight your way through the brush to see it, but it is worth the effort.

The path continues uphill, curving left, nearly overgrown by brush, for 200 m/yd to where another dirt road connects from the right. On the left, is a dam, which you cross, then you

Fish Ladder

What happens when you build a dam across a river with a salmon population? Salmon only give birth in the river where they were born, returning near the river's source after years roaming the Atlantic Ocean.

The answer: a fish ladder, a series of low steps built around the barrier that fish can easily leap up. Liscomb River contains a fine example; if you are there during the peak of the run in early July you might see it in use.

follow the distinct footpath. Shortly after that, you find yourself crossing a suspension bridge, traversing a narrow, 10 m/yd deep gorge. This is one of the few bridges of its type in the province, and the hike is worth undertaking for this reason alone.

Once on the west side of the river, the path follows the river downstream until crossing Long Lakes Brook, 1.6 km (1 mi) from the suspended bridge. The trail leaves the river and climbs a hill, reaching a lookoff 500 m/yd later. The trail also becomes wider, and surfaced with crushed stone.

Level at first, the path soon begins a steady descent, reaching a junction with the Crooked Falls Trail 850 m/yd from the lookoff. Turn left; you reach the river in less than 100 m/yd at a wonderful spot with massive rocks allowing easy access to the water.

Once back on the main trail, turn left, then left again 100 m/yd later at the next junction, onto a trail signed "No Bikes." This wanders close to the river again, emerging next to Chalet 10, under another gate, 450 m/yd later. From here, you can either continue down the road to Highway 7 and cross the road bridge back to your car, or follow a paved walkway underneath the highway to the main lodge complex.

Ruffed Grouse

At risk of a heart attack? Then be careful while hiking on any wooded trail, because if you pass close to a ruffed grouse it is likely to remain very still until you are almost upon it, then explode into noisy flight through the brush.

In the spring, however, should you appear to threaten her brood of chicks, a mother grouse might charge towards you, puffing her feathers to double her normal size and hissing menacingly. Since we are talking about a bird that looks like a wild chicken, I have never been worried about injury. Nor has any grouse ever done more than flutter close in an aggressive display.

The ruffed grouse is not migratory, so it might be encountered at any time of year. It is relatively abundant and a popular game bird. In fact, one of its Latin names, *Bonasa*, means "good when roasted"!

7. North Granite Ridge Trail

◄--- ► 17.5 km (10.9 mi) return

🕐 : 5+hrs

🥾 : 4 [rugged terrain]

Type of Trail: natural surface, compacted earth

Uses: walking, biking*, snowshoeing, cross-country skiing*

⚠ : Animals. Rugged terrain. Cliffs. Remote location. Hunting is permitted in season.

🔖 : Adequate throughout.

Facilities: outhouses, benches, covered picnic tables

Gov't Topo Map: 11D14 (Musquodoboit Harbour)

Trailhead GPS: N 44° 53' 28.4" W 63° 15' 00.4"

Access: From the end of Highway 107, turn right onto Highway 7, towards Musquodoboit Harbour. Drive 2.6 km (1.6 mi), turning left onto Highway 357, and follow it for 15.5 km (9.7 mi). Turn right at the trail sign into the parking lot.

Introduction: The Wilderness Trails of the Musquodoboit Trailways Association have been designed for those who enjoy a challenge. No compromises have been made on the route selection; if there is a hill nearby, you will climb it, whether it is a gentle ascent or a nearly sheer rock face. Wear sturdy footwear for this one, and carry lots of water. Do not forget either binoculars or camera and expect sore muscles afterward.

A volunteer association created this wonderful trail network. Their first project was the 14.5 km (9.1 mi) rail trail that is part of the Trans Canada Trail. Then in 2000 they opened the 9 km (5.6 mi) Admiral Lake Loop — short but tough. These were followed by the Bayers Lake Loop, the Gibraltar Rock Loop, and finally, the North and South Granite Ridge trails.

With The Bluff Wilderness Hiking Trail and the Crowbar Lake system, the Musquodoboit Trailways Wilderness trails are a fantastic hiking resource, less than an hour's drive from downtown Halifax.

Route Description: You begin on the rail trail, turning left onto the Gibraltar Rock Loop almost as soon as you pass the metal gate. The next several hundred metres give fair warning of the type of experience you are undertaking; the path heads straight up a steep hillside littered with large granite

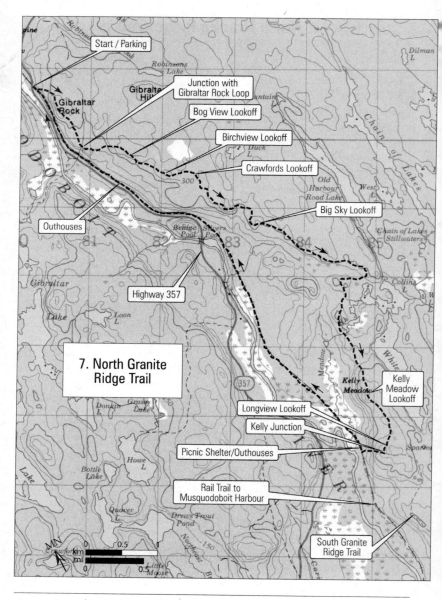

Start / Parking

Junction with
Gibraltar Rock Loop

Gibraltar
Rock

Bog View Lookoff

Birchview Lookoff

Crawfords Lookoff

Big Sky Lookoff

Outhouses

Highway 357

7. North Granite
Ridge Trail

Kelly Meadow
Lookoff

Longview Lookoff

Kelly Junction

Picnic Shelter/Outhouses

Rail Trail to
Musquodoboit Harbour

South Granite
Ridge Trail

boulders. The lookoff is welcome, and not just for the splendid views of the Musquodoboit River and valley.

The trail makes its way along the ridge for several hundred metres/yards, passing another lookoff, before descending slightly, where it reaches a junction with the Gibraltar Rock Loop just after crossing a small brook, 1.3 km (0.8 mi) from the start. The sign says that Kelly Junction is 9 km (5.6 mi) farther.

Right away the path becomes rougher, due as much to the fact that far fewer people tackle it than the Gibraltar Rock Loop. This path is almost never level, constantly working up over toothy granite ridges and down into narrow, thickly forested creek beds. Watch for red metal markers affixed to trees to ensure you are on the correct route. But for the first 600 m/yd or so it is mostly uphill — and steeply at that — as it climbs to the Bog View Lookoff. (There is a sign, and a view of the bog in the distance.)

Leaving Bog View, the trail descends slightly, then turns left and traces the crest of the ridge overlooking the Musquodoboit Valley, giving you occasional glimpses of the hills opposite. The path frequently has to contort itself around a huge boulder or past a sheer rock face, and always it is climbing a little and descending. You might notice that one

of the red markers is labelled "2 km" (1.25 mi) About 350 m/yd later, you emerge onto the Birchview Lookoff, about 3.7 km (2.3 mi) from the start.

The trail turns sharply left and drops to cross another brook, then climbs the next rocky knoll, where the trees have been flattened by storms and the trail is forced to pick a convoluted route through the debris. Crawfords Lookoff is only about 750 m/yd past Birchview, but the view here (in June) was disappointing.

The section between Crawfords and Big Sky lookoffs may be the most challenging you have yet faced. It is very rocky, and has some steep hillsides to traverse, but worst of all is the massive amount of deadfall from storm damage, which in some places appears like clear-cuts. So many trees are down that there are extended gaps in the signage; challenging, especially when the trail has had to be rerouted around the worst of the piles.

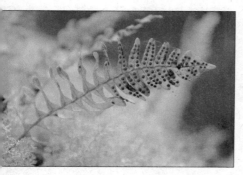

I have to confess that I lost track of my distance travelled here, as I picked my way over deadfall, through extensive wet areas, and walked several times off the trail. It is at least 1 km (0.6 mi) between the two lookoffs.

The view from Big Sky, which is a huge, almost treeless rock face, is impressive, with a large bog directly beneath and long sightlines between a number of burly-looking knolls. I rested here awhile before resuming my trek.

From Big Sky, the trail follows the ridge above the bog for several hundred metres/yards before dropping — steeply, of course — into it and turning back in the direction of the Musquodoboit River. The trail turns left again, however, plunging onward through the thick forest.

You sight a nearby pond, on your left, just before reaching the bridge crossing Meadow Brook. Follow the portage route to your left; in 200 m/yd you will reach the pond, where hunters often camp.

The next section, the remaining 1.6 km (1 mi) to Kelly Junction, is quite pleasant walking, even if there is still more climbing. However, when you reach Longview Lookoff, with its bench, the path works its way directly beneath the sheer granite cliff on which Longview sits. There, in a fantastic jumble of granite boulders, you reach Kelly Junction, where there is a map bolted to one of the rocks.

The sign directs you down the hillside, a rapid descent of 250 m/yd over the craggy hillside under a thick hemlock canopy. The forest floor of brilliant green sphagnum moss covers everything but your route.

You emerge at the covered picnic table at the halfway point of the rail trail, after a punishing 9 km (5.6 mi) on backcountry footpaths. The level, grass-covered track looks indecently easy after your recent experiences.

Turn right, and follow this gentle walkway 7 km (4.5 mi) to return to the trailhead. En route there are other rest areas and even outhouses to further ease your passage.

8. Queensport Road

◄---► 18 km (11.25 mi) return

⏱: 5+ hrs

🏃: 5 [distance, navigation challenges]

Type of Trail: crushed stone, natural surface, compacted earth

Uses: walking, biking*, horseback riding*, ATVing*, snowshoeing, snowmobiling*

⚠: Animals. Remote location. No signage. Rugged terrain. Variable weather

conditions. Hunting is permitted in season.

: None at trailhead, or until the top of the barrens. Good thereafter, except for some dead zones near Southwest Pond Brook.

Facilities: gazebo, interpretive panels, picnic table

Gov't Topo Map: 11F06 (Chedabucto Bay)

Trailhead GPS: N 45° 16′ 04.5″ W 61° 16′ 20.8″

Access: Turn off Highway 104 at Exit 37, driving towards Canso. Drive on Highway 4 for 1.2 km (0.75 mi), then turn onto Highway 16. Continue for 63 km (39.4 mi) to the junction with Highway 316. Turn right and follow Highway 316 for 20 km (12.5 mi). Look for a large gravel parking lot on the right 1 km (0.6 mi) past the turnoff to Cole Harbour.

Introduction: The dirt road connecting Cole Harbour on Tor Bay with Queensport on Chedabucto Bay fell into disuse after the nearby parallel route from Port Felix to Halfway Cove was paved. By the 1970s it was no longer maintained by the Department of Highways. Since then the path has gradually grown over, and it now offers a wonderful, wild walk across a remarkable landscape. Despite bi-

cycling and horseback riding being permitted, thick growth effectively hinders these activities beyond the radar station. I recommend this trail only for experienced hikers.

Much of the land this trail passes through is part of the 10,846 ha (26,790 ac) Bonnet Lake Barrens Protected Area, part of the Canso Coastal Granite Barrens landscape. Composed of granite and forming headlands and knolls with elevations of up to 200 m (650 ft), the barrens are thinly covered by a sandy loam soil that leaves almost 50% of the surface as exposed bedrock. Much of the area looks like a bleak moonscape, with large boulders deposited by the glaciers littering the landscape.

Route Description: The first part of the walk is misleadingly easy, because it has only recently (2010) been developed as a walking route to the site of a former RCAF radar station situated here during WWII. So at the trailhead, there is a large gravelled parking lot, a commemorative plaque, and even flags flying.

A large sign directs you onto "#5 Radar Unit Trail," a crushed-stone pathway that starts by climbing a shallow ravine, reasonably steeply, for about 650 m/yd, where the grade lessens substantially and there is a picnic table. About 200 m/yd later you should glimpse small First Cow Lake to your left, followed quickly by some rusting machinery, a side trail off to the right, and at 1.1 km (0.7 mi), a gazebo marking the location of the radar station.

This is off to the left, and there is a building plan of the former base, which was situated between First and Second Cow lakes. In 2011, it was still possible to explore among the ruins on paths that had been cleared to permit such viewing. By Second Cow Lake, the barrens become visible on your left, although you descend into thick vegetation almost immediately.

However, this spot also marks the end of the maintained trail, and when I hiked this in September 2011, I faced an almost completely overgrown road blocked by a thicket of low, dense vegetation. For the next 3 km (1.9 mi), you fight through the brush, the trail distinct, but not easy. The track is frequently wet, especially when you cross Smelt Brook 600 m/yd later. Between there and Otter Run Lakes, a distance of 2 km (1.25 mi), the footing gets rougher. Rivulets run down the path and the brush grows so thick that Blackberry Run Lakes is sensed rather than seen, though it is only 100 m/yd on your right. Note the numerous sumac trees in this stretch.

After crossing a tiny stream feeding Otter Run Lakes, on your right, the trail becomes easier. It is still overgrown, and still occasionally resembles a creek, but compared to the previous section, it seems wonderful.

Then, 900 m/yd beyond Otter Run Lakes, you suddenly climb out of the brush and onto the barrens. The transformation is dramatic, particularly when you reach the crest and gain views across Chedabucto Bay to Cape Breton and Isle Madame. To your right, you can gaze far across the barrens back towards Tor Bay, the landscape littered with abundant rocks and scattered with clumps of scrubby spruce and tamarack. Expect the wind to be cooler and harsher on this bleak hilltop. Pitcher plants thrive in this harsh environment.

Crossing the top of the barrens all too quickly, the trail, now much more distinct and walkable, falls rapidly down the steeper north slope.

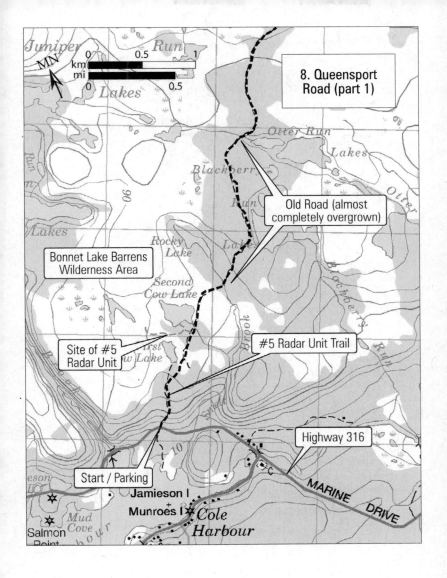

8. Queensport Road (part 1)

Otter Run Lakes

Old Road (almost completely overgrown)

Blackberry Run

Bonnet Lake Barrens Wilderness Area

Rocky Lake

Second Cow Lake

Site of #5 Radar Unit

#5 Radar Unit Trail

Highway 316

Start / Parking

Jamieson I

Munroes I Cole Harbour

Salmon Point

Mud Cove

MARINE DRIVE

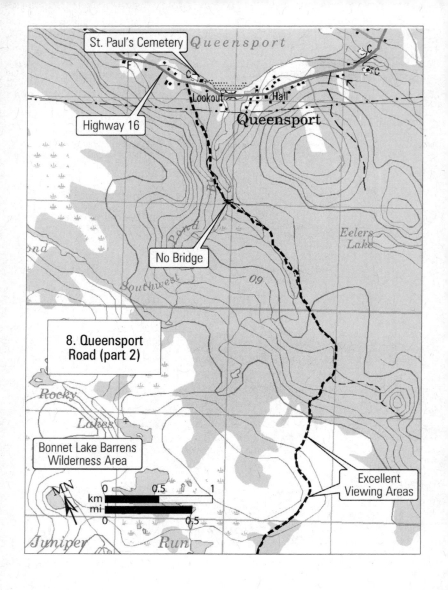

St. Paul's Cemetery

Queensport

Highway 16

Lookout

Hall

Queensport

No Bridge

Pond

Eelers Lake

Southwest

09

8. Queensport Road (part 2)

ond

Rocky

Lakes

Bonnet Lake Barrens Wilderness Area

MN

| km | 0 | 0.5 | 1 |
| mi | 0 | | 0.5 |

Excellent Viewing Areas

Juniper *Run*

Pitcher Plant

In the acidic bogs of the barrens can be found one of the most interesting residents of Nova Scotia, the entirely passive — yet carnivorous — pitcher plant. Bogs are unbalanced systems where more organic matter is produced than decomposes. Pitcher plants, to supplement their meagre diet, have learned to capture and digest insects.

The pitcher plant's green, red-veined leaves are shaped into open-topped cups that fill with water. Insects that venture inside the pitcher-shaped cup in search of pollen drown after finding that tiny leaf hairs obstruct their escape. The plant releases enzymes into the water that break down the insect's body into compounds that can be easily absorbed.

In early June and July, pitcher plants sport large purple flowers with fleshy tepals (not petals). Look inside and you might find their lunch.

ATVs use this route to drive from Queensport to the top of the barrens, which is just outside the Wilderness Protected Area.

Milder here, and in better soil, the trees are more robust and taller. Keep left at a junction 500 m/yd below the open ground, and follow the ravine as it continues 2 km (1.25 mi) downhill to Southwest Pond Brook. There is no bridge, although the ruins of the original structure remain. ATVs have created a new route to the right about 400 m/yd before the river; keep straight.

Beside the brook there is a lovely spot to take a break, and despite a little ravine the water is easily crossed. On the other side, the old road follows the ravine, then passes a gravel pit and under a power line to emerge on Highway 316, about 100 m/yd from St. Paul's Cemetery in Queensport, 1.5 km (0.9 mi) from Southwest Pond Brook.

Retrace your route. The return walk will be steeper, but you get to see the barrens one more time, and that will be worth the effort.

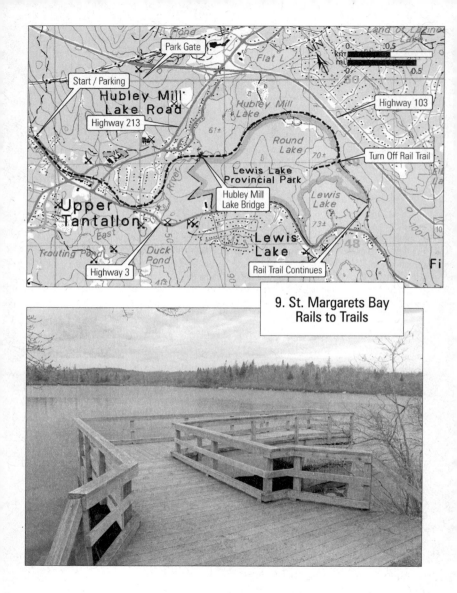

Park Gate

Start / Parking

Hubley Mill
Lake Road

Highway 213

Hubley Mill
Lake

Round
Lake

Highway 103

Turn Off Rail Trail

Lewis Lake
Provincial Park

Hubley Mill
Lake Bridge

Lewis
Lake

Upper
Tantallon

Lewis
Lake

Highway 3

Rail Trail Continues

9. St. Margarets Bay Rails to Trails

9. St. Margarets Bay Rails to Trails

◄---► 10 km (6.25 mi) return

⏱: 2+hrs

🚶: 2

Type of Trail: crushed stone, natural surface

Uses: walking, biking, horseback riding, ATVing, snowshoeing, cross-country skiing, snowmobiling

⚠: Animals. Motorized vehicles. Road crossings.

📱: Adequate throughout.

Facilities: benches, picnic tables, outhouses

Gov't Topo Map: 11D12 (Halifax)

Trailhead GPS: N 44° 41' 37.8" W 63° 53' 10.9"

Access: Take Exit 5 off Highway 103 onto Highway 213, in the direction of Highway 3 (Peggys Cove). Follow Highway 213 for 2.3 km (1.4 mi), turning right onto Highway 3. After 1 km (0.6 mi), turn right into the parking lot next to "Bike and Bean," 5401 Highway 3.

Introduction: The St. Margarets Bay Rails to Trails Association, a decidedly ambitious group of volunteers, has developed the 33 km (20.6 mi) section of abandoned rail line between Hubley, the end of the Beechville–Lakeside Timberlea (BLT) Trail, and Hubbards, where it connects to the Aspotogan Trail, as a shared-use recreational trail.

I thought that a 66 km (41.25 mi) hike might be too much for most walkers, so have chosen to focus on a section of the trail that starts at a café

and connects to a provincial park. At 10 km (6.25 mi), it can be completed easily by most healthy walkers.

Route Description: The trail starts at the former French Village Station, which was built in 1904 by the Halifax and Southwestern Railway, before the community's name changed to Upper Tantallon. It is now home to a combined bike shop and café, which provides you with a wonderful opportunity for a coffee and/or pastry either at the start or conclusion of your walk.

Start your walk back in the direction of Halifax. The wide, crushed-stone pathway is unmistakable, and on a busy weekend you are likely to find yourself sharing it with cyclists, horseback riders, ATVers, and other walkers especially. There is little signage on such an obvious

route, although the association tries to maintain — too often unsuccessfully against vandalism — kilometre markers. If there, you might see the 4-8 km (2.5-5 mi) signs.

For the first 1.8 km (1.1 mi), until you cross Fox Hollow Drive, the trail is squeezed into the small space between Highway 3, on your right, and French Village Station Road, on your left. There are many houses and businesses — including a Superstore — near or right beside the trail, with innumerable access points. Once Highway 213 is crossed, about 1 km (0.6 mi) from the station on the former rail bridge above the road, most of the houses on the left disappear,

Trans Canada Trail

One of the most exciting recreational developments in the world is the construction of a nationwide, multi-use pathway connecting all ten provinces and three territories. In Nova Scotia, the main route of the trail runs from Amherst to North Sydney.

The former rail line from Halifax to Lunenburg is part of the Trans Canada Trail system, which will eventually exceed 23,000 km (14,375 mi) when completed. Several routes profiled in this book, such as Chain of Lakes, Guysborough Shoreline, and St. Margarets Bay Rails to Trails are part of the Trans Canada Trail network.

Trans Canada Trail
Sentier Transcanadien

but the sounds of traffic on busy Highway 3 are still loud.

But as you approach a small stream, the East River, the trail curves left, away from Highway 3, and crosses Fox Hollow Drive. It also begins to climb. For 800 m/yd beyond, the road follows the river through an attractive wooded area, the water bubbling over exposed rocks on the right, slightly lower than the path. There are still houses nearby, but far fewer, and on larger, tree-covered lots.

At 2.6 km (1.6 mi), the trail crosses a bridge over the East River on the Hubley Mill Lake Bridge; the lake is that large body of water to the left. There is even a bench on the far side. One house on the lake is quite close to the bridge, and you can see many structures on the far side; these are the last houses you will see on this route.

For the next 350 m/yd the trail curves around the lake, your forest a cover of healthy hardwoods. For the next 550 m/yd you climb away from the lake, the forest dense on both sides, and shortly after the path crosses a small brook it begins to level out. By 3.5 km (2.2 mi), the trail is following the brook, and the forest is gradually giving way to a large bog, on your right.

You parallel this large open area, past another bench, for about 500 m/yd before re-entering the forest. You might notice automobile sounds again; the trail passes within 100 m/yd of Highway 103, which is to the left, and there is an informal side trail that will take you roadside. It can be quite noisy.

The trail has been in a right-hand curve for almost 1 km (0.6 mi), when you cross a bridge over a small brook and the path straightens somewhat. About 150 m/yd past the bridge, you come right beside Round Lake, and you can see some of the park structures in the water there.

Just after the rail trail passes the end of the lake, watch for a footpath leading off to the right. Turn here, and follow it over the rocky ground. This is unsigned, but easy to follow, and Round Lake should always be close on your right. Within 150 m/yd you should reach the crushed-stone pathway of Jerry Lawrence (formerly Lewis Lake) Provincial Park at a lake lookoff. Follow this for another 200 m/yd, and you will arrive at the wheelchair accessible pier that extends into Round Lake. It is meant for fishing, not swimming; the lake is stocked several times throughout the season with brook and rainbow trout.

There are many picnic tables available, as well as outhouses. This makes the park a wonderful spot to relax and have a picnic before beginning your return trip.

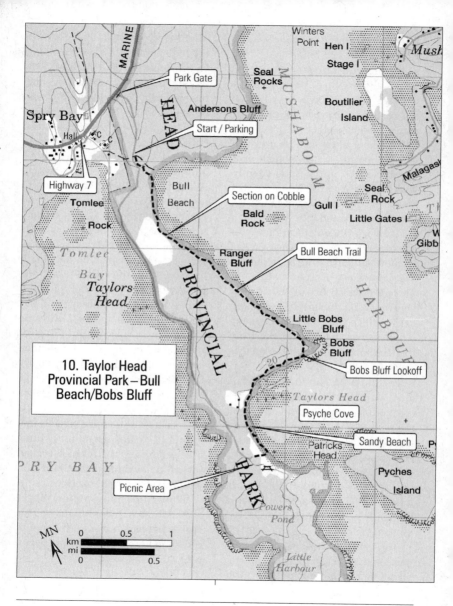

Park Gate

Andersons Bluff

Start / Parking

Bull Beach

Section on Cobble

Bald Rock

Ranger Bluff

Bull Beach Trail

Little Bobs Bluff

Bobs Bluff

Bobs Bluff Lookoff

Psyche Cove

Sandy Beach

Patricks Head

Picnic Area

Powers Pond

Highway 7

Tomlee

Rock

Tomlee

Bay

Taylors Head

Spry Bay

Hall

HEAD

PROVINCIAL

PARK

PRY BAY

Little Harbour

MARINE

MUSHABOOM

Winters Point

Hen I

Stage I

Seal Rocks

Boutilier Island

Seal Rock

Gull I

Little Gates I

Mush

Malagash

Gibb

W

HARBOUR

Taylors Head

Pyches Island

10. Taylor Head Provincial Park – Bull Beach/Bobs Bluff

MN

0   0.5   1
km
mi
0   0.5

10. Taylor Head Provincial Park – Bull Beach/Bobs Bluff

◀- - -▶ 11.5 km (7.2 mi) return

⏱: 3+hrs

🏃: 3

Type of Trail: natural surface

Uses: walking, snowshoeing

⚠: Animals. Variable weather conditions.

⛺: Adequate throughout.

Facilities: change houses, interpretive kiosk, picnic tables, outhouses, water

Gov't Topo Map: 11D15 (Tangier)

Trailhead GPS: N 44° 50′ 16.4″ W 62° 34′ 42.1″

Access: Taylor Head Provincial Park is approximately 100 km (62.5 mi) from Halifax on Highway 7, and 11 km (6.9 mi) from Sheet Harbour. A large road sign marks the entrance; turn onto a dirt road and drive 800 m/yd to the Bull Beach trailhead, on the left. Watch for a sign.

Introduction: Situated on Nova Scotia's rugged Eastern Shore, Taylor Head is a rocky finger projecting 6.5 km (4.1 mi) into the Atlantic Ocean. Encompassing more than 16 km (10 mi) of coastline, including more than 1 km (0.6 mi) of magnificent white-sand beach, the headland is littered with glacial erratics deposited throughout the peninsula.

I have selected this route because the Bull Beach Trail may be one of the least hiked in the park, yet combined with the Bobs Bluff Trail it is very scenic. In additional, because it starts only 800 m/yd from the highway gate,

it can be much more easily accessed for those long months when the park in not officially open.

This might be a bit long for a family hike, but except for its length it is a fine choice for new hikers.

Route Description: The trail does not follow the old road down to the beach, but heads into the forest to its right and meanders through the spruce, crossing over a moss-covered stone wall, to arrive at the water 400 m/yd from the trailhead. To your left is Bull Beach, which is worthwhile exploring, but the footpath goes right.

The path parallels the shoreline, and begins as a well-defined footpath, bordered by bright green sphagnum moss, beneath a canopy of thick white spruce. For the next 750 m/yd you are in this forest, although you pass through some openings where all the spruce have recently died.

At this point your hike takes you

right out onto the rocky cobble bordering Mushaboom Harbour, the ocean having pushed the shoreline inland, killing the coastal trees and washing away the path. As there is a huge bog just inland here, there is no option but to walk along the rocks.

After only 200 m/yd, the path leaves the cobble. This entire next section is very wet; my feet sank ankle deep in the sponge-like sphagnum moss. So when you find two little boardwalks about 100 m/yd later, you will likely find their appearance somewhat amusing. Equally droll is the signage system, usually yellow metal markers on the trees in the direction you are heading, and usually red for the opposite direction, but not always. Not to mention that there are sometimes orange markers too.

But the most important consideration is that the trail is signed, although it is sufficiently well defined that there should be no confusion as to your route. And there are many boardwalks as well, such as the long one at 1.8 km (1.1 mi), but when I hiked in October 2011, there was always much more bog than boardwalk.

Shortly after this, the path climbs behind a small headland, Ranger Bluff, and is out of sight of the water. The terrain is a little hillier through here, requiring some minor climbs, and the trail does not rejoin

Mushaboom Harbour again for almost 650 m/yd.

For the next 1.1 km (0.7 mi), the path continues to follow the coastline. Then, in an area of dead spruce and coming up to a large hill, it turns 90° to the right. Just 65 m/yd later, you reach the junction with the Bobs Bluff Trail, where there is a map, 3.5 km (2.2 mi) from the start.

To your left 50 m/yd away is an exceptional lookoff perched on the massive exposed granite rock of Bobs Bluff, with broad views including Psyche Cove and the beach that is our final destination. A bench is available there.

Returning to the junction, turn left onto the Bobs Bluff Trail. This will be a somewhat rougher walk, with more rocks in the path and far more hilly. You are constantly climbing and descending, often through dense white spruce, though with regular views of the water.

Then, 700 m/yd from Bobs Bluff, you reach a steep rock face. Fortunately, a set of stairs assists you to the top where, appropriately, there is a lookoff. You do not remain this high for long, however, before you descend again, this time helped by two staircases. The vertical granite walls to your right force the trail to work around them.

Barely 200 m/yd later, an informal footpath leads out to the water, where

Boreal Chickadee

Curious and very comfortable around people, chickadees, with their easily recognizable *chik-a-dee-dee* call, are a frequent hiking companion. In the softwood forests of Nova Scotia, the boreal chickadee, distinguished by its brownish-grey head and the least common of the two varieties living in Nova Scotia, is often found.

Stand motionless and make a low, steady *pish-pish-pish* sound; this should soon result in several of the little birds lighting in nearby trees to get a closer look. Both species of chickadee remain throughout the year and in winter can often be seen in company with golden-crowned kinglets and red-breasted nuthatches.

you get attractive views of a sheltered cove, especially in the late-afternoon sun. Only one more hill remains, at the far side of which you emerge from the woods onto the main beach, barely 1 km (0.6 mi) from the Bobs Bluff Lookoff. You will find a map and a trailhead sign here.

Descend the small stairwell and continue along the gorgeous white-sand beach. The cottages you see on your right are private property, so keep moving. Likewise, continue past the first picnic tables you see about 400 m/yd from the stairwell. About 200 m/yd beyond this you will find a path through the dunes; leave the beach here, as this will take you to Taylor Head's main parking area, where there are covered tables, interpretive panels, outhouses, and other amenities.

Either lunch here or on the beach. Retrace your route to return to your car.

12. Blomidon Provincial Park

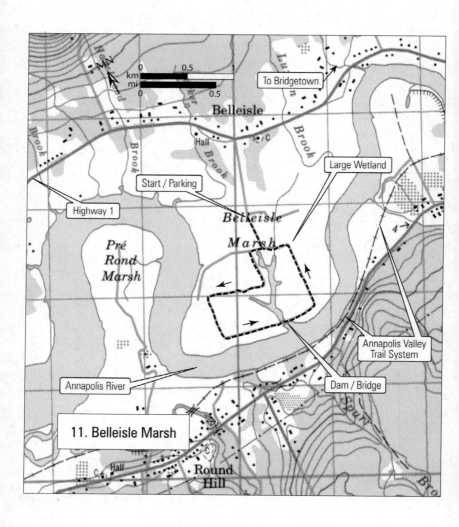

To Bridgetown

Belleisle

Large Wetland

Highway 1

Start / Parking

Belleisle
Marsh

Pré
Rond
Marsh

Annapolis Valley
Trail System

Annapolis River

Dam / Bridge

11. Belleisle Marsh

Round
Hill

11. Belleisle Marsh

◄--► 4.5 km (2.8 mi) return

🕐 : 1+hr

👥 : 1

Type of Trail: compacted earth

Uses: walking, biking, snowshoeing, cross-country skiing

⚠ : Yield to farm equipment. Hunting is permitted in season. Ticks.

🔽 : Adequate throughout.

Facilities: interpretive panels

Gov't Topo Map: 21A14 (Bridgetown)

Trailhead GPS: N 44° 47′ 39.2″ W 65° 24′ 01.6″

Access: From Exit 20 on Highway 101, head through Bridgetown on Highway 1 and continue for 12 km (7.5 mi). Watch for a sign for Little Brook Road. Continue on Highway 1 for 400 m/yd, turning left onto an unnamed dirt road. The Visitor Parking area is 900 m/yd on the right.

Introduction: The Belleisle Marsh Wildlife Management Area Project was initiated in 1990 as part of the North America Waterfowl Management Plan. The province purchased 283 ha (700 ac) of the broad low marsh to be protected as a waterfowl habitat. However, located on the rich alluvial plain of the Annapolis River, Belleisle Marsh includes some of the most productive agricultural land in the Nova Scotia. So, 69 ha (170 ac) were left as wetlands, and 135 ha (333 ac) are being managed as upland habitat, but 79 ha (195 ac) are being used for agricultural production.

There is no formal trail at Belleisle Marsh, but the wide, soft earth roads used by the farmer's machinery describe a loop that passes through rich farmland, adjacent to the Annapolis River, and next to several wetlands. This is an easy and scenic pastoral walk, although it can be punishing in the summer because no trees shade you from the scorching Annapolis Valley sun. I recommend it in the spring and fall.

Route Description: This is a short, flat walk around a broad grassy marshland that is a wonderful birdwatching location. At the parking area, a large interpretive panel features a good map of the small peninsula, which looks almost like a thumb pressing into the Annapolis River, forcing the water to flow around it.

Although the parking area sits at a four-way junction, begin your walk by continuing along the extension of the road you drove in on. The area around you is flat and extensively cultivated; expect to see some farm equipment in action somewhere along your route.

After about 400 m/yd you reach a T-junction; turn right. You will cross a small, sluggish brook in about 50 m/yd, where you might startle your first waterfowl, and reach the next junction about 50 m/yd beyond that. Expect ducks and even herons to be lurking in the shallow watercourse.

Either direction will do, but I turned left and followed the more distinct track as it parallels the creek, which flows towards the Annapolis River. There is a bit of an embankment on the left, which is grass covered, so you rarely see the water. To your right are large fields with grasses ripening in the intense heat. (I hiked this in June.)

After a straight section of 400 m/yd, the road turns right 90°. It continues another 150 m/yd before making a little dip and curving to cross another, smaller outflow that in the late summer is choked with thick vegetation. When you make your next 90° turn in 350 m/yd, this time to the left, you will have walked almost 1.5 km (0.9 mi) from the trailhead.

To your right you can catch glimpses of the lower Annapolis Valley, as you continue another 500 m/yd until you reach the dike sep-

arating the shallow marsh from the river. The hills of South Mountain on the far bank appear quite close, and if you climb to the top of the dike you can see the rail trail on the shore opposite, barely 300 m/yd away. The view along the river is extensive, the lines of North and South mountains disappearing into the distance in both directions.

Turning left again, 250 m/yd later the trail bridges a substantial brook that bisects the marshlands. This bridge also acts as a dam to regulate the flow of water between river and marshlands. The path continues for a further 600 m/yd before it turns left again and away from the perimeter of the marsh, about 3.2 km (2 mi) into your walk. You are leaving the Annapolis River behind, so take this final opportunity to climb the embankment and savour the rich blue of the water, richly contrasting with the vibrant summer greens.

The treadway of the next section is almost completely grass covered, and stays more in the interior of the protected area. Expect quite a bit of birdlife in the surrounding bushes and grasses. Continue straight, past another gate, for 700 m/yd. Here, on your right, is a large wetland, home to a wide variety of waterfowl. If you have not done any birdwatching before, now is the best opportunity.

Turn left from this junction, hav-

ing walked almost 4 km (2.5 mi). About 150 m/yd later you cross one final stream, and 150 m/yd farther you complete the loop when you reach the first T-junction. Turn right, and finish the final 400 m/yd back to the trailhead. Side trips up embankments or around the perimeters of wetlands may have added a few hundred metres/yards to your walk, but the loop described is slightly more than 4.5 km (2.8 mi).

Aboiteau

When the French settlers arrived in Acadie in Nouvelle-France, they decided that farming the salt marshes was preferable to clearing the dense forests. In order to do so, they built dikes to protect the land from the ocean and devised an ingenious mechanism to drain the fields.

Their creative solution was a wooden sluice containing a hinged door, called an aboiteau. At low tide it opened to allow fresh water to drain, but at high tide the advancing water shut it tightly and prevented salt water from flooding the fields.

The aboiteau was so effective that it is still used on dikelands today.

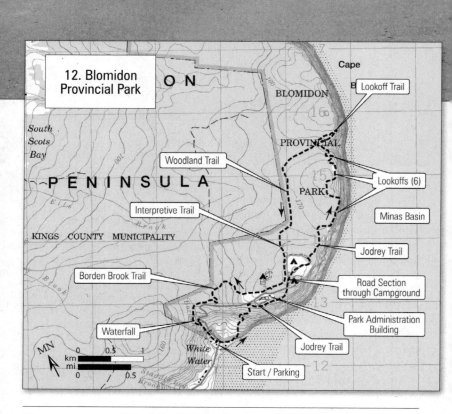

12. Blomidon
Provincial Park

Cape

BLOMIDON

Lookoff Trail

South
Scots
Bay

PROVINCIAL

Woodland Trail

Lookoffs (6)

PENINSULA

PARK

Minas Basin

Interpretive Trail

KINGS COUNTY MUNICIPALITY

Jodrey Trail

Borden Brook Trail

Road Section
through Campground

Park Administration
Building

Waterfall

MN

km
mi

White
Water

Jodrey Trail

Start / Parking

12. Blomidon Provincial Park

◄- - -► 12.5 km (7.8 mi) return

🕐 : 4+hrs

🧗 : 4 [steep hills]

Type of Trail: natural surface, compacted earth, crushed stone

Uses: walking, snowshoeing

⚠ : Animals. Poison ivy. Road crossing. Steep cliffs.

📱 : Good throughout except on the Woodland Trail.

Facilities: camping, firewood, garbage cans, outhouses, picnic tables, playgrounds, showers, water

Gov't Topo Map: 21H08 (Parrsboro)

Trailhead GPS: N 45° 15′ 26.1″ W 64° 21′ 05.0″

Access: From Highway 101, take Exit 11 north to the junction with Highway 1 and Highway 358. Follow Highway 358, through Canning, for 13.6 km (8.5 mi), turning right onto Bessie Road. Continue 1.8 km (1.1 mi), turning left onto Pereau Road. Follow Pereau Road for 10 km (6.25 mi), turning right into the parking lot at the park entrance. The trail starts at the far end of the lot.

Introduction: Blomidon Provincial Park is positioned on the top of an impressive 183 m (600 ft) cliff that both overlooks and dominates the skyline of the Minas Basin. The brick red of the sandstone slopes is mirrored in the broad mud flats that are exposed by the retreat of the highest tides in the world, an elevation change of 12 m/yd.

The views of the Minas Basin and the Parrsboro shores from this trail's lookoffs are breathtaking, and the area has long been considered one of the most scenic on the mainland of Nova Scotia. Blomidon Provincial Park, 759 ha (1,875 ac) in size, was established in 1965 after the land was donated to the province for preservation. The park, usually open from mid-May to early September, includes seventy campsites and picnic areas both at the top and at the bottom of the hill.

People who want a shorter, easier walk should drive to the picnic area at the top of the hill and begin their hike from there.

Route Description: At the start there is an excellent map of the park's trail network and a sign indicating the direction of the Jodrey Trail. Walk down the staircase, cross the small brook, and turn right as soon as you are across and in the field. In barely

100 m/yd you reach a junction where you turn left. A sign warns you of a steep cliff, but a steel mesh fence, on your right, limits your access in that direction.

Your path is a wide cleared strip through a grassy field, passing some picnic tables, to your left, about 400 m/yd after you started. Very quickly you gain excellent views of the coastline to the south. Once you enter the forest, the trail immediately becomes narrow, rocky, and strewn with tree roots. Red flashes of paint on the trees (yellow in the opposite direction) sign your route.

The climb also becomes steeper, the path switching back and forth across the hillside to reduce the grade. This is the most challenging section of your hike, as you plow right up the steep hillside — although assisted by at least three stair systems. Finally, just after it almost levels, about 1 km (0.6 mi) from the start, you reach a lookoff where there is a picnic table.

Less than 10 m/yd later you reach a junction, where a blue hiker sign directs you right where you work through the trees near the top of the steep slope. To your left is the upper picnic area, where there are outhouses and drinkable water, and the park administration building. There are a few exits, including one at about 1.7 km (1.1 mi) that has a trail map.

Signs indicate the route of the Jodrey Trail, which soon comes into an area where all the trees have died. Wooden posts tipped in red paint mark the route, which works its way up to a grassy field about 2 km (1.25 mi) into your walk.

The trail has been rerouted from what was shown on the map at the trailhead. The blue hiker "Jodrey Trail" signs direct you onto the campsite road, heading in the direction of sites 28-70. Follow this about 200 m/yd before turning right (there is a Jodrey Trail sign); continue another 400 m/yd through the campground, passing a playground, outhouses, and a large field with grand views to your right. Just before leaving the field, there is a map on the right.

About 100 m/yd past the map sign you leave the road, to the right; signs direct you on the Jodrey and towards the Lookoff Trail. The trail heads through very attractive forest, well back from the cliff face, and is quite wide. After 600 m/yd, it narrows back into a footpath, and 200 m/yd later you reach a pond, where the path turns right about 90°.

Perhaps 300 m/yd later, about 3.8 km (2.4 mi) from the start, you reach the first major lookoff, a large wooden platform with an interpretive panel and an impressive view of the Minas Basin. For the remainder of the Jodrey Trail the path meand-

ers through the forest, curving out to the cliff to a lookoff — there are six — then turning back among the trees. The views are all worthwhile, and the forest through which the trail passes is lush. In the spring, expect to find carpets of red trilliums.

After another 1.6 km (1 mi) you reach the junction with the Lookoff Trail, about 5.4 km (3.4 mi) from the start. Turn right, crossing a small gully; in less than 100 m/yd you will find the Indian Springs monument. The Lookoff Trail continues about 400 m/yd through mature spruce stands to a final cliffside panorama, two viewing areas facing northeast

and southeast, then returns on a different route to finish almost at the end of the Jodrey Trail.

The return trip follows the Woodland Trail, completely forested except for a rapidly regenerating clear-cut area just outside the western boundary of the park the path — but no lookoffs. After almost 3 km (1.9 mi), the trail widens as you approach the campground and the entrance to the Interpretive Trail.

Continue for less than 250 m/yd, then turn right at the junction with the Borden Brook Trail. This works past the campground and picnic area, staying in the forest, crossing

Red Trillium

In late May or early June, before leaves have spread on the overhanging rich deciduous trees, small deep red, three-petalled flowers poke through the brown carpet of dead leaves and give proof to the end of winter with a riot of powerful colour.

Look, but do not smell! Pollinated by flies, the red trillium, also known as "Stinking Benjamin," is reputed to have a scent like rotting meat. (Personally, I have never checked.) Instead, just enjoy the welcome contrast they provide to the still bleak-looking forest floor.

the road to the Group campsite about 1 km (0.6 mi) later and emerging onto a large field 100 m/yd later. (By the way, on Borden Brook we are following yellow paint flashes.)

The trail follows the edge of the forest for 300 m/yd before returning under the trees, then it descends steadily. There are several turns and junctions with old woods roads, but all are well signed. After leaving one

ATV track, 1.5 km (0.9 mi) after leaving the field, you face an extremely steep, rocky descent for the next 350 m/yd down to Borden Brook.

Once across the bridge, turn left towards the waterfall. You can only go 135 m/yd; all of it is challenging, cut into the slope of a narrow, steep ravine. Back on the main trail, a much easier 500 m/yd is all that remains. (Look for a carved owl about 100 m/yd from the bridge.) You follow the brook for a time, soon reaching a pathway surfaced in crushed stone. You emerge from the woods in sight of the parking lot, where a crosswalk directs you over the park entrance road, where you began.

Hypothermia

Teeth chattering? Shivering uncontrollably? Hands numb? You may be entering Stage 1 Hypothermia, and are in danger. Hypothermia is a condition in which a person's temperature drops below that required for normal metabolism and bodily functions, and it can happen in spring and fall as well as winter. If you experience these symptoms, end your hike immediately. If you are far away from the trailhead, a mildly hypothermic person can be effectively re-warmed through close body contact and by drinking warm, sweet liquids.

Layering

Instead of having a separate outfit for each weather condition, put together a variety of clothes for different purposes: base (underwear), insulation, and outer shell. Mix and match according to conditions, adding, removing, or changing items as you warm up or cool down and if weather conditions change. Synthetic clothes for layering tend to be lighter, more durable, and provide greater flexibility.

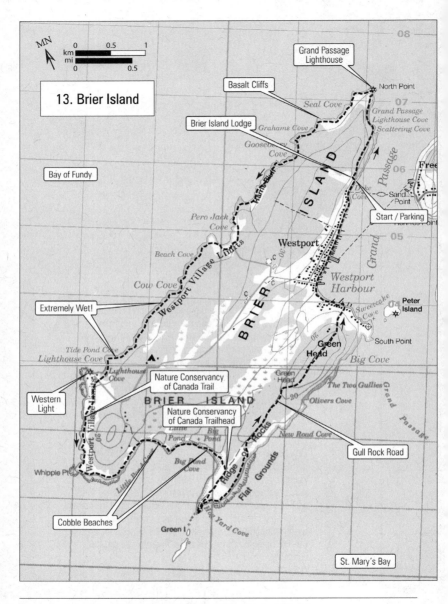

13. Brier Island

Grand Passage Lighthouse

Basalt Cliffs

Brier Island Lodge

Start / Parking

North Point

Seal Cove

Grand Passage Lighthouse Cove
Scattering Cove

Grahams Cove

Gooseberry Cove

Harris Bluff

Pero Jack Cove

Bay of Fundy

Sand Point

Menzies Point

Beach Cove

Westport Village Lights

Westport

Cow Cove

Westport Harbour

Extremely Wet!

Peter Island

Sweetcake Cove

South Point

Tide Pond Cove
Lighthouse Cove

Green Head

Big Cove

Western Light

Lighthouse Cove

BRIER ISLAND

Nature Conservancy of Canada Trail

Nature Conservancy of Canada Trailhead

Green Head

The Two Gullies

Olivers Cove

Ridge of Rocks

New Road Cove

Gull Rock Road

Whipple Pt.

Westport Village Lights

Little Pond

Big Pond

Big Pond Cove

Flat Grounds

Cobble Beaches

Green I.

Tide Yard Cove

St. Mary's Bay

MN

km
mi

0   0.5   1

0   0.5

Bay of Fundy

13. Brier Island

◄---► 20 km (12.5 mi) return

⏱: 5+hrs

🏃: 5 [distance, rugged terrain]

Type of Trail: natural surface, compacted earth, asphalt

Uses: walking, biking*, horseback riding*, ATVing*, snowshoeing, cross-country skiing*, snowmobiling*

⚠: Motorized vehicles. Road crossings. Variable weather conditions. High winds and waves.

📵: No reception from 1 km (0.6 mi) after North Point to Little Pond Cove. Good otherwise.

Facilities: garbage cans, interpretive panels, picnic tables

Gov't Topo Map: 21B01 (Meteghan), 21B08 (Church Point)

Trailhead GPS: N 44° 05′ 34.6″ W 66° 01′ 43.1″

Access: From Exit 26 on Highway 101 at Digby, continue on Hwy 101 for 3.9 km (2.4 mi), turning right onto Middle Crossing Road. At the junction with Highway 217, in 4.1 km (2.6 mi), turn left and continue 41 km (25.6 mi) to Digby Neck/Long Island Ferry. Cross to Tiverton, and follow Highway 217 for 17.5 km (10.9 mi) to Westport/Freeport Ferry. Cross to Westport; turn right and drive 1 km (0.6 mi) to Brier Island Lodge, 557 Water Street, and park there.

Introduction: Brier Island is an exceptional place, in a province crammed with special places. It is Nova Scotia's westernmost point; its symmetrical basalt cliffs resemble the Devil's Causeway in Ireland; it hosts one species of rose, *Geum peckii*, found nowhere else in Canada; and bird-watchers come from all over the world each fall to view the migration, particularly of many species of hawks.

Because it is an island, vehicular traffic is light, permitting roads to be comfortably incorporated into a walk. Most trails are privately owned, and unmaintained, although the Nature Conservancy of Canada has recently constructed a 5 km (3.1 mi) footpath on its 485 ha (1200 ac) property. Considering the scenery through which you will pass, I consider the occasional meander through boggy barrens or over unmarked rocky coastline a fair price.

Only people comfortable trekking through occasionally challenging terrain should attempt the full hike around the island; most should

content themselves with the Nature Conservancy's trail.

Route Description: The Brier Island Lodge is very welcoming to hikers, so this is a good place to use as your base, both for lodging and to start your hike. From there, turn left and continue up Water Street to the road's end at North Point and the Grand Passage Lighthouse, about 1.4 km (0.9 mi).

The view, when there is no fog, is impressive, across the Bay of Fundy to New Brunswick. A picnic table is available if you wish to snack. From here, head left along the coastline. There is no sign, but there are several distinct tracks; I recommend keeping close to the coastal fringe.

Continuing over the treeless shore, within 350 m/yd you have rounded a point and are in Seal Cove. Expect to see seals — seriously, they are usually there. The exposed basalt rocks work in steps down to the water, although in some places there is a vertical cliff.

The coastline through Grahams Cove, Gooseberry Cove, and over Harris Bluff is lovely, and the paths distinct but unsigned and unmaintained. Your route is likely to meander as you dodge wet areas and explore headlands. I only saw one house on this section, about 2 km (1.25 mi) from North Point.

Rounding the rocky and challenging headland into Pero Jack Cove, about 3.8 km (2.4 mi) from North Point, you encounter the remains of a gravel pit, where a road accesses the coastline and you can return to Westport if you choose.

Continuing along the shoreline, the trail gets somewhat rougher, with more wet ground and the trees pushing out almost to the water. Dense thickets of rose bushes block the path, and even the ATV tracks seem barely able to fight through them. Also, there are numerous "decorations" set up along the coastline, wooden spars festooned with fishing floats — very interesting.

Cow Cove, at 5.4 km (3.4 mi) from North Point, is quite distinct, a shal-low indentation in the coastline boasting a cobble beach. But the trail from here to the Western Light is extremely messy, with frequent large bogs and even ponds, making walking along the rocks and cobble your only dry option — unless it is stormy and the waves are high.

You see the Western Light long before you reach it, which you do 7.6 km (4.75 mi) from North Point. The trail actually reaches a road and continues across; a short diversion is required if you want to go to the brightly striped lighthouse.

As soon as you cross the road, heading towards Whipple Point, walking conditions improve. The route is higher above the ocean,

situated on a rocky base, and it is a treeless barren. Barely 200 m/yd from the road you reach a Nature Conservancy interpretive panel about the birds of Brier Island.

This is a gorgeous area, with numerous rocky outcroppings, high coastal cliffs, and jagged fingers of basalt reaching into the ocean. These gradually diminish as you approach Whipple Point, which is actually quite low, 1.6 km (1 mi) from Western Light.

Here you turn left almost 90°, as the path follows the coastline into Little Pond Cove. The route keeps improving, now even being surfaced with stones. After another 1 km (0.6 mi) you connect to Camp Road; keep right. You start walking along cobble beach, and about 200 m/yd later cross the barrier beach at Little Pond, then the one at Big Pond 700 m/yd after that.

The Big Pond barrier beach is almost 500 m/yd long, and once across

you find some rope barriers lining one of the paths. If you follow those, in 200 m/yd you reach several interpretive panels and the trailhead for the Nature Conservancy's hiking trail, 4.2 km (2.6 mi) from Western Light.

Continue to follow the coastline. This works its way around a slender, barren peninsula called "Ridge of Rocks," with more splendid views of basalt coastline, and the shore of the Nova Scotia mainland in the distance. After an additional 1.7 km (1.1 mi), I ended up leaving the shoreline and returning to Gull Rock Road.

From here, follow the dirt road uphill over Green Head, then down to Westport Harbour, about 2.8 km (1.75 mi). Turn left and follow the now asphalt road around the harbour and through the village of Westport back to the Brier Island Lodge, a final 2.3 km (1.4 mi). There are several stores and other businesses in the village where refreshments are available if you choose to tarry.

Basalt Shield

Acting as a shield from the ravaging tides of the Bay of Fundy to the softer soils of the Annapolis Valley, the dark, grey basalt rocks of the North Mountain were created as a result of repeated lava flows when the North American and African continental plates began separating about 200 million years ago.

Their columnar shape has created distinctive features such as the Balancing Rock, on Long Island on the Digby Neck, or the symmetrical eastern cliffs on Brier Island.

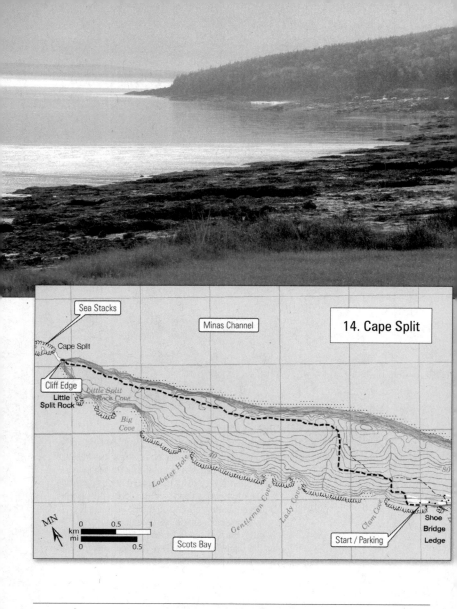

Sea Stacks

Minas Channel

14. Cape Split

Cape Split

Cliff Edge
Little Split Rock

Little Split Rock Cove

Big Cove

Lobster Hole

40

80

Gentleman Cove

Lady Cove

Clam Cove

Shoe Bridge Ledge

Start / Parking

Scots Bay

MN

km
0   0.5   1

mi
0   0.5

14. Cape Split

◄---► 16 km (10 mi) return
🕑: 4+hrs
🏃: 4 [distance]
Type of Trail: natural surface
Uses: walking, biking, ATVing*, snowshoeing

⚠: Animals. Motorized vehicles. Ticks. Cliffs. Hunting is permitted in season. Variable weather conditions. No signage.
🔷: Adequate throughout.
Facilities: none
Gov't Topo Map: 21H08 (Parrsboro)

Trailhead GPS: N 45° 18′ 52.8″ W 64° 25′ 45.9″

Access: From Highway 101, take Exit 11 north to junction with Highway 1 and Highway 358. Follow Highway 358, through Canning to its end in Scots Bay, for 30 km (18.75 mi). Turn left onto Cape Split Road, and follow it to its end in 2.6 km (1.6 mi).

Introduction: If mainland Nova Scotia contains an iconic hiking destination, it is Cape Split. Although it has never been a maintained trail, and only since 2007 has the land been owned by the public, nevertheless it seems as if every person you speak to wants to trek to the cape.

Once you are there it is easy to see why its fame has spread. You are perched on the grassy top of near-vertical cliffs, more than 122 m (400 ft) high, at the tip of a slender spear of land where the Bay of Fundy tides, constricted by the Minas Channel, roar past Cape Split in staggering volumes at unbelievable speeds.

This hike contains several dangers: the route is unsigned, and there are many informal paths that every year cause people to become lost. The cliffs, naturally, are quite dangerous, but the hilltops are deceptive, covered in thick grass that spills over the edge, with ground that slopes towards the cliff: you can literally walk off the edge without noticing you have reached it. Finally, because the tides expose a considerable amount of seabed, people try to find a way to the waterline. This is difficult; getting back up is even more so, and at high tide the coastal shelf is flooded. Exercise extreme caution on this hike.

Route Description: From the small parking area, where there is a sign with a trail map, you head immediately into the mostly softwood forest, skirting a small field to your right. You will immediately notice that the unimproved footpath is rocky, criss-crossed by roots, and often wet.

After about 250 m/yd you leave the field behind, and begin your climb. After about 500 m/yd you connect with an ATV track, soon crossing a small brook that often uses the trailbed as its course. In this next section, as you curve left and parallel the slope, there are even minor descents.

You do not remain on this shared track for long, and at 1.5 km (0.9 mi) your path makes a sharp turn right and begins to seriously climb again. After about 500 m/yd, in a lovely vale, the trail works left again and ascends its most steep climb of the hike.

There is only about 200 m/yd of sharp ascent, however, before the grade starts to lessen. You are now close to the Minas Channel, and when there are few leaves in the mostly hardwoods surrounding you, by 2.5 km (1.6 mi) you should be able to view the far coastline.

I particularly enjoy this section in the early spring. Needing to blossom before their sunlight is cut off by tree leaves, purple trillium and spring beauties literally carpet the hilltops. When the sun reflects off them, it can be a dazzling display, especially so soon after the winter greys.

In some respects there is little to remark about the next 5 km (3.1 mi). The path stays close to the north side of the cape and it undulates up and down, but never to an extreme climb or descent. Occasional views are available to your right; there are even one or two side tracks to a vantage point.

It is only when you near Cape Split that the trail begins to change. The first thing you notice is a sound, a growing murmur that builds to a roar. That is the ocean; the tide flows past Cape Split at speeds up to 40 kph (25 mph), racing in opposite directions every six hours and thirteen minutes. The sound of its passage is audible.

When you reach a deep notch in the hillside to your right, which requires the path to veer left around it, you have almost arrived. A glimpse into the deep gully on your right shows how high you are, and how sheer are the hillsides. Little more than 150 m/yd beyond that point, you leave the trees and enter a grassy field.

When you emerge from the forest, the view is first disorienting, then staggering. You appear to have reached the end of the earth, which, in a local sense, you definitely have. The grass seems to merge with the ocean, which stretches away to the horizon.

You do not notice the cliffs right

Cliffs

Trails such as Cape Split are popular because of their extraordinary views. But their dangers are often just as impressive. These particular cliffs, more than 100 m (300 ft) high, not only have no guardrails, but they also feature a downward-sloping verge, an actively eroding edge, and slippery vegetation (particularly with the morning dew or frost). Enjoy the view, but respect the risks.

away; it is only when you advance that the full realization of your position becomes clear. You are perched on a small grass platform, rounded uncomfortably towards the precipices. The ground falls away abruptly in front and to your right, and the final tip of Cape Split has been carved into several free-standing rocky sea stacks, each smaller the farther into the Minas Channel they reach, whittled remorselessly by the powerful tidal currents.

The view, as you wander (cautiously) around your privileged perch, is truly magnificent. There are no other sights quite the same in Nova Scotia.

Side trails work down the coastline to your left, in the direction of Little Split Rock. Under the spruce here you will find evidence of previous campers. Explore in this direction if you wish, but return to the grassy tip and retrace your route to return to your car.

4. Crowbar Lake

7. North Granite Ridge Trail

8. Queensport Road

15. Delaps Cove

16. Gaspereau River

17. Hectanooga

15. Delaps Cove

◄---► 9.5 km (5.9 mi) return

🕐 : 2+hrs

🏃 : 2

Type of Trail: natural surface, compacted earth, crushed stone

Uses: walking, mountain biking*, ATVing*, snowshoeing, cross-country skiing*, snowmobiling*

⚠ : Animals. Motorized vehicles. Ticks. Poison Ivy. Hunting is permitted in season.

📱 : Adequate throughout, except for some inland portions of the Charlies Trail.

Facilities: benches, interpretive panels, outhouses, picnic tables

Gov't Topo Map: 21A12 (Digby), 21A13 (Granville Ferry)

Trailhead GPS: N 44° 45' 39.2" W 65° 38' 55.6"

Access: From Exit 22 on Highway 101, turn onto Highway 8 (north) and follow for 5.8 km (3.6 mi) to the junction with Highway 1. Turn right, and follow Highway 1 for 2 km (1.25 mi) to Granville Road. Turn left, and follow for 9.5 km (5.9 mi), turning right onto Hollow Mountain Road. After 6.5 km (4.1 mi), turn left onto Shore Road. After 950 m/yd, a road sign directs you left onto a steep dirt road. Follow for 2 km (1.25 mi) to the parking lot: 2077 Shore Road West, Delaps Cove.

Introduction: Situated on the ocean side of North Mountain, exposed to the harsher weather of the Bay of Fundy and located on infertile basalt rock, Delaps Cove was typical of the poor lands granted to Black Loyalist immigrants. The 1871 census listed 70 inhabitants here, with all the families but one being black. Despite their disadvantages, some managed to become fairly prosperous; James Francis owned 125 acres of land, twelve sheep, two oxen, a house, a barn, and a boat. Just one house remains occupied today, and only the rock walls, apple trees, and foundations remind us of this former community.

The Municipality of Annapolis County opened the Delaps Cove Trail in 1985, making it one of the oldest municipal wilderness paths in the province. There is much to see on this walk: the remains of the former settlement, a waterfall, interesting plant life, the Bay of Fundy itself, and possibly seals and whales!

Trail Description: A large interpretive display at the trailhead contains a map of the path network, and there

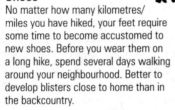
are outhouses at the parking lot. You will also find a guest book waiting for your signature. Turn right; the 2.2 km (1.4 mi) Bohaker Trail quickly takes you downhill to the ocean over a well-maintained footpath, covered in crushed stone and with frequent boardwalks and good drainage.

Following the coastline, the trail overlooks exposed basalt ridges running from the forest edge into the water, their rectangular shape making it look like a coastal staircase leading into the Bay of Fundy. An interpretive panel explains more about the distinctive rock formations along this coastline. This section along the shoreline is frequently very wet, and rocks have been placed to provide dry footing.

After 400 m/yd you reach Bohaker Brook, where a small cliff-lined cove has been etched into the basalt, and tidal action has jammed it with driftwood. There might even be a rope to allow the adventurous to descend down the steep slope into the cove.

At the back of the hollow is the 13 m (43 ft) Bohaker Falls. The trail heads inland now, although a side path crosses the brook, ends in a lookoff at the top of the waterfall, and provides one of the most scenic views of the hike.

Leaving the coast, you move inland through lovely spruce and balsam fir stands paralleling the brook. Well-constructed bridges lead you to the other side. At a junction, turn left and cross a bridge to return to the parking lot, crossing an impressive old stone wall en route. Those wishing to continue the trek, head right, where the sign indicates to the Charlies Trail.

After a challenging 300 m/yd on a hilly, much more rugged footpath, the right-hand track connects to the Shore Road, the remains of the former highway that once ran the length of North Mountain. There is no sign here, and it looks like an old woods road, not a footpath. Turn right.

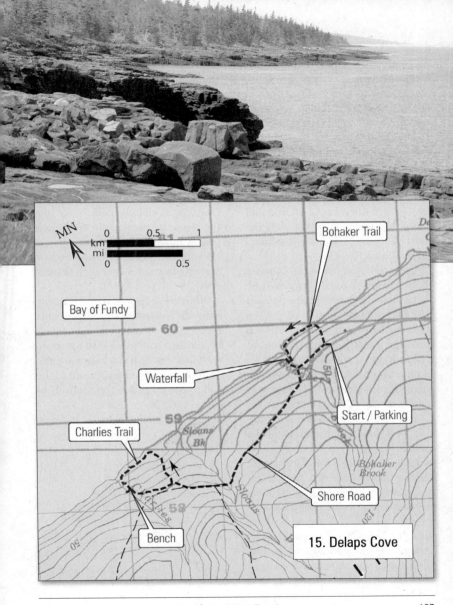

MN

Bay of Fundy

Bohaker Trail

Waterfall

Charlies Trail

Start / Parking

Shore Road

Bench

15. Delaps Cove

Sloans Bk

Bohaker Brook

There is little shade along this 2.7 km (1.7 mi) stretch, so wear a hat and carry lots of water on hot, sunny summer days. It is on the Shore Road that ATVs, mountain bikes, or snowmobiles (although there is rarely enough snow) might be encountered.

Few landmarks are available on the Shore Road, and there is little to see except the ever-changing pattern of logging in the woods alongside. The descent to the crossing of Sloans Brook, at about 2 km (1.25 mi), and the climb up the other side, is the most distinctive characteristic found on the Shore Road.

One small sign marks the entrance to the 1.9 km (1.2 mi) Charlies Trail; do not miss it. Goldenseal, a popular folk remedy for mouth pain, grows abundantly among northern beech fern, bracken fern, and bunchberries. There is no map here, and the path is on a natural surface. Almost immediately you encounter a junction; a green arrow directs you right.

You pass through attractive, mature forest, the trail dropping down a gentle slope towards the ocean. This section is only about 500 m/yd, and the last 50 m/yd are very soggy! The path stays in the forest and parallels the coastline. Several side trails take you to lookoffs at the water's edge, with the last spur featuring an observation deck overlooking Charlies Cove and the coastline towards Digby

Gut. On a clear day you might even sight the Digby–Saint John Ferry.

From here, you head away from the water and uphill, where you encounter the foundation of the Pomp household and an interpretive panel giving the history of the area. Just beyond that there is a second, smaller site.

Anyone wanting a rest, or a few moments of contemplation, should take a side trail across Charlies Brook. Only 100 m/yd long, it descends into the steep, narrow ravine to a bench beside and above the cascading waters enfolded by mature softwoods, a perfect place for a sandwich or even a nap.

Returning to the main trail, the footpath leaves the stream and cuts through the forest, crossing several little ridges and gullies, to return to the Charlies Trail entrance on the Shore Road. From here, return to the parking lot at the Bohaker Trail, about 3 km (1.9 mi).

Coyote

Nova Scotia's most recently arrived large mammal resident is also one of its most elusive. Clever, adaptable, and unbelievably resilient, coyotes arrived in Nova Scotia as a continuation of their eastward migration across the continent. The first coyote kill was in 1977, and today they are widespread throughout the province.

Eating almost anything, including plants and berries, coyotes prefer snowshoe hare and other small mammals, including domestic pets.

Rarely exceeding 30 kg (65 lb), coyotes resemble large brownish-grey dogs. Accustomed to being shot on sight by farmers and hunters, coyotes are quite shy about being seen. Usually all you will find is scat in the middle of the trail, with the fur of recent kills mixed through it.

If you do sight a coyote nearby, slowly walk away, never turning your back. If it approaches, try to scare the animal away by making noise, swinging sticks, and generally acting aggressive.

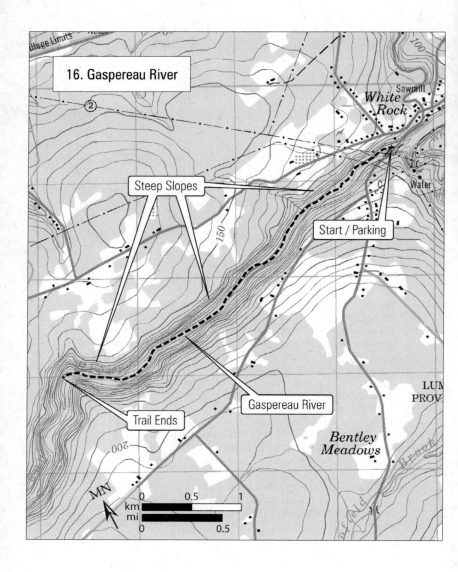

16. Gaspereau River

Steep Slopes

Start / Parking

Gaspereau River

Trail Ends

Bentley Meadows

White Rock

Sawmill

Water

LUM PROV

MN

0   0.5   1
km
mi
0   0.5

16. Gaspereau River

◄- - -► 9 km (4.5 mi) return
⏱: 2+hrs
🧍: 3
Type of Trail: natural surface
Uses: walking, snowshoeing

⚠: Animals. No signage. Hunting is permitted in season. Seasonal flooding.

🔋: Minimal at the trailhead; none in the gorge.

Facilities: none

Gov't Topo Map: 21H01 (Wolfville)

Trailhead GPS: N 45° 02′ 53.8″ W 64° 24′ 53.2″

Access: Take Exit 11 off Highway 101 and turn uphill towards the Old Orchard Inn. Drive 1.5 km (0.9 mi) to the intersection with Ridge Road. Turn right, and drive 2.5 km (1.6 mi) to the village of White Rock. Turn right at the first stop sign, and left at the next sign less than 100 m/yd later, towards Black River. About 500 m/yd later, park on the left, after crossing a bridge over the Gaspereau River.

Introduction: This route is an informal track used by fishers that follows a river up a narrow, steep-sided canyon. I loved it, and even though there are farms at the top of the slopes on both sides of the river, I found this always felt much more isolated than it actually is.

Although Kings County has developed a number of other good trails, I so enjoy this that I had to include it in this edition.

Route Description: The path begins on the far side of the bridge from the parking lot, on the opposite side of the road. There might be notices posted for fishers on some of the trees, but otherwise no signage.

The track is not difficult to find, however, as there is only a narrow band of earth at the bottom of the steep slopes next to the river. The distinct path parallels the river, which is to your left.

Within 200 m/yd you reach your first obstacle, an area where, at high water, the track is submerged. But even then a short wade of a few steps takes you back onto the dry trail.

The hill slope on your right is quite steep and high, and as you continue, rocky outcroppings are frequent. As a result, about 400 m/yd into the walk you reach an area where water from the slope has turned the dirt track into a quagmire.

The Gaspereau River is shallow

but fairly wide, especially in the summer and fall. Expect to find king-fishers, eagles, and herons in the little pools in the bends in the stream. The area is densely forested, with mostly large hardwoods on the valley floor and equally thick softwoods on the slope. During the summer, you should always be sheltered by a solid leafy canopy.

At 500 m/yd you cross a small, un-bridged brook that is deeply etched into the hillside, and 100 m/yd beyond that you may find a plank (I did) laid across the next wet area, and 50 m/yd later an even more substantial bridge.

Through this section the path is quite wide and distinct, and passes through an attractive level area for another 200 m/yd before trail and hillside reconnect. For the next while the trail stays close to the slope, somewhat far from the river, and crosses numerous wet areas.

Again, there is no signage, and there are no structures, but some small bridges have been built and stone walkways have been placed in many of the wet areas. At times, the pathway is wide enough for two to walk side by side, and there is evidence that recent deadfall has been removed from the path.

At about 1.2 km (0.75 mi), the path climbs slightly above river level on the slope and passes through an area

of hemlock. To your left, there is access to a little point that extends into the river. Barely 100 m/yd farther, the trail climbs onto a slate outcropping with views of the river, about 5 m (16 ft) below.

The path looks more like an old road now, wide and level. At 1.5 km (0.9 mi) you should notice that the river side of the trail has been stabilized with an extensive slate wall. The slopes on the right are gorgeous, covered with large trees and very little understorey, providing long views uphill. Every fold in the ground is home to a tiny stream, which bubbles across the path.

In about 300 m/yd, the path drops back down to river level, onto another flat area, where the slope recedes off to the right. In the spring, the ground is carpeted by thousands of ferns, and the hardwoods are quite high. This lasts only another 300 m/yd, when you must climb again to pass a narrow section where the Gaspereau River has pushed close to this bank.

At 2.4 km (1.5 mi), a most attractive brook descends the slope on your right, the stream a series of cataracts visible far up the hill. The path is often very easy, with few roots or rocks. The most challenging section, so far, was the first 500 m/yd.

On the next flat shelf, about 400 m/yd later, you cannot even see the Gaspereau River, but you always hear it. When you rejoin the river, at about 3 km (1.9 mi), the path begins another climb. It also changes, narrowing into a single track footpath. The valley constricts as well, with the ridges closing in on both banks.

For the remainder of the walk, the path no longer looks like a road. In autumn, falling leaves from maple, beech, and birch can completely obscure the trail. This next hill is more challenging, and the rugged section lasts for nearly 500 m/yd before descending into the largest, flat area of the walk.

This was my favourite spot, the next 600 m/yd very attractive, raised slightly above the river and covered by healthy, mature hardwoods. It was also deep in shade, even at only 6 p.m. on one of the longest days of the year. Unlike other flat areas, the path remains closer to the steep slope, but the river is not too far — maybe 20 m/yd — to see or to reach through the open forest.

But once again the valley narrows, and you must scamper up the hillside. This time it is somewhat different; you climb perhaps 10 m/yd above the river on a very narrow, rocky footpath. Footing is difficult; the most challenging yet.

Fortunately, this section lasts only 200 m/yd before you reach another — the final, and not very wide — flat area. The river is much closer, and

you have several views of the canyon walls on the far bank.

After 150 m/yd, at 4.5 km (2.8 mi), the walkable trail ends. The path becomes virtually impassable because of deadfall and the disappearance of any shelf at the bottom of the hillside. There is some evidence that the route may continue on the far back, but there is no bridge and it is not possible to proceed without fording. Retrace your route back to your car.

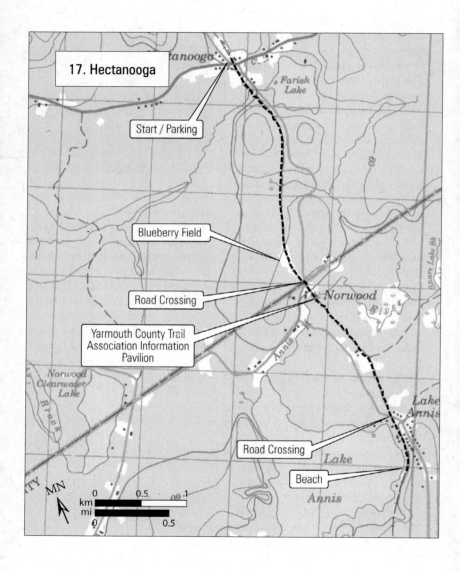

17. Hectanooga

Start / Parking

Blueberry Field

Road Crossing

Yarmouth County Trail Association Information Pavilion

Road Crossing

Beach

MN

km
mi

0   0.5   1

0   0.5

17. Hectanooga

◄---► 10 km (6.25 mi) return

⏱: 2+hrs

🚶: 2

Type of Trail: compacted earth, crushed stone

Uses: walking, biking, horseback riding, ATVing, snowshoeing, cross-country skiing, snowmobiling

⚠: Animals. Motorized vehicles. Road crossings. Ticks.

🧭: Adequate throughout.

Facilities: bench, interpretive panels

Gov't Topo Map: 21B01 (Meteghan)

Trailhead GPS: N 44° 05' 34.6" W 66° 01' 43.1"

Access: Take Exit 32 off Highway 101 onto the Hectanooga Road. Drive in the direction of Hectanooga for 11 km (6.9 mi), into the village. The parking lot and trailhead pavilion are on the left where the trail crosses the road.

Introduction: When the Dominion Atlantic Railway was abandoned from Kentville to Yarmouth in 1990, trail advocates dreamed of developing it into a recreational corridor. On October 26, 2011, the Annapolis Valley Trail System, a 200-km (125-mi) long network of trails, was officially opened. Although a few gaps remain, mostly around the huge bridges at Bear River and Weymouth, the majority of the former rail line is available for use by everything from walkers to ATVs.

I enjoyed and profiled this section, partly because the vegetation through most of the route is so attractive, partly because of the benches and interpretive signage, but mostly because the beach at Lake Annis was so welcome, and makes a very pleasant destination.

Route Description: You begin at a trailhead of the Sentier de Clare, in Digby County. The elaborate pavilion there includes a map, detailed information about the trail's development and construction, emergency numbers, and a considerable amount of historical information about the former railway. The first 3 km (1.9 mi) of the route is managed by this group.

Cross the Hectanooga Road, and proceed along the long straight track. To your left are some houses and cleared lands, and you can see the paved Norwood Road, running parallel. The former rail bed is elevated above the surrounding lands, providing a good view.

You might notice the lushness of the hardwood trees in this area. Massive oak and maple tower overhead, and there are many more pines than spruce. When I hiked in mid-September, the brush alongside the trail was thick and tall grass grew right to the fringe of compacted earth of the treadway.

When you approach the first road crossing, 500 m/yd from the trailhead, you will be warned by a sign, In addition, metal posts have been mounted in the middle of the path to slow motorized vehicles, with yellow-painted rocks flanking it on both sides. Shortly after passing this point, sheltered by a high canopy of mature hardwoods, you should notice Farish Lake to your left.

After about 800 m/yd, the path begins a long, gradual curve to the right. By 1.1 km (0.7 mi) you have settled into another long straightaway, now lower than the ground to your left, and also distinctly, but gently, descending. There is no human habitation visible, and the trail feels quite isolated.

At 1.8 km (1.1 mi) there is a slight turn to the left, followed by another straight section. The land has changed somewhat, with occasional bogs found on both sides of the track.

A field glimpsed on your right is a commercial blueberry farm; signs warn you not to sample. The path curves left, and at 2.75 km (1.7 mi) crosses the Norwood Road through an elaborately signed, rock-lined lane. On the far side of the road there is a trail etiquette sign.

There is also another blueberry field, this time on the left. Facing it, just in front of an abandoned farmhouse, is a sturdy concrete bench. Also, in sight just 250 m/yd farther, the entire distance lined by large yellow-painted rocks, is a quite substantial bridge, crossing the modest (in summer, at least) Annis River.

On the far side of the bridge is another trail pavilion, this one announcing that you have entered the area of the Yarmouth County Rails to Trails Association. This large eight-sided structure contains a plethora of natural, historical, and trail development information, and also informs you, as does a sign on a nearby concrete bench, that it is 30 km to Yarmouth. (But not for this hike!)

From the bridge, there is an 800 m/yd straight section that is thickly forested on both sides. Just before you begin another gradual right-hand turn, you should see a field and two houses on the right. Those are the only signs of habitation, at least for another 700 m/yd, when you abruptly

Hiking with Dogs #2

Just as you need supplies for yourself, you will need some for your dog. Water and food are critical — there is no guarantee that you will find any on the trail — as is a small pet first aid kit, including flea and tick protection. And make sure that your dog's tags are securely attached, in case you become separated.

reach, and cross, the Lake Annis Road — where there is yet another concrete bench.

Where before there was seeming wilderness, suddenly there are houses all around you. Even the treadway changes, with it now covered in crushed stone. On your right, Lakeside Lane parallels your route and the waters of Lake Annis are visible through the trees.

You cross Lakeside Lane 200 m/yd after the Lake Annis Road, and now there are numerous entrances to the trail from adjoining houses. The path curves gently right, coming closer to the lake, the houses ending.

At almost exactly 5 km (3.1 mi) from Hectanooga you should find a distinct side trail that leads down the insignificant embankment to the lakeshore. Leave the rail trail here and follow this; you reach a small, but exquisite, sandy beach, which is a popular swimming area and a place for residents to dock their boats.

Stop here; snack, swim, and relax for a while. When you are ready, retrace your route back to Hectanooga.

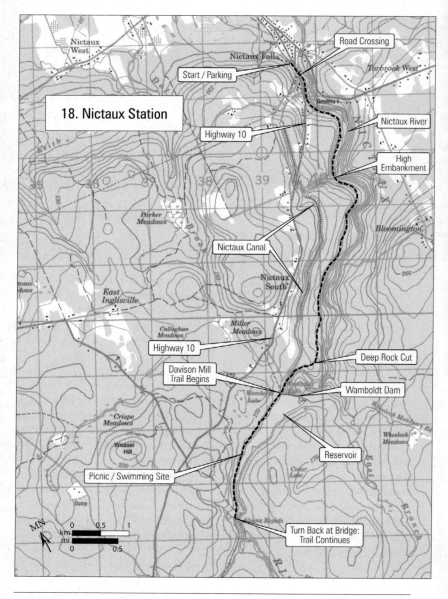

18. Nictaux Station

Road Crossing

Start / Parking

Highway 10

Nictaux River

High Embankment

Nictaux Canal

Highway 10

Deep Rock Cut

Davison Mill Trail Begins

Wamboldt Dam

Reservoir

Picnic / Swimming Site

Turn Back at Bridge: Trail Continues

Nictaux West

Nictaux Falls

Torbrook West

Parker Meadows

Bloomington

East Inglisville

Nictaux South

Callaghan Meadows

Miller Meadows

Crispe Meadows

Wheelock Meadows

Weasel Hill

Cedar Lake

Dump

MN

km
mi

0   0.5   1

0   0.5

18. Nictaux Station

◄---► 21 km (13 mi) return

🕐: 5+hrs

🏃: 4 [distance]

Type of Trail: compacted earth, crushed stone

Uses: walking, biking, horseback riding, ATVing, snowshoeing, cross-country skiing, snowmobiling

⚠: Animals. Ticks. Road crossing. Motorized vehicles.

📱: Good throughout except between km 2 (mi 1.25) and km 5 (mi 3.1).

Facilities: none

Gov't Topo Map: 21A14 (Bridgetown)

Trailhead GPS: N 44° 54′ 24.2″ W 65° 01′ 55.7″

Access: From Exit 18A on Highway 101, turn onto Victoria Road, and follow for 1.2 km (0.75 mi) to Highway 1. Turn right onto Highway 1, and follow for 1.9 km (1.2 mi) to the junction with Highway 10 in Middleton. Turn left, and continue for 5.5 km (3.4 mi) towards Nictaux Falls; a large parking area is on the right.

Introduction: In 1889, the Nova Scotia Central Railway offered service between Bridgewater and Middleton, which continued until the line was abandoned by Canadian National in 1984. Since that time snowmobilers and ATVers have increasingly used this corridor. Although the walk from Nictaux Falls as far as Alpena Rapids is fairly long, this is a relatively easy hike and many people should be able to complete it. The most difficult por-

tion is at the start, so the return will be much less challenging.

The section climbing the Nictaux River is extremely attractive. Erosion has carved the deep valley through the Ordovician slate bedrock of the South Mountain Foothills. The granite of the South Mountain Rolling Plain, which you will find up around Alpena Rapids, is much more resistant to weathering.

Route Description: From the parking lot, the trail runs in both directions. There is a large sign that indicates that this trail was developed by the South Shore Annapolis Valley Recreational Trails Association, and that this spot is Nictaux Station. Turn left, and walk the 200 m/yd to Highway 10, which you cross.

Road and trail separate almost

immediately, with the highway climbing the slope of the hillside while the wide, compacted earth pathway heads into beckoning gap of the Nictaux River gorge. The slope on the right soon looms steeply to tower over the path, and 300 m/yd from the road crossing a small brook seeps down from the road. You will be able to hear cars above you to the right and the roar of Nictaux River to your left and below.

Hugging this steep hillside, the trail begins to climb gently, but noticeably. You might spot tiny Smiths Island in the river below, and at about 1 km (0.6 mi) you cross a small bridge across a steep stream cascading down the almost vertical cut. Trees from the right bank lean overhead, providing shade on most days, those on both slopes being primarily hardwoods. About 200 m/yd beyond that a track separates to the left and heads down to the Nictaux River.

As it climbs, the trail curves back and forth. It sometimes crosses embankments high above the ground on either side; sometimes it passes between rock cuts about twice as high as the average person. The elevation gain is appreciable, more than 70 m (230 ft). The far side of the valley is sometimes visible when the trail skirts near the edge of the cliff, but the dense foliage of the hardwoods

that mostly cover the hillside usually blocks any views.

After nearly 6 km (3.75 mi) from the trailhead you enter the most extensive rock cut, about 250 m/yd in length. The trail association has surfaced the trail here with crushed stone. Just beyond that, you get a good view to the left, and shortly afterward the vegetation gives way on the right.

If you climb up the small, grassy hillside, you will find the Nictaux Canal. Continuing another 500 m/yd along the trail, you reach Wamboldt Dam and the beautiful reservoir it created by blocking the Nictaux River gorge. A walk is possible to the far end of the 400 m/yd earthen embankment of Wamboldt Dam, and this is worthwhile both for the views of the reservoir and the outflow at the far end. The small deep lake is long and narrow, and canoeists and kayakers are often found on its placid surface.

At the junction of the trail, dam, and Nictaux Canal, a dirt road heads right and uphill 1 km (0.6 mi) to Highway 10. Directly ahead, a small bridge crosses over the sheer rock walls at the mouth of the canal and a sign announces that we are starting on the 33 km (20.6 mi) long Davison Mill Trail. (Don't worry, you won't be doing all of it.) You are 7 km (4.4 mi) from Nictaux Station.

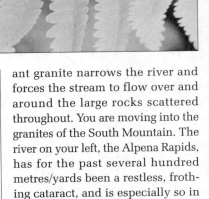

Canadian Tiger Swallowtail

From late May to early July, one of the most colourful sights in the air along many of the inland trails will be the large Canadian Tiger Swallowtail butterfly. As it enjoys living along the edge of deciduous and mixed forests, the corridors created by the wider rail trails make a perfect habitat.

Although usually seen singly, I noticed that fresh coyote droppings in the middle of the path could attract a surprising number in an apparent (and faintly disgusting) feeding frenzy.

For the next 2 km (1.25 mi) the trail follows the shore of the reservoir, staying quite close to the water's edge. About 1.5 km (0.9 mi) from the dam you will find a favourite camping and swimming site of the local residents, the sandy ground sheltered by towering pines. This is a good place to rest, then turn back, because alongside the reservoir, the path is no longer climbing.

If you continue, the surroundings become more rugged; erosion-resist-ant granite narrows the river and forces the stream to flow over and around the large rocks scattered throughout. You are moving into the granites of the South Mountain. The river on your left, the Alpena Rapids, has for the past several hundred metres/yards been a restless, froth-ing cataract, and is especially so in the spring runoff.

I suggest continuing another 1 km (0.6 mi), stopping at the junction of Oakes Brook and the Nictaux River, about 10 km (6.25 mi) from the start. The hearty could follow this trail all the way to New Germany, 45 km (28 mi) farther. However, for most I recommend that you turn back and retrace your route to Nictaux Station.

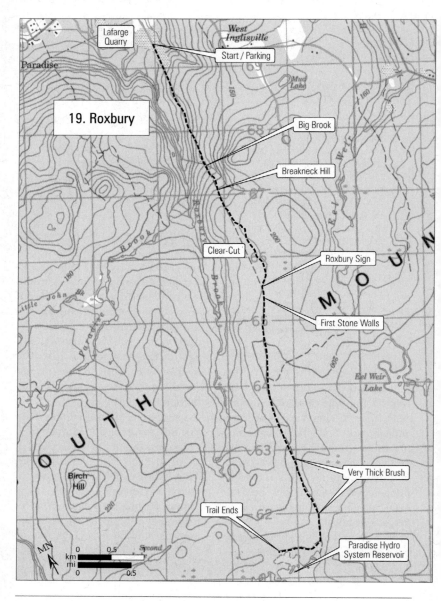

Lafarge Quarry

Start / Parking

West Inglisville

Paradise

Mud Lake

19. Roxbury

Big Brook

Breakneck Hill

Clear-Cut

Roxbury Sign

First Stone Walls

M O U N

Eel Weir Lake

Very Thick Brush

Birch Hill

Trail Ends

Paradise Hydro System Reservoir

S O U T H

MN

km
mi

0   0.5

0   0.5

19. Roxbury

◄--- ► 18 km (11.25 mi) return

⏱: 5+hrs

🏃: 5 [distance, remoteness]

Type of Trail: compacted earth, natural surface

Uses: hiking, biking, horseback riding, ATVing, snowshoeing, cross-country skiing, snowmobiling

⚠: Animals. Ticks. Hunting is permitted in season. No signage.

📱: Adequate reception for first 7 km (4.4 mi); poor beyond that. Good at the reservoir.

Facilities: none

Gov't Topo Map: 21A14 (Bridgetown)

Trailhead GPS: N 44° 51' 16.6" W 65° 11' 19.1"

Access: Turn off Highway 101 at Exit 19, turning onto the Elliot Road towards Highway 1 and Lawrencetown. Travel 2.3 km (1.4 mi), turning left onto Highway 1. After 700 m/yd, turn right onto Lawrencetown Lane and cross the Annapolis River to the junction with Highway 201 in 850 m/yd. Turn right, and drive 3.5 km (2.2 mi) to West Paradise, turning onto a dirt road on your left, at the "Roxbury Road" sign. Continue on the narrow lane, past the Lafarge Paradise asphalt pit, about 1.1 km (0.7 mi) from Highway 201. Park on the left, and continue on foot.

Introduction: Near the end of this old road we will discover some of the remains of the abandoned settlement of Roxbury. This isolated community once boasted its own school, two lumber mills, a grist mill, and numerous farms and orchards. Today, all that remains of the settlement are graveyards, apple orchards, foundation depressions, and moss-covered stone walls, although some ramshackle hunting cabins have been erected on former homesteads.

Roxbury Road leads into a surprisingly remote area of the province; I have done this hike three times, and seen a bear on two occasions — once less than 10 m/yd away. I recommend this route for experienced outdoor persons only.

Route Description: Where the road becomes too difficult for ordinary cars, you will find a small grassy parking area. Your path continues along the rocky and eroded track, which heads straight uphill. You will climb almost 150 m (500 ft) in this hike, most of it in the first 2.5 km (1.5 mi).

From the beginning you see evidence of logging in the woods flanking the road. There are numerous side trails created by logging equipment, and there are downed trees everywhere. The first 700 m/yd is uphill, then there is a short respite where larger logging roads split off. About 300 m/yd later, at the far end of a large clearing, there may be a sign mounted on a tree saying that you have reached "D. Gaul Landing."

You continue to see evidence of logging, but even so, many of the surrounding trees are quite tall and should provide some shade. The road is rough, but there are a few strips of broken asphalt on some of the steeper hillsides.

At 2 km (1.25 mi) you cross a small bridge, where there is a sign telling you that this is Big Brook. After this, the climb becomes even steeper for the next 500 m/yd. Another sign, on the right, tells you this is Breakneck Hill. (I also saw a sign, at about 1.8 km (1.1 mi), saying that it was 3 km (1.9 mi). I suspect that is the distance from Highway 201.)

Once the path (nearly) levels the vegetation includes many more hardwoods, including some old maples. Several species of fern cover the ground beneath them. About 600 m/yd beyond the brook there is a grassy clearing large enough to make a reasonable campsite.

At 2.8 km (1.75 mi) you emerge from the forest into a massive clearcut, which has removed everything in a broad swath on your right. Your route keeps close to the vegetation boundary on your left, and actually may no longer be on the original route of the Roxbury Road.

After the attractive forest through which you have been walking, the clear-cut looks horrible. However, due to the removal so many trees, you actually gain a view of the surrounding hills and the contours of the land.

For the next 1.7 km (1.1 mi), the clear-cut continues on your right, except for slender strips of vegetation left where tiny creeks flow past, and the trail hugs the treeline on the left. Even the road looks grim, with large puddles that must be waded suddenly appearing.

Then, about 4.5 km (2.8 mi) from the start, the trees on the left are also

Black Bear

Everyone's greatest fear while hiking, the black bear is an impressive and dangerous animal. Growing to 215 kg (470 lb), it is capable of climbing trees and of bursts of speed up to 30 kph (19 mph). It is primarily nocturnal and usually solitary, except for a brief time during mating season and when a mother is caring for cubs.

However, the black bear is itself usually frightened of encountering people. From the beginning of human settlement in Nova Scotia, bears have been hunted and driven from nearby habitations. Making noises while you are walking will announce to a bear that you are nearby, and it will almost certainly withdraw before you see it.

Opinions differ on the best course of action to take should you actually come face to face with a bear. Always remember that they are wild and unpredictable animals that are capable of causing you serious injury or even death, and behave accordingly.

Then the road becomes a creek bed, and the track narrows considerably, suitable only for walking. The tread-way is now almost completely grass covered, and alders crowd in from both sides of the old road. Occasional stone wall remains can still be seen, and even a well sign or two. ATV tracks separate on either side, fairly frequently.

The path begins to descend, and clear-cuts reappear on both sides of the road. At 8.4 km (5.25 mi) you reach a junction; turn right, and within 200 m/yd you will reach the shores of Paradise Hydro System Reservoir. You will find the remains of numerous campfires: this is a popular overnight destination for fishers. The route ends at 9 km (5.6 mi), at a concrete retaining wall at the edge of the water. Return along the same route.

clear-cut, and you end up passing through a bleak looking landscape. After about 500 m/yd you reach what appears to be a roadside quarry where sand and gravel was excavated to help surface the road.

Fortunately, at 5.3 km (3.3 mi) you should sight a sign on a tree to your right welcoming you to "the community of Roxbury." There will be a guestbook in an orange mailbox. Another sign announces "Roxbury, 1865, population 67." The stone fences of the community begin shortly afterward, and the beautiful, thick forest resumes — immediately and dramatically.

For the next 1.5 km (0.9 mi) the walls border both sides of the road, and small signs put up by the historical society indicate where wells and other former structures can be found. You may notice several hunting cabins, maintained by descendants of the original settlers.

20. Uniacke Estate

◄ --- ► 12 km (7.5 mi) return

⏱: 3+hrs

🚶: 3

Type of Trail: compacted earth, natural surface, crushed stone

Uses: walking, snowshoeing, cross-country skiing*

⚠: Animals.

📱: Good throughout.

Facilities: benches, garbage cans, interpretive panels, outhouses, picnic tables

Gov't Topo Map: 11D13 (Middle Sackville)

Trailhead GPS: N 44° 54' 06.7" W 63° 50' 39.4"

Access: Turn off Highway 101 at Exit 3 and drive 200 m/yd to Highway 1. Turn left, and follow for 7.5 km (4.7 mi), through the village of Mount Uniacke, to the Uniacke Estate Museum Park entrance. Turn left, and follow the dirt road for 200 m/yd to the parking area.

Introduction: One of Nova Scotia's two "Great Roads" required for movement of troops and cattle after the founding of Halifax, the Halifax-Windsor road featured weekly stage service by 1801, with mail and passenger service offered by 1815. Mount Uniacke, located halfway between the communities, made a convenient watering place.

Uniacke Estate Museum Park is a great place to visit on a weekend and stretch your legs, and their walking routes are a fine addition to Nova Scotia's trail network. This is an ex-cellent site for novices to try shorter distances over varied terrain.

Each trail is well marked with coloured wooden triangles affixed to trees, a different colour for each named trail. In addition, maps are posted at all trail junctions, and usually found at the halfway point of longer routes, such as the Post Road.

Route Description: Several walking opportunities begin from the parking lot. An interpretive panel located next to the estate house contains a map showing the trail network. The walks vary in difficulty with all fitness levels being accommodated, including a wheelchair accessible walk.

From the parking lot, walk behind the main estate building and follow the wide, gravelled path as it leads into a field past several other buildings. This is the formal trailhead. Turn right here; the Hot House Trail

Trails Are Not Always Easy to Follow

Even official trails, if they have not been maintained recently, can be difficult to follow. Brush and other vegetation can obscure the route. Animal or unofficial trails may also be in the same area, making it hard to determine which path is the correct one. Novices should rethink their trip if uncertain. It's safest to backtrack (head back the way you came) than risk losing the trail.

loops around a small hill, passing alongside some attractive moss-covered stone walls, and connects to the Post Road Trail, where you turn left. There is also a bench here, tucked away in the thick spruce.

The Post Road Trail, the Old Windsor Road, continues in a virtually straight line almost to the far end of the property, where the old track rejoins Highway 1. This has more rugged footing than the paths near the estate building, but is still easy walking. In the thick young spruce, there is little to note until you reach a map at the halfway point, about 1.9 km (1.2 mi) from where you left the parking lot.

The track is mostly grass covered at this point, and, except for frequent wet areas much of the year, pleasant walking for the 400 m/yd until

you reach the bridge crossing Black Brook and the first junction with the Wetlands Trail.

Keep straight on the Post Road Trail, which seems a little rougher once past the junction, although I found this one of the most pleasant of the entire walk. There are several small climbs, but the 900 m/yd to its end passes too quickly.

Turn left onto the Wetlands Trail, marked with forest green triangles. This is the most remote and challenging walk on the estate. A narrow footpath over alternatively rocky and boggy ground, most people will find it requires good footwear.

The 300 m/yd to Clark Lake are challenging; it looks as if the area has been clear-cut, but it is only the result of storm damage, and the path is forced to pick its way around the

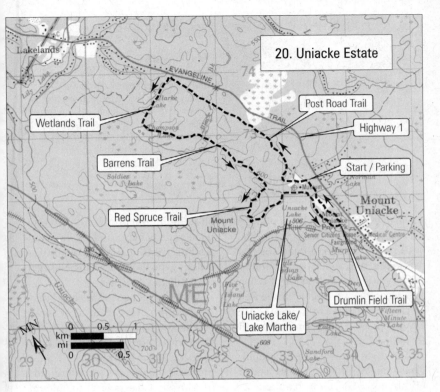

20. Uniacke Estate

Post Road Trail

Highway 1

Wetlands Trail

Barrens Trail

Start / Parking

Red Spruce Trail

Mount Uniacke

Drumlin Field Trail

Uniacke Lake/ Lake Martha

many downed trees. The small pond is a welcome sight, and the forest improves somewhat after that. And 950 m/yd after leaving Clark Lake the path delivers you to a rocky outcropping perched above the water of Thompson Lake.

The Wetlands Trail turns sharply left now, and traces the shore of the small lake to a small cove about 150 m/yd later, about 4.5 km (2.8 mi) from the start. It leaves the water, and

climbs a small ridge, heading back in the direction of the estate. After 400 m/yd you connect with Black Brook, which is on your right, and the trail follows it for a short distance before turning left away from it to connect with the Barrens Trail, about 1 km (0.6 mi) from Thompson Lake.

Turn right onto the Barrens Trail, which immediately descends to cross Black Brook on a decidedly homemade looking bridge. Once across,

Mayflowers

The floral emblem of Nova Scotia since 1901, the delicate, pink mayflower blossoms even before the last winter snows have melted. But do not look for huge stems and large blossoms. The tiny mayflower, also known as trailing arbutus, is found in clusters of tiny blossoms huddled on the forest floor.

the path leaves the brook and plunges through the most difficult part of the walk: rocky, heaps of dead spruce, and extensive sections of flooded pathway. (I hiked this in May.) When you reach the junction with the Red Spruce Trail, 1.5 km (0.9 mi) after leaving the Wetlands Trail, you will be relieved.

Turn right onto Red Spruce; conditions improve quickly, drying as you climb, and heading into an area of magnificent mature spruce stands. In only 700 m/yd you reach a sign telling you that continuing forward is "Not a Trail," while your path curves sharply left and descends to the shore of Lake Martha, a steep drop.

Red Spruce finishes paralleling the shoreline, connecting to the Lake Martha Loop 800 m/yd from the turning point, 8.5 km (5.3 mi) total distance so far. Continue on the crushed-stone pathway along the

shore, which features interpretive panels and benches and is the easiest walking, until you reach the bridge crossing the brook draining Norman Lake 400 m/yd farther.

Continue along the lakeshore, now the Drumlin Field Trail. After about 600 m/yd, this path curves left, away from the water, and 200 m/yd later connects to the Murphy Lake Trail, a trailhead outside the estate grounds on Murphy Lake, behind the Mount Uniacke fire hall. The Drumlin Field Trail keeps left, climbing the hill and emerging from the forest onto a grassy field with a superb view of Uniacke Estate.

Simply walk the 600 m/yd back to the parking area, completing your total hike of 12 km (7.5 mi).

Richard John Uniacke

Born in Ireland in 1753, Richard John Uniacke established himself as a lawyer in Halifax in 1781, eventually rising to Attorney General of Nova Scotia in 1797. In 1786, Uniacke acquired his first property, a grant of 305 ha (753 ac). Eventually acquiring, by 1819, consolidated holdings of 3,460 ha (8,546 ac), Uniacke developed a working farm and built what has been described as "one of Canada's finest examples of colonial architecture ... a grand country house in the Georgian tradition." Richard John died in his bed at Mount Uniacke in 1830.

In 1949 the remainder of the estate, approximately 900 ha (2,223 ac), was sold by the family to the Province of Nova Scotia, and in 1960 the property became part of the Nova Scotia Museum. Since 1951 the estate has been open to the public, with the main building being the principal attraction. Over the last several years, however, there has been a re-evaluation of use of the extensive property, culminating in the Landscape Management Plan in 1993. Under this ambitious multi-year strategy, the Uniacke Estate landscape will be restored to a period of 150 years ago and protected as an important cultural resource. Increased access to the property will be encouraged through recreational trail development.

23. Cape Chignecto Provincial Park

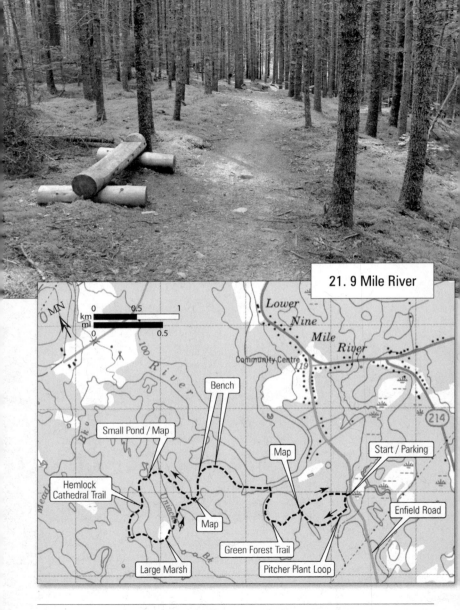

21. 9 Mile River

km
mi

Lower
Nine
Mile
River

Community Centre

Bench

Small Pond / Map

Hemlock
Cathedral Trail

Map

Large Marsh

Green Forest Trail

Map

Start / Parking

Enfield Road

Pitcher Plant Loop

21. 9 Mile River

◄---► 10 km (6.25 mi) return

⏱: 2+hrs

🏃: 3

Type of Trail: crushed stone, compacted earth, natural surface

Uses: walking, biking, snowshoeing, cross-country skiing

⚠: Animals.

📱: Adequate throughout.

Facilities: benches, garbage cans

Gov't Topo Map: 11E04 (Kennetcook)

Trailhead GPS: N 45° 00′ 35.0″ W 63° 33′ 20.3″

Access: Take Exit 7 off Highway 102, turning onto Highway 2 in the direction of Enfield. Continue for 2.2 km (1.4 mi), turning left onto Old Enfield Road. At 2.3 km (1.4 mi), keep right on Enfield Road. Continue 5.8 km (3.6 mi); turn left into the trailhead parking lot (signed).

Introduction: A number of small walking trails have been developed along the Halifax–Truro corridor. Most of these, such as those found in Milford and Brookfield, are less than 2 km (1.25 mi) in total length, well below the threshold of what I consider a "hike." One of the reasons for these shorter distance trails, other than the fact that they have been developed primarily for community recreation, is that the heavily settled Halifax–Truro corridor contains few large parcels of Crown land.

One notable exception to this is the fine network of paths developed near the community of Enfield in Hants County (East). This ambitious system, intended for mountain bikers as much as for walkers, is projected to eventually be made up of five "stacked" loops. (A stacked loop system is one where the trail is designed as a series of loops, each one attached to the far end of the nearer. This enables walkers to chose short, long, or a variety of intermediate lengths.)

In 2011, not all the paths were completed, so I assembled a route from what was available.

Route Description: A colourful trailhead map sign provides an overview of the eventual intended trail system. The walk starts on the Green Forest Trail, but as soon as you enter the forest, on an excellent treadway of crushed stone, you encounter a junction with the Pitcher Plant Loop.

Turn left, and for the next 700 m/yd you work your way on the wide trail over multiple boardwalks on the crushed-stone path until it reconnects with Green Forest. You will probably notice that the ground is very wet, with many boggy areas (hence the many bridges and boardwalks). Signage is good, with red metal markers attached to trees about 1.5 m (5 ft) high.

Turn left at the next junction, where there is another map. The crushed stone ends here and the trail narrows. Soon you encounter many small wooden boardwalks/bridges and almost as many wet and muddy spots in between them. (I hiked this in mid-May and it was very sloppy; I returned at the end of August and it was much drier.) The path crosses an ATV track 300 m/yd from the junction, and enters a lovely stand of hemlock less than 200 m/yd later.

Just after crossing a small bridge, you reach a T-junction, where the crushed stone resumes, roughly 800 m/yd from the last junction. There is no sign, and this is actually your closest point to the Nine Mile River, although you probably cannot see it through the thick vegetation lining the riverbank. Turn left, following what now appears to be an old road, ignoring several side tracks.

Within 150 m/yd the crushed stone ends again, and you find yourself on a narrow footpath. The land here slopes away to the right, and the trail works along the sloping ridge. Bridges are occasionally required to cross some deep gullies. Nearly 500 m/yd from the T-junction you reach an area where all the trees have been knocked over and are all stacked in the same direction; this was not done by human agency but by the oft-amazing power of nature.

You soon pass into undamaged forest, where the ground is a vast carpet of green sphagnum moss. When you reach a rough long bench overlooking a woodland meadow, you have walked 2.1 km (1.3 mi). (This will also be a junction for the yet-uncompleted Forest Glade Trail.)

Your route swings left, working its way through a thickly forested hilltop; the ground slopes away to the right. The dense spruce roof almost blocks the sun from the path, which is a brown earthen stripe crossing a blanket of brilliant green. Another bench — at which you may rest but will likely only feed mosquitoes — has been situated in these woods at 2.7 km (1.7 mi).

Continuing through the forest, the trail crosses an old road (again, well signed) 500 m/yd past the bench, then over a long boardwalk and to the next junction, where there is a map. Keep straight along the path as it works along the side of the low hill. The land falls off to the left. Only 650 m/yd after crossing the old road, Green Forest turns left, crosses another boardwalk, and reaches the junction (with the unfinished Witches Cauldron), where there is another map, beside a small, unnamed pond, 4 km (2.5 mi) from the start.

Inexperienced walkers should retrace their route back to the trailhead. For those who do not mind walking on a less-travelled path, I turned left at the pond, adding the unopened Hemlock Cathedral Trail to the route. It begins easily, following an old road around the pond. After only 150 m/yd the trail leaves the old road at a well-signed spot.

This is a much more challenging route, with few markers and a much less distinct treadway. Even though there are a number of boardwalks, many quite long, there was also considerable deadfall obstructing the path. Only confident navigators should attempt this section.

Mosquitoes

Between May and first frost, no hike will be entirely free of these tiny, annoying, blood-sucking pests. Forget bears; mosquitoes are the most common threat found on most trails, and if you do not take adequate precautions, your walk will turn into a running fight where the scenery is forgotten while you slap frantically at biting bugs and flail the air vainly trying to drive them away.

There are more than twenty-seven species of mosquito in Nova Scotia, and they prefer blood to develop eggs, even though their primary food source is nectar from flowers. Some species carry diseases such as St. Louis encephalitis and the West Nile virus, which they can transmit to humans.

To limit your exposure to these ubiquitous nuisances, wear long sleeves and pants, especially during dawn and dusk, and use insect repellents with up to 35% DEET for adults and 20% for children over six months of age.

On a positive note the trail does pass through several hemlock-covered hillsides and alongside a very large, scenic meadow. After a testing 2.5 km (1.6 mi) meander, the Hemlock Cathedral Trail rejoins the Green Forest Trail at the junction 3.5 km (2.2 mi) from the trailhead. Turn right, and retrace your route to the start.

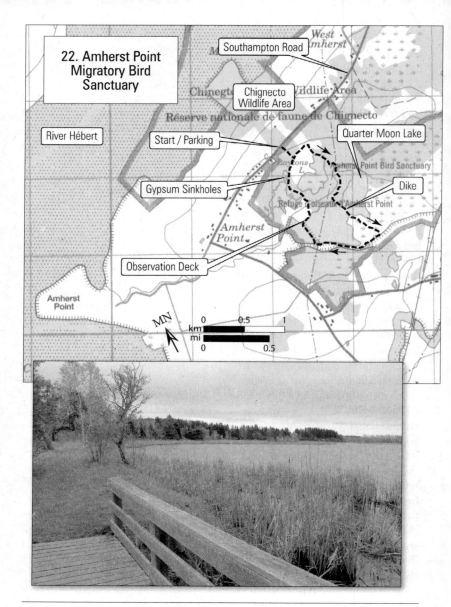

22. Amherst Point Migratory Bird Sanctuary

Southampton Road

Chignecto Wildlife Area

River Hébert

Start / Parking

Quarter Moon Lake

Gypsum Sinkholes

Dike

Observation Deck

Amherst Point

MN

km
mi
0   0.5   1
0   0.5

22. Amherst Point Migratory Bird Sanctuary

◄---► 6 km (3.75 mi) return

⏱: 1+hr

🚶: 2

Type of Trail: natural surface, compacted earth, crushed stone

Uses: walking, snowshoeing, cross-country skiing

⚠: Animals.

🔦: Good throughout.

Facilities: benches, garbage cans, interpretive panels, observation decks

Gov't Topo Map: 21H16 (Amherst)

Trailhead GPS: N 45° 47′ 50.1″ W 64° 15′ 36.8″

Access: Take Exit 3 off Highway 104, and drive southwest, away from Amherst, on Southampton Road for 3.1 km (1.9 mi). Turn left into the parking lot opposite house #947.

Introduction: Designated a Migratory Bird Sanctuary in 1947 at the request of neighbouring landowners, the Amherst Point Migratory Bird Sanctuary assumed its present size of 433 ha (1,070 ac) in 1980, and together with the 600 ha (1,480 ac) John Lusby Marsh makes up Chignecto National Wildlife Area. A surprising variety of habitats lie within the sanctuary, but 66% of its area is open water, marsh, and bogs, or controlled water-level impoundments, an environment ideal for waterfowl.

The enclosed wetlands, specifically the impoundments created by the dikes and sluices built by Ducks Unlimited in the 1970s, are among the best breeding grounds in Nova Scotia. More than two hundred bird species have been observed at Amherst Point, which is a regular nesting site for regionally rare varieties such as gadwall, redhead, ruddy duck, Virginia rail, common gallinule, and black tern.

Gypsum deposits underlie the entire area, and from 1935 to 1942 a commercial mine operated near the sanctuary. The distinctive sinkholes of karst topography are found throughout the area.

Route Description: There is a trailhead pavilion in the parking area that includes a poor map of the trails. A crushed-stone path traverses the 200 m/yd tree-covered section from the parking lot to a three-way junction at the top of a grass-covered hill overlooking Laytons Lake.

Turn left, and continue along the

---

crushed-stone-surfaced path along the top of the hill, through abandoned upland fields, for about 400 m/yd. No sign marks the right turn downhill, where the crushed-stone surface ended in May 2011, and a distinct track continues straight, but at this junction descend towards the woods and Laytons Lake.

A beautiful spruce canopy provides shade as the trail follows the water's edge; a solitary rough-hewn bench looks out on a tiny cove.

Following a ravine inland, and crossing over a tiny bridge, the trail wends through the forest. To the left, depending upon the season and the thickness of foliage, you should have occasional views of Quarter Moon Lake. Rejoining Laytons Lake, the path follows its bank fairly closely until it connects to an abandoned rail line.

Turn left and follow this track to the power line. Continue straight for 300 m/yd to the dike separating impoundments 2a and 2b. Follow this, where for the next 2 km (1.25 mi) you will walk on the narrow dirt causeways through the best waterfowl breeding areas. Birch trees shield you somewhat from the water on both sides, and for 800 m/yd the path continues straight until it reaches the far shore.

A dirt road heads over a hill directly ahead, but remain on the dike system, turning right. This soon becomes a narrow unsheltered dirt track, and it continues this way, with some tree cover, for another 800 m/yd to the next junction. Here you will find a monument dedicating the Amherst Point II Bird Sanctuary and a bridge. However, on the far side is a "Trail Closed" sign, so turn right and continue back to higher and drier ground, about 400 m/yd further.

Continue a further 50 m/yd; you should find an observation deck tucked among the trees overlooking the marshes through which you just hiked. This is a worthwhile place to linger, especially if you brought your binoculars and camera.

Walk 200 m/yd beyond this and you will arrive at another junction; turn left here, keeping on the edge of the forest, with a field to your left. At the next junction, reached very quickly, turn left again and almost immediately you encounter a small bridge spanning a brook. Laytons Lake is once again on your right.

Just beyond this bridge is an X-junction; right leads up the hill 500 m/yd to the start, left goes into the field back towards the dikes. Continue straight instead, and 300 m/yd later you will find another observation deck overlooking "The Cove" on your left. Another bridge separates two ponds, and on the other side you re-enter stands of gorgeous eastern hemlock, and encounter a trail junction and another directional sign, this one directing you to the right.

You have reached what is probably the most challenging area for walking of this entire route. Note the sudden and dramatic change in the land; erosion of the soft gypsum underlying this area has created a cratered landscape of deep sinkholes and razor-thin ridges separating them. The trail traces the narrow crest of these ridges, and occasional handrails assist the climb up some of the steepest sections.

You only have a few hundred metres/yards of this undulating terrain before you climb up onto a ridge where the ground falls off steeply on both sides. The surface is now crushed stone.

You complete the loop only 200 m/yd farther along this path, when you reach the initial junction on the top of the hill. Turn left again, after maybe one more look around, to return to the parking lot.

Sea Stacks

The ferocious tides of the Bay of Fundy constantly attack the shoreline between Economy and Cape Chignecto, and they affect the two main soil groups of the area quite differently. Where soft sandstone is exposed, it erodes rapidly, creating wide tidal platforms. When volcanic basalt is present, high, steep-sided coastal cliffs result.

Eventually, the relentless ocean wears away all the softer material, and only columns of basalt remain. These offshore pillars are known as sea stacks. Isle Haute, visible far out in the Bay of Fundy; the well-known Five Islands, near Economy Mountain; and the Three Sisters (shown here) in Cape Chignecto Provincial Park are outstanding examples.

23. Cape Chignecto Provincial Park

◀---▶ 51 km (31.9 mi) return

⏱: 3 days

🥾: 5 [distance, rugged terrain]

Type of Trail: natural surface

Uses: walking, snowshoeing

⚠: Animals. Rugged terrain. Remote location. Cliff edge. Steep climbs. Variable weather conditions. Exposed coastline.

📱: Good on high ground facing south; none in ravines or inland.

Facilities: benches, camping, garbage cans, outhouses, picnic tables

Gov't Topo Map: 21H07 (Cape Chignecto)

Trailhead GPS: N 45° 21' 01.1" W 64° 49' 27.4"

Access: Take Exit 12 off Highway 104 onto Highway 2 at Glenholme. Drive in the direction of Parrsboro for 74 km (46.25 mi) to the junction with Highway 209. Turn left and drive west along Highway 209 for 45.7 km (28.6 mi), through Advocate Harbour, turning left onto West Advocate Road. Drive 1.7 km (1.1 mi) to the Park Administrative Centre and parking area at the end of the paved road.

Introduction: Cape Chignecto Provincial Park is a 4,200 ha (1,374 ac) natural environment park on a dramatic coastal peninsula jutting into the Bay of Fundy. The park offers wilderness camping in secluded coves and ravines along this remote shoreline, on a trail that wanders over high cliffs and into deep canyons. However, the maximum elevation is only around 175 m (575 ft), whereas Mt. Katahdin in Baxter State Park (Maine) climbs 1220 m (4,000 ft) in 9.6 km (6 mi).

Cape Chignecto officially opened on July 25, 1998, and right from its opening it has enjoyed a deserved reputation as one of the most difficult, and also one of the most scenic, trails in Nova Scotia. I recommend taking three days to hike the complete loop, and if you just wish to visit Refugee Cove, camp overnight there.

Cape Chignecto Provincial Park charges both camping and day-use fees; these are paid at the Administration Centre.

Route Description:

Day 1: From the trailhead, your route heads across the Christy Field picnic area; there is a large interpretive panel (and outhouses), before you reach the forest 500 m/yd from the start. A large sign says Mill Brook is 6 km (3.75 mi) away, Eatonville 14 km (8.75 mi).

The path, an old woods road marked with bright red metal flashes, climbs. After 600 m/yd you reach the junction with the McGahey Canyon Trail (signed); keep left. This is great path, clearly marked with frequent metal tags mounted on trees. Puncheons (plank roads) cross wet spots, and numerous small bridges reduce the difficulty navigating the frequent deep and narrow cuts in the hillside.

For the first 2 km (1.25 mi), forest enfolds you, until the first coastal lookoff provides a magnificent view of Advocate Bay, the Minas Channel, Cape d'Or, and a sizable length of the Annapolis Valley coastline. (Ignore any lookoffs to the right.) Soon afterwards, the path descends steeply into the first of the deep ravines slashing into these coastal cliffs.

To reach and cross McGahey Brook requires you to take a flight of wooden stairs and cross a bridge; immediately after the trail climbs again, regaining lost elevation. Just over the bridge you will pass the second junction for the McGahey Canyon Trail; keep left. More stairwells aid the ascent, but this next hill is exceptionally long and steep.

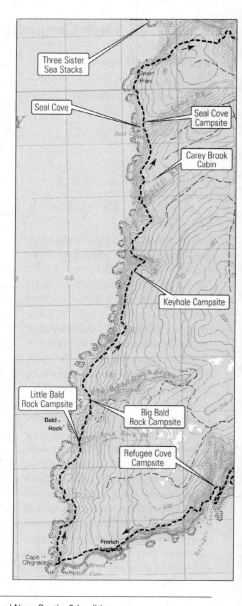

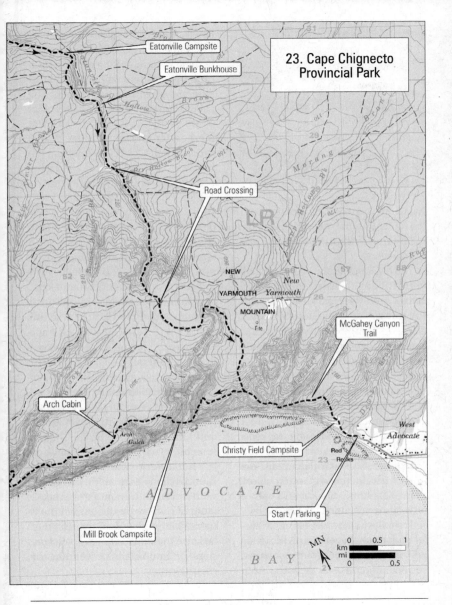

23. Cape Chignecto
Provincial Park

Eatonville Campsite

Eatonville Bunkhouse

Road Crossing

LR

NEW
YARMOUTH   New
Yarmouth
MOUNTAIN

Fire

McGahey Canyon
Trail

Arch Cabin

Arch
Gulch

Christy Field Campsite

Red
Rocks

West
Advocate

Mill Brook Campsite

A D V O C A T E

Start / Parking

MN

km
mi

B A Y

0   0.5   1

0   0.5

Brook, 8 km (5 mi) from the start. At 11.5 km (7.2 mi), another long, steep descent begins, ending at the mouth of Refugee Cove, where there is an attractive stone and sand beach. The path turns right, and camping sites are 500 m/yd inland, above the high water mark, after crossing Refugee Cove Brook, about 12 km (7.5 mi) from the trailhead. For most, this will be a good place to finish the first day's walk.

Day 2: The day starts with a steep climb, up to French Lookout, where there are excellent views of the coastal cliffs, Cape d'Or, and maybe even Cape Split! Continuing through meadows and around Broad Cove, the path descends gradually until it reaches a signed junction at 4.5 km (2.8 mi). Turn left to reach Cape Chignecto — not much of a view, actually — 100 m/yd later. Continuing right, towards Spicers Cove, the main path becomes rougher, working up and down the coastal cliffs as it gradually descends towards Stoney Beach and Little Bald Rock Brook, 3.5 km (2.2 mi) away. (Note that signage on the trail refers to Bauld rather than Bald.) This is a fantastic coastline, with lookoffs built onto every headland. In some respects the walking is more challenging than the first day, because the route is never level, constantly climbing and descending the rugged slopes.

At its top, you reach the junction with the route to Eatonville, which is to the right. You continue towards Cape Chignecto.

In similar fashion, you next drop into Mill Brook. Amazingly, the descent is even steeper. At the bottom of the hill you find the first campsite, 6 km (3.75 mi) from the trailhead. A sign says that Refugee Cove is 6 km (3.75 mi) farther.

Perhaps the most taxing section of the trail is found in the climb on the other side of Mill Brook. At one point, a smooth rock face forms the wall for the narrow trail. Stones and tree roots have been used as stairs as the trail sharply scales the hillside, and the tops of nearby trees are often below the weary hiker. Quads and calves protest the sustained labour.

From the top the walk is much easier and almost level. You will notice one of the new backcountry cabins, and an outhouse, near the top of Arch

At Little Bald Rock Brook you will find an outhouse and campsites next to a tiny brook in a narrow gorge, as you will at Big Bald Rock Brook, 2.2 km (1.4 mi) farther. Anyone too energetic to stop at Refugee Cove might choose one of these isolated sites to spend their first night.

It is difficult to adequately describe the next 8 km (5 mi), some of the finest coastal hiking in mainland Nova Scotia. Rugged, scenic, and of breath-stealing beauty, this section is an unending succession of dramatic views. The climbs out of Keyhole Brook (campsite) and Carey Brook (cabin) are particularly memorable,

and there is one inland climb you will not forget either! You will end your second day at the Seal Cove Brook campsite, 19 km (11.9 mi) from Refugee Cove.

Day 3: After Seal Cove, the cliffs are perhaps only half as high, but they are impressive nevertheless. You cross some wonderful barrens for 1 km (0.6 mi) before the path begins to curve away from the ocean. If you are lucky you will sight the famous Three Sisters, a row of tall, narrow basalt sea stacks. Once away from the water, you face one more challenging climb before the path descends to reach

Eatonville Brook, crossing on a large, new bridge about 4 km (2.5 mi) from Seal Cove. The path follows the river for another kilometre (0.6 mi), then crosses again and climbs a long gentle hill through beautiful woods to reach the Eatonville campsite, perhaps 6 km (3.75 mi) from Seal Brook.

The sign there says it is 14 km (8.75 mi) to the trailhead at Red Rocks. Your path now is through the interior of Cape Chignecto. There are few views, with the path first roughly paralleling the Eatonville Road, then after the bunkhouse following Eatonville Brook for several kilometres/miles. After the dramatic beauty of the coastline, I was sur-

prised by how much I enjoyed the gentle saunter on a leaf-covered old woods road alongside a small brook. I did not enjoy the climb at the end of the brook, as the trail ascends the back of the coastal cliff.

After a confused meander over the hillside, where you actually cross Mill Cove Brook high upstream, the path works down a stunningly beautiful hardwood-covered hillside to reconnect with the main trail on the climb above McGahey Brook. Turn left, and retrace the initial 4 km (2.5 mi) of your trek to return to the trailhead.

24. Cobequid Trail

◄---► 14 km (8.75 mi) return

🕐: 3+hrs

🚶: 3

Type of Trail: crushed stone, asphalt

Uses: walking, biking, snowshoeing, cross-country skiing

⚠: Road crossing. Yield to farm equipment.

🗑: Adequate throughout.

Facilities: benches, garbage cans, interpretive signs, picnic tables

Gov't Topo Map: 11E06 (Truro)

Trailhead GPS: N 45° 21' 58.5" W 63° 19' 35.1"

Access: Take Exit 14 off Highway 102 and turn onto Highway 236 west in the direction of Old Barns. Continue for 650 m/yd; the parking area is on the right (signed).

Introduction: The Cobequid Trail is a system of paths running through the communities of Bible Hill, Truro, and the County of Colchester. In total length it comprises 16 km (10 mi) of trails. However, not all the various sections are linked. Two of the sections, the Marshlands and the Old Barns, pass through the dikelands along the Salmon River just west of Truro.

The Cobequid Bay Lookoff is a good place from which to watch the tidal bore, and the entire length is an excellent location for birdwatching; ducks, geese, and hawks are among the many species you should be able to find while on your walk. Ringed-neck pheasants are another common sight, especially in the grassy fields of the dikelands.

Route Description: From the small parking lot, the Cobequid Trail runs in both directions. However, a sign says that Old Barns is 7 km (4.4 mi) to your left. Head that way. There is also another sign advising you that you will be passing through a working agricultural area, which means 1) there might be dangerous machinery about, so stay on the trail, and 2) fertilizer smells might assault your delicate olfactory senses.

The path is brilliantly good, wide, and covered in a slate-grey layer of crushed stone. The rich green grasses of the dike lands grow right to the edge of the stone, providing a pleasing contrast. For the next 3.5 km (2.2 mi) the path stands out in the open, crossing through the treeless farm-

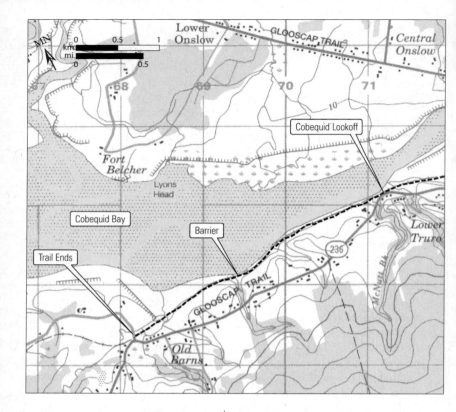

lands protected by the dikes lining the Salmon River, and providing long views in almost every direction.

For the first 900 m/yd you travel with the road close to your left and farmland on your right. You pass a sign that indicates that you should yield to farm equipment, so that means you might encounter heavy machinery on the trails as well as walkers and bikers. Then the trail suddenly becomes a paved road, the track having been used to build a road to the new Central Colchester Waste Water Treatment Facility. For 500 m/yd road and trail share the same route before the road splits off to the left.

When road and trail diverge there is a bench, and two more interpretive panels, one talking about the potential agricultural activities found

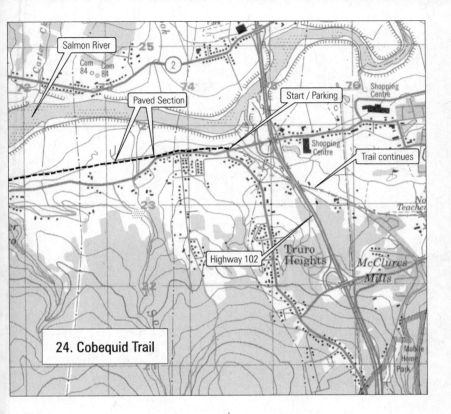

24. Cobequid Trail

on the marsh between April and November, and the other explaining what crops might be sighted. For the next 1.7 km (1.1 mi) the trail continues on a straight line through the marsh, slightly elevated from the lands on either side.

You have walked nearly 3 km (1.9 mi) and have almost reached the ocean. The trail curves to the left and you are about 100 m/yd from

a small bridge when you encounter another interpretive panel, this one explaining the aboiteaux that drained the salt marshes that these lands once were.

You should notice that Highway 236 is getting much closer on your left. Little more than 300 m/yd past the bridge you reach the Cobequid Lookoff, where there is another parking area, bench, and garbage can.

You also now have the ocean, the Cobequid Bay, immediately beside the path on your right, with extensive views far down towards the Minas Basin, but also of the extensive mud flats exposed at low tide.

This is an excellent site for observing shorebirds, especially during the spring and fall migratory seasons, when they visit these mud flats to build up their reserves for their long flights.

The trail continues beyond the lookoff, still an excellent crushed-stone surface. No doubt because the ocean is so close, you pass benches frequently, one 400 m/yd from the lookoff, another 850 m/yd later, and another 300 m/yd beyond that. This is a marvellous walk for a summer

Shorebirds

Anyone walking on one of Nova Scotia's beaches will invariably sight flocks of sparrow-sized birds apparently engaged in some sort of game with the ocean. Skittering rapidly across the sand, they advance or retreat up and down the beach just ahead of the leading edge of the waves. This is because their main diet is composed of mud-flat invertebrates, such as the small worm *Heteromastus filiformis*, which is found only in the intertidal zone.

Dozens of varieties can be found along the coastline, especially during the fall migration period of July-September. Some, such as the whimbrel, are crow-sized, and minute variations of beak or leg colouring are often all that distinguish the various species.

evening, as the view down Cobequid Bay is facing west. The land on the left is often higher than the trail, and sometimes there are animal dens dug into the soft-soiled hillside.

After almost 1.5 km (0.9 mi) following the shoreline, the trail begins to slowly move away from the water. Just at the point that it does, there is a fence on both sides of the path and two posts in the crushed-stone treadway. There is also another bench there.

As you continue, there is an increasingly large mud flat to your right between the trail and the water. About 800 m/yd after the barrier, where you actually have trees on both sides of the path, there is another covered bench.

From here you can actually see, beyond the end of the trail, a large white church. Nearly 200 m/yd after the bench you pass through another gate, and 250 m/yd beyond that you cross the largest bridge on the route. Only 200 m/yd remain; you arrive at Shore Road close to Highway 236 and just across from the church. There is a stop sign and the crushed stone simply ends.

You have reached the end of the Cobequid Trail. When you turn around to retrace your route, you will see a sign that tells you it is 7 km (4.4 mi) to Lower Truro. Enjoy the walk.

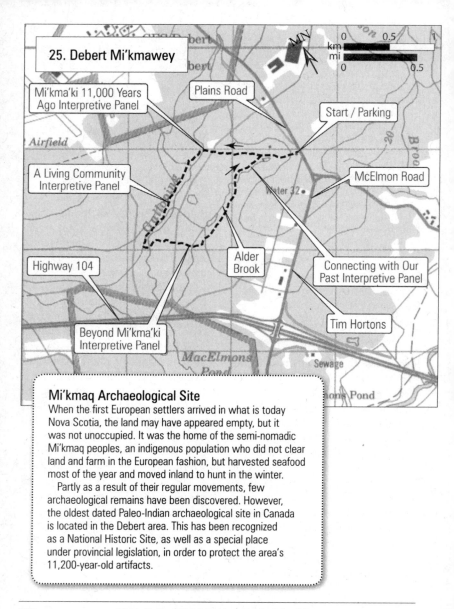

25. Debert Mi'kmawey

Mi'kma'ki 11,000 Years Ago Interpretive Panel

Plains Road

Start / Parking

McElmon Road

A Living Community Interpretive Panel

Highway 104

Alder Brook

Connecting with Our Past Interpretive Panel

Tim Hortons

Beyond Mi'kma'ki Interpretive Panel

Mi'kmaq Archaeological Site

When the first European settlers arrived in what is today Nova Scotia, the land may have appeared empty, but it was not unoccupied. It was the home of the semi-nomadic Mi'kmaq peoples, an indigenous population who did not clear land and farm in the European fashion, but harvested seafood most of the year and moved inland to hunt in the winter.

Partly as a result of their regular movements, few archaeological remains have been discovered. However, the oldest dated Paleo-Indian archaeological site in Canada is located in the Debert area. This has been recognized as a National Historic Site, as well as a special place under provincial legislation, in order to protect the area's 11,200-year-old artifacts.

25. Debert Mi'kmawey

◄----► 4.5 km (2.8 mi) return

⏱: 1+hr

🏃: 1

Type of Trail: natural surface, compacted earth

Uses: walking, biking, ATVing*, snowshoeing, cross-country skiing

⚠: Animals. Motorized vehicles. Poison ivy.

🌲: Adequate throughout.

Facilities: benches, interpretive panels, picnic tables

Gov't Topo Map: 11E06 (Truro)

Trailhead GPS: N 45° 24' 47.8" W 63° 25' 36.7"

Access: Take Exit 13 off Highway 104, turning onto McElmon Road in the direction of Debert. Follow for 1.5 km (0.9 mi), keeping left as it merges with Plains Road. The parking area for the trail is on the left 200 m/yd past the intersection (signed). The trailhead is at the far end of the clearing.

Introduction: The Mi'kmawey Debert Interpretive Trail is a short path through a forested area that was an important hunting area for the Mi'kmaq and predecessor peoples for perhaps 11,000 years. This trail is managed by the Confederacy of Mainland Mi'kmaq, in recognition of the discovery near this site of some of the oldest First Peoples artifacts in Canada.

This is a short, pleasant walk without too many hills that crosses several sluggish streams — on bridges. Along the way, a number of illustrated in-terpretation panels tell of the known history of this site and its significance to the Mi'kmaq people. This should be a good family stroll, especially in the fall.

Route Description: At the trailhead there is a picnic table and the first of the large, colourful interpretive panels that make this route an education in history as well as nature, this one titled "Connecting with Our Past." As with all the signage along this route it is bilingual: Mi'kmaq and English.

Just past the large sign is a smaller one, containing a map; the natural surfaced footpath distinctly cuts through the grass beside it. Crossing tiny Tupsiey Sipu'ji'j (Alder Brook) in the first 100 m/yd, you reach a junction, where a number of signs indicate that this is to be walked counter-clockwise.

As you stroll along, you need to

be mindful of roots and rocks in the path, but small bridges have been installed to cross even minor gullies, and benches and "stump" chairs are located in several places. The forest is very attractive, particularly the many red pine, which become more numerous as you proceed. After perhaps 900 m/yd you reach a dirt road, which you follow briefly before turning back into the woods, where there is a small bridge.

You also reach the next large interpretive panel: "Mi'kma'ki 11,000 Years Ago." Immediately after the panel, the trail descends a wooden staircase and crosses the first brook. Once across, the path meanders up an attractive sphagnum moss-covered hillside, under thick spruce and fir. Again there are more "stump" seats, and 300 m/yd later railings line the path as it descends to cross another gully and small stream.

On the far bank, wooden steps built into the hillside assist the ascent back up to the ridge line. When I passed a remarkable gnarled and twisted old pine, 300 m/yd later, I wondered if the path was deliberately routed that way. The next panel, "A Living Community," is reached 200 m/yd later.

Again, immediately afterwards the path drops to cross another small stream. This time there is a bench beside the water. The trail continues over the uneven hillside for only 400 m/yd more before reaching a quite elaborate stairwell and boardwalk/bridge structure. The route turns sharply left here and descends to cross Galloping Brook (although I have never seen it moving anything but sedately).

Once across, there are benches in a small open, grassy area by the brook. The path climbs the bank, at the top crossing a small dirt road, then plunging into a thick copse of pine. Another small road is crossed in 200 m/yd, then a very busy-looking dirt track 100 m/yd later. There may or may not be signs at each of these crossings.

Another lovely area of pine is entered, and about 100 m/yd later you reach the next panel, "Beyond Mi'kma'ki," situated beneath a magnificent white pine. There is also a bench here — an attractive spot. Continuing, you drop down to cross Alder Brook. Interestingly, the bridge has no railings, but the climb up the hillside, probably the steepest of the entire walk, does.

On the top of the bank the footpath connects to a quite wide dirt road, which it follows, turning left. The soil is very sandy and dry, and the trees surrounding you are almost all red pine. This level route continues for more than 750 m/yd, through several junctions, before a sign directs you

Cellphones

Cellphone batteries — particularly those for smartphones — have an extremely short life. Battery strength fades quickly with use or if you leave the phone on in areas of poor service, where the phone continually searches for access. If you carry your phone for emergency purposes, start the hike with it fully charged and leave it turned off. If you can, carry a freshly charged spare battery as a backup. However, many remote areas have poor or no cell reception.

Do not rely on your cellphone as your only communication/safety resource.

left and down the hillside to recross Alder Brook.

For the remainder of the route, the trail follows the ridge with Alder Brook below and to the right. Benches and "stump" chairs are frequent. After about 500 m/yd you reach the final interpretive panel, "Connecting with our Past." Just beyond it, you return to the first junction. Turn right, cross Alder Brook one final time, and walk the 200 m/yd back to the trailhead.

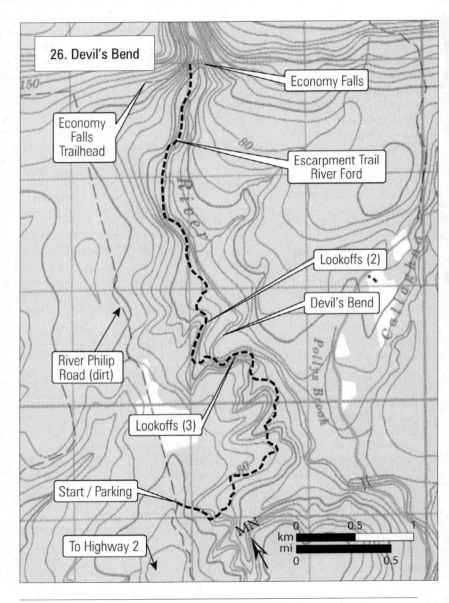

26. Devil's Bend

Economy Falls

Economy Falls Trailhead

Escarpment Trail River Ford

River

Lookoffs (2)

Devil's Bend

River Philip Road (dirt)

Pollys Brook

Lookoffs (3)

Start / Parking

To Highway 2

MN

km
mi

0   0.5   1

0   0.5

26. Devil's Bend

◄---► 13 km (8.1 mi) return

⏱: 4+hrs

🚶: 4 [rugged terrain]

Type of Trail: natural surface

Uses: walking, snowshoeing

⚠: Animals. Rugged terrain. Steep climbs. Cliffs. Remote location. Hunting is permitted in season.

📱: Good reception at trailhead and at the top of the canyon; no reception at the bottom of the ravine.

Facilities: benches, outhouses, picnic tables,

Gov't Topo Map: 11E05 (Bass River)

Trailhead GPS: N 45° 24' 36.1" W 63° 55' 15.0"

Access: Take Exit 12 off Highway 104 onto Highway 2 at Glenholme. Drive in the direction of Parrsboro for 36.4 km (22.75 mi) to the village of Economy. Turn right onto River Philip Road (dirt) and travel 3 km (1.9 mi) to the trailhead parking area, on the right.

Introduction: The Kenomee Trail Society developed an impressive system of hiking trails in the Cobequid Mountains centred around Economy Falls. Since 2000, these have been among the best wilderness hiking experiences available in Nova Scotia, yet the trails are not heavily used.

The Devil's Bend Trail, at 13 km (8.1 mi) for the return trip, is within the range of most fit people. However, hikers should be aware that this is a backcountry experience. For most of its length the trail is a narrow foot-path that passes through the rugged landscape of a steep-sided ravine, which it climbs several times. This route is much more challenging than most mainland Nova Scotia hikes.

Route Description: From the trailhead, where you might notice a "6 km" sign, the path begins with a descent. The well-defined footpath swings left after 200 m/yd to follow a spur, with steps and a handrail to assist in the steepest section.

At about 500 m/yd you cross a woods road, then begin to climb; there is another staircase, then the trail drops into another ravine, where there is a small bridge at the bottom. That is the pattern of this trail, to be frequently repeated.

These narrow ravines are forested mainly in softwoods, and the hillsides are carpeted in thick, green mosses. Most of your walk will be shaded by the high forest canopy, making nightfall arrive much earlier in this deep canyon.

After about 1.6 km (1 mi) from the start, you pass alongside a steep sandstone cliff, on your left, and for the first time find yourself almost at the level of the Economy River. However, the trail curves left, to another rock face, and climbs an elaborate, railed staircase then back up to the crest. The trail has been designed so it passes at the foot of these splendid walls.

Higher up the ridge, you pass the "4 km" marker, but you have still more climbing to do, as the trail contours over the hillside, dropping briefly in little gullies then climbing on the spurs. About 200 m/yd past the sign you work around another rock face, the trail clinging to the cliff and supported by a wooden railing, then cross a bridge over a small gully before resuming your climb.

At 2.4 km (1.5 mi) you climb to the first lookoff, perched high above Devil's Bend. From this spot you gain wide views of the Economy River Valley. A jutting elbow of land has forced the river into several 90° turns beneath this vantage point, providing a dramatic vista of the river and the 50 m (164 ft) sandstone bluff opposite, sculpted by wind and rain.

Two more lookoffs follow in quick succession. Scan the waters in the river below; deer and bears sightings are common, while raptors enjoy the convenient perch on the tall trees overlooking this open part of the valley.

The hike becomes even more challenging during the next kilometre (0.6 mi), climbing and descending as it traces the narrow gorges cutting deeply into the hillside. (A bench is thoughtfully provided halfway up one hill.) At 3.3 km (2.1 mi) you reach the best viewing station yet, perched high above Devil's Bend on the top of the sandstone bluff. A second lookoff 100 m/yd later has less of a view.

About 150 m/yd the trail intersects a woods road and follows it right, downhill, keeping right at another junction — it is well signed — 150 m/yd later. After another 250 m/yd on the woods road, a footpath splits from it to the right. Crossing a small bridge 150 m/yd later, you find yourself on the banks of the Economy River, about 4 km (2.5 mi) from the start.

For the remaining 2.5 km (1.6 mi) the trail stays relatively close to the water, although it occasionally moves inland for short stretches. It continues its pattern of climb and descent, although it is much gentler in comparison with the trail earlier.

The principal highlight of this section is at the crossing site for the Cobequid Escarpment Trail. You will

find a sign, but no bridge over the wide river. This is shallow most of the year, and usually easily forded, but during the spring runoff it is best avoided. Fortunately, your route continues along the same side of the river.

With only 400 m/yd remaining, you arrive at another lookoff, although the falls are still hidden by the hills. The Devil's Bend Trail ends in the middle of the Economy Falls Trail; turn right and descend through 105 steps to end your walk at the base of the falls, a 6.5 km (4.1 mi) walk from the trailhead.

You may return by the same route, but if you prefer an easier, although much less scenic, return walk, follow the stairs (approximately 180!) at Economy Falls up the hill and from there to the River Philip Road. Turn left; about 4.5 km (2.8 mi) of mostly level walking is required to get back to the Devil's Bend trailhead.

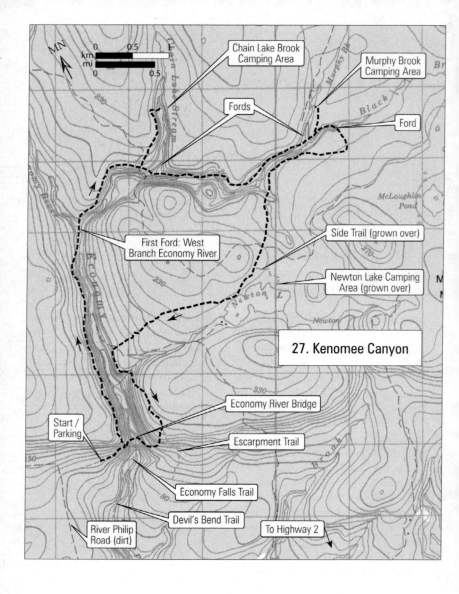

MN

km
0   0.5   1
mi
0   0.5

Chain Lake Brook Camping Area

Murphy Brook Camping Area

Fords

Ford

First Ford: West Branch Economy River

Side Trail (grown over)

Newton Lake Camping Area (grown over)

McLaughlin Pond

Newton L.

Newton

27. Kenomee Canyon

Economy River Bridge

Escarpment Trail

Start / Parking

Economy Falls Trail

Devil's Bend Trail

River Philip Road (dirt)

To Highway 2

27. Kenomee Canyon

◄---► 21 km (13.1 mi) return

⏱: 6+hrs

🏃: 5 [rugged terrain, distance]

Type of Trail: natural surface

Uses: walking, snowshoeing

⚠: Animals. Rugged terrain. Remote location. Hunting is permitted in season.

📱: No reception anywhere, except near the trailhead and on the east hillside above the falls.

Facilities: campsites, garbage cans, outhouses, picnic tables

Gov't Topo Map: 11E05 (Bass River)

Trailhead GPS: N 45° 26′ 39.4″ W 63° 55′ 39.3‴

Access: Take Exit 12 off Highway 104 onto Highway 2 at Glenholme. Drive in the direction of Parrsboro for 36.4 km (22.75 mi) to the village of Economy. Turn right onto River Philip Road (dirt) and travel 7 km (4.5 mi) to the Economy Falls Trailhead parking area.

Introduction: The Kenomee Canyon Trail, opened in 2002, is one of the most uncompromising hikes in the province, requiring five different fordings of streams. Signage is limited, and minimal work was performed to improve the treadway to minimize the impact on the terrain. Kenomee was one of the first (deliberately) wilderness-standard treks developed in Nova Scotia and is a must for any person who wants an outdoor challenge.

The basic loop is about 18 km (11.25 mi), but adding the side trip and the approach walk adds about 3 km (1.9 mi). If you intend to camp, permits can be obtained at the Interpretive Centre, 3248 Highway 2, in Economy (tel 902-647-2600, May to September); reserve ahead.

Route Description: From the parking area, follow the wide, well-signed path towards Economy Falls. Continue straight at the junction, where there is a bench, and the trail descends to the right to the base of Economy Falls. (You will get quite enough climbing without adding this.) About 700 m/yd from the parking lot, with views of the river valley to your right and a rail fence for protection, you encounter a junction.

Turn left, and follow the route signed "Kenomee Canyon via Chain Lake Stream." You immediately begin

a punishing 500 m/yd climb along a narrow footpath, although assisted by occasional steps cut into the slope. If you had any lingering doubts about the type of hiking experience you will have, this section should dispel them. Of course, the hillside is forested by magnificent mature hardwoods, and the Economy River, down the slope to your right, roars with potent strength.

The next 4 km (2.5 mi) are a good warm-up, as the trail follows the gorge, the steep-sloped hillside bordering Economy River. Reasonably well signed, it is a combination of footpath and old woods road, alternatively climbing and descending, but always with the river downhill to your right. It wanders a little, but makes its most distinct turn to the right, and its longest descent, to bring you the bank of the West Branch Economy River.

This is your first ford, and for most of the year it is no more than knee deep. In the spring or for a day following a rainstorm, however, it is usually higher. Once across, the path climbs onto a ridge above the East Branch Economy River, which it now follows. Nearly 2 km (1.25 mi) from the ford you encounter a junction. There is a map here, with the side trail to the Chain Lake Stream Camping Area. This is a worthwhile diversion. Not only are the woods attractive, particularly in an area of white spruce carpeted with lush sphagnum moss, but at the end of this 1.1 km (0.7 mi) spur is a small and pleasant waterfall that has created an attractive swimming hole.

However, unless you are planning to camp, you are probably in a hurry and don't wish to pause, so continue on the main trail. You very quickly drop down the ridge, briefly using an extremely rocky former ATV track, and within 200 m/yd come to the ford of Chain Lake Stream, within sight of its connection with the Economy River. In summer you might be able to step from rock to rock here.

The next 3 km (1.9 mi) are quite pleasant, the trail following the course of the East Branch Economy River, though working upstream. Although the terrain occasionally forces the path to climb as high as 30 m (100 ft) above the water, much of this section is almost at water level — at the start and near its end.

Your next ford, Murphy Brook, is not very wide, and almost immediately after that you reach the junction with the side trail to the Murphy Brook camping area. (The sign says it is 1.2 km [0.75 mi], but I found it to be much shorter.) This was my favourite campsite; the falls are the smallest you will see, but the tent pads are better sited.

The main trail continues only a short distance past the junction before turning right and reaching the most challenging of the fords, Black Brook. It might be higher than knee-deep here.

The far bank is very different, rugged and rocky. The trail works uphill following a tiny creek that has split through the ridge wall. You clamber along for a few hundred metres/yards, it becoming easier as you advance, with the route turning right, crossing the creek, and returning its path following the river, but now high above it on a very steep ravine.

When the trail turns left to work through the forest, maybe 1 km (0.6 mi) later, you are leaving the Economy River behind, until you return to the gorge and Economy Falls. You continue along at roughly the small elevation — with minor variations, of course — past Newton Lake. (In August 2011, when I hiked Kenomee Canyon, the spur to the Newton Lake Camping Area was overgrown and the sign missing.)

The trail does come close to Newton Lake, briefly, then turns away onto another maple-covered hill. This soon levels, and you cross a distinct woods road about 1.6 km (1 mi) from Newton Lake. Beyond this, the footpath works its way left and begins to gradually, and steadily, descend. About 1.3 km (0.8 mi) after crossing that road, the track turns sharply left into a narrow, deep ravine, where you cross the brook that drains Newton Lake.

The climb of the opposite bank is perhaps the steepest yet, but mercifully short. For the next 1.7 km (1.1 mi), the path works along the broken ridge above the gorge; you can hear the river's roar. When you reach a junction, on top of a small knoll, turn right in the direction of the Economy Falls Trailhead.

Immediately you drop down, suddenly and steeply. Stairwells and railings assist in negotiating this narrow footpath switching back and forth down a very steep canyon wall. Only 450 m/yd from the junction you reach the impressive bridge spanning the Economy River above the falls. Cross and turn left; you pass a lookoff, then complete the loop barely 100 m/yd later. Only 700 m/yd straight ahead remain to the trailhead.

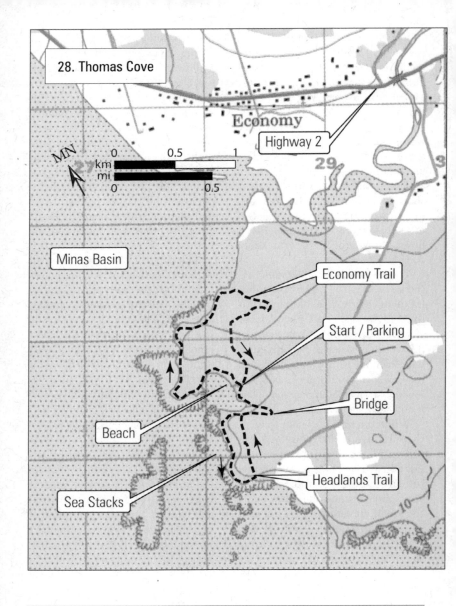

28. Thomas Cove

Economy

Highway 2

MN

0   0.5   1
km
mi
0   0.5

Minas Basin

Economy Trail

Start / Parking

Bridge

Beach

Headlands Trail

Sea Stacks

28. Thomas Cove

◀---> 7 km (4.4 mi) return

⏱: 2+hrs

🏃: 2

Type of Trail: natural surface

Uses: walking, snowshoeing

⚠: Cliffs (actively eroding). Animals. High (Bay of Fundy) tides.

☌: Good throughout.

Facilities: benches, picnic tables

Gov't Topo Map: 11E05 (Bass River)

Trailhead GPS: N 45° 21′ 45.9″ W 63° 54′ 56.6″

Access: Take Exit 12 off Highway 104 onto Highway 2 at Glenholme. Drive in the direction of Parrsboro for 35 km (21.9 mi) to the village of Economy. Turn left onto the dirt Economy Point Road. Continue until the road ends, approximately 4 km (2.5 mi) further.

Introduction: Thomas Cove, near Lower Economy in Colchester County, has trails that are perfect for a hot summer weekend. The network is organized in two loops, both beginning and ending at the same spot, which is the parking area and also has beach access.

Each of the loops is approximately 3.5 km (2.2 mi). So, if someone becomes tired more quickly than they expected, they get an opportunity halfway through to stop and rest. There are also some picnic sites near the parking area, and the beach makes a good place to wait as well.

Unfortunately, the Thomas Cove trails may not be open to the public

much longer. Built on private land, the original owner has passed away and the current owner may sell the property. As this route shows some of the best views available of the eroding coastline and the fantastic shapes carved by the tidal action, I suggest that you visit Thomas Cove as soon as possible.

Route Description: Our walk starts at the trailhead in Thomas Cove, on Economy Point. A small parking lot has been cut out almost at the high water mark. The trail's entrance is well marked, with an old road on the right. If the tide is low, however, you can walk from your car directly onto the exposed beach.

The Economy Trail loop follows the old road for only a few minutes before turning off to follow the shoreline, allowing frequent views of the Minas Basin and the Walton Shore across the bay. Several lookoffs have been created, and log barriers established wherever the view overlooks a hill or cliff. Economy Mountain and the Five Islands dominate the view to the right, while in the centre of the basin the rocky spire of the Brick Kiln (a hill so named on the topo map) stands out even at high tide. During WWII, Brick Kiln was used as a target for bomber training.

Roughly halfway through the walk, where the land curves back towards the mouth of the Economy River, a stairway provides access to a rocky beach. From here, you can view either inland or — on a very clear day — sight Cape Blomidon. At low tide, several kilometres/miles of sandy beach extend out from Economy

Point. Clam digging is popular, and it is this exposed sand with its abundant life that attracts waves of shorebirds during the fall.

The trail follows the shoreline until it reaches Paddys Cove. The final ocean view is of the beach stretching out towards Economy, with the hills of the Cobequids climbing above the village. The final kilometre (0.6 mi) is a narrow, winding trail through spruce bog, quite wet, but this should in no way detract from your experience.

The second loop, the Headlands Trail, begins on the left side of the parking area, initially following an old cart track. A small footpath on your left redirects you before the old route ends in the water, but watch closely for it — it is not well marked. This track skirts a deep indentation of tidal overflow, and follows the water's edge inland for several hundred metres/yards before rounding the water's final advance to return to the headland.

Upon reaching the top of this small bay, you are presented with three options: on your right, a slight descent to a small, sandy beach, on your left, a trail inland, and ahead a path along the water's edge. I recommend following this last option.

For the next 1.5 km. (0.9 mi), the trail follows the perimeter of Economy Point as it curves to the left and

towards Truro. At first your view is down the Minas Channel, but as you continue it changes to include the shore from Walton and Tennycape to Burntcoat Head.

In addition, the shoreline of Economy Point is composed of soft, quite highly erodable rock. There are several places where columnar fragments, known as sea stacks, are standing alone separated by the ocean from the rest of Economy Point. Some still have tufts of vegetation on their tops.

After reaching a final viewing platform, from where you can also see cleared fields not too much farther

Call of Nature

No, not a wolf howl. When you do need to . . . "s**t in the woods," remember that the trail is a public place. Move well off the path, stay 25 m/yd away from water, and if you can, dig a scat hole. When finished, cover it up. Toilet paper, sanitary napkins, tampons, and disposable diapers should be packed out, because other chemicals used in their production will leach into the soil.

along the point, the trail turns sharply into the trees, and quickly returns to the junction near the small beach. From here, you return along the path you entered.

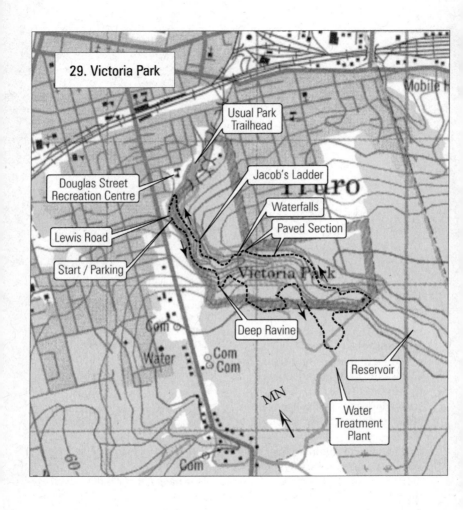

29. Victoria Park

Usual Park Trailhead

Jacob's Ladder

Douglas Street Recreation Centre

Waterfalls

Paved Section

Lewis Road

Start / Parking

Deep Ravine

Reservoir

Water Treatment Plant

MN

29. Victoria Park

◄---► 5.5 km (3.4 mi) return

⏱: 1+hr

🏃: 1

Type of Trail: crushed stone, compacted earth, asphalt

Uses: walking, biking, snowshoeing, cross-country skiing

⚠: Animals. Cliffs.

🔋: Adequate throughout.

Facilities: benches, firepits, garbage cans, gazebo, interpretive panels, outhouses, picnic tables, playgrounds, water

Gov't Topo Map: 11E06 (Truro)

Trailhead GPS: N 45° 21' 19.5" W 63° 16' 31.8"

Access: Take Exit 13 off Highway 102 in the direction of Truro. Drive 1 km (0.6 mi) to the junction with Highway 2/Willow Street. Turn left and follow for 800 m/yd, turning right onto Arthur Street (street lights). Follow it for 900 m/yd, turning right on Young Street. Continue 800 m/yd before turning left onto Fairview Drive. Park on the street near the corner 65 m/yd further; the trail starts on the right (signed).

Introduction: Victoria Park in Truro is one of the oldest protected places in Nova Scotia, the first 10 ha (25 ac) having been donated to the municipality in 1887. Since then it has grown, both in size and in community affection. Its superbly developed pathways, particularly in and around the Lepper Brook gorge, are popular year-round.

This is an outstanding location for novices and families. I have outlined a roughly 5.5 km (3.4 mi) route, but any combination of the intricate trail network can be made to provide a walk of whatever length you prefer.

Route Description: There is a map at the entrance to a wide, dirt track known as the Lewis Road. A metal gate blocks motorized access, but this is used for service vehicles. Thick forest lines your left, but on the right what was until recently a large field is being rapidly filled with houses and a church. A thin buffer of trees sits between trail and buildings.

Follow Lewis Road for about 600 m/yd to a junction. A trail enters from the housing on the right, but you turn left, plunging immediately into a hemlock-shrouded hillside on a crushed-stone pathway. Instantly this becomes a very different experience: mature hemlocks, no understorey, and steep-sided slopes.

There are many paths, formal and otherwise, on the hillside. Keep straight, and 125 m/yd after leaving Lewis Road you reach the edge of a deep ravine. Looking over the wood-rail fence, you should notice water issuing from a stone cairn. Turn right; the path works around this ravine, fenced along its entire length with benches. Where the trail crosses, turning almost 180°, there is a bench underneath a protective canopy.

After barely 200 m/yd along-side the ravine, you reach another junction, where you turn right and head away from the crest, working gradually uphill, still on a crushed-stone treadway. As you continue, the mature hemlock gives way to more hardwoods and younger trees, and the forest floor is covered by vegetation.

At a T-junction about 300 m/yd from the ravine, turn right, continuing uphill on the road-width track. Just 200 m/yd later you reach a five-way intersection. There is no map here, oddly, only a garbage can. Keep to the leftmost path; this 500 m/yd stretch, more grass covered than any thus far, transports you through thick, young vegetation to the next junction.

Here you turn left. The route forks immediately, but the two reconnect shortly at the next junction less than 150 m/yd away. Located here is a bench and a map, which tells us that we have connected to the Dr. Jim Vibert Memorial Trail. Turn right here, and proceed through the thick forest — no views — for 600 m/yd to the next junction, where there is another map and a bench. This is next to the Town of Truro's water treatment plant and a dirt road.

The path turns left and parallels the road for about 100 m/yd before turning back into the forest, where it quickly returns to a very steep, hemlock-covered slope. Turning sharply right, you reach a junction, with a bench, 275 m/yd from the road. Keep straight/right; almost immediately you emerge from the woods back at the dirt road, but this time with a view of the earthen Lepper Brook Dam and the reservoir above it.

If you wish, you may walk across the dam on the road, which crosses its top, or make your way to the edge of the water. The Vibert Trail, how-ever, parallels the road for less than 100 m/yd, then descends the steep hillside alongside the spillway to drop down to brook level, crossing it on a large bridge about 300 m/yd from the road.

For the first time you are at the bottom of the hills, with Lepper Brook to the left and the tree-covered slope on the right. Very little sunlight penetrates this part of the trail. Continue straight/left at the next junction 250 m/yd later, after which the trail curves to the left and the slope on the right grows progressively steeper.

About 600 m/yd from the bridge, you leave the Vibert Trail, coming onto an asphalt road. To the left, a trail crosses Lepper Brook and heads up the opposite hillside, and other trails head uphill on your right; you continue straight on the wide road, which is lined with picnic tables. When you reach the next bridge, 125 m/yd later, take a detour to walk onto it and view the brook; it is already at least 10 m/yd below the level of the trail. From now on there is a railing on the left of the trail.

Less than 200 m/yd beyond the bridge, a gravel track splits left from the asphalt. Follow this to a long, steep staircase, which you descend to reach the base of Waddell Falls. This is usually a very busy area, and there are observation decks, benches, and railings everywhere. But it is, especially in winter and during the spring runoff, an attractive spot.

Turn right, following the trail along the river. In the next 450 m/yd you will pass many sights: the plaque commemorating the donor of the land, the Observation Gallery, the Witches Cauldron, the Gazebo, and Holy Well. Just continue with the river on your left until you reach

the bridge at the base of the Jacob's Ladder staircase. Cross Lepper Brook here.

With the brook on your right, and virtually a cliff on your left, follow this path downstream for 300 m/yd to a junction just across Lepper Brook from the picnic pavilion. Head there if you wish, or keep left and climb the steep hill. At its top, 200 m/yd later, you come out of the park on Lewis Road next to the Douglas Street Recreation Centre. Turn left, almost 180°, and follow Lewis Road the 200 m/yd back to your car.

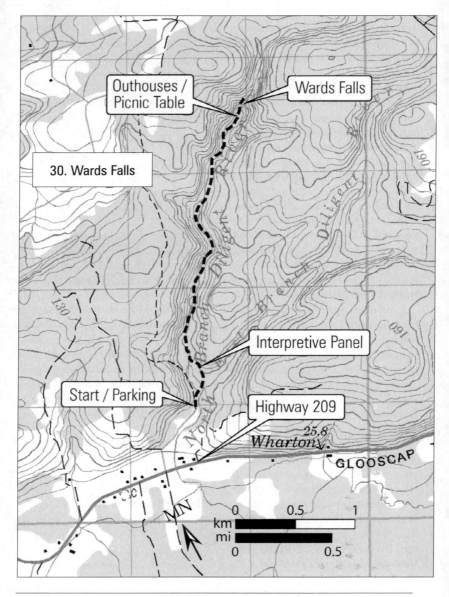

Outhouses / Picnic Table

Wards Falls

30. Wards Falls

Interpretive Panel

Start / Parking

Highway 209

Wharton

25.8

GLOOSCAP

km

mi

0   0.5   1

0   0.5

30. Wards Falls

◄- - -► 7 km (4.4 mi) return

⏱: 2+hrs

🏃: 2

Type of Trail: natural surface, compacted earth

Uses: walking, biking, snowshoeing, cross-country skiing

⚠: Animals. Hunting is permitted in season.

📱: Adequate at trailhead, no reception in the ravine.

Facilities: benches, garbage cans, interpretive panels, outhouses, picnic tables

Gov't Topo Map: 21H08 (Parrsboro)

Trailhead GPS: N 45° 25' 24.3" W 64° 25' 28.2"

Access: Take Exit 12 off Highway 104 onto Highway 2 at Glenholme. Drive in the direction of Parrsboro for 74 km (46.25 mi) to the junction with Highway 209. Turn left and drive west along Highway 209 for 7.1 km (4.4 mi) to Wharton. A green and yellow sign on your right directs you onto the dirt access road. Follow it for 200 m/yd, turning right at the junction. Follow it another 400 m/yd to the parking area.

Introduction: The North Branch Diligent River carves a narrow (4 m/yd wide) gorge nearly 40 m/yd long and 20 m/yd deep through the Cobequid Hills. In summer, water barely trickles from the opening, and it is possible — depending upon whether there is a ladder or a rope to help you — to climb into the gorge without getting wet. During the spring, however, the narrow aperture is sometimes insufficient to accommodate the water pressing through, with incredible results. There are few similar sites in Nova Scotia.

Wards Falls belongs to lumber and building supply company C. Ernest Harrison & Sons Ltd. of Parrsboro. In memory of founder C. Ernest Harrison, they have taken the land around the falls out of production and perform regular trail maintenance. All the company's lands are open for recreational use, and snowmobile clubs have many kilometres/miles of groomed track in other locations.

Route Description: A sign in the parking lot stands at the entrance to the walk, which looks like a continuation of an old road. In August — when I hiked it — the young, thick brush crowded towards the centre, making it more of a single-person footpath. In any case, within 100 m/yd the trail separates right off the old road and crosses the brook on a bridge, the first of several.

The trail heads up the valley with the North Branch Diligent River, at this flat area more of a meandering brook, on your right. Once over the bridge, and a second 75 m/yd later, the route crosses abandoned fields choked with thorny raspberry and blackberry bushes. About this point I regretted wearing my shorts.

There are a few old signs in this section, but these were difficult to spot in the thick undergrowth. However, if you remain close to the river, by 250 m/yd you reach an area of planted red pine; here the route is very distinct. And barely 50 m/yd later, you should sight a picnic table off to your right and a large, colourful, if somewhat tattered, interpretive panel.

Once past this sign, the trail begins once again to resemble an old woods road, and the river is close to your left. From this point on, the trail moves under a high spruce canopy, maintained for the remainder of the walk. As you approach the third bridge, an unrailed structure with several stairs at either end about 650 m/yd from the parking lot, you should be able to see that you are already well inside the narrow steep-sided ravine.

As if unable to make up its mind, the path crosses back and forth over the brook on several more of these well-constructed bridges — there are too many crossings to count, and certainly too many bridges to mention each one. (Okay, I did count: nineteen bridges, although a couple are pretty small.) Also throughout the route are a few rough benches and seats carved from tree stumps, and several small interpretive signs, although the only ones still legible when I was there read "Spruce" and "Yellow Birch."

The farther up the increasingly steep-sided valley you go, the older and larger the trees become. On fall mornings, when a light mist rises from the brook and fills the ravine with its smoky translucence, the moss-covered rocks and old trees look enchanted — or haunted! If you walk quietly you might sight a blue heron fishing.

Encountering two large outhouses on your left indicates that you have nearly reached the end of the walk, almost 3.5 km (2.2 mi) from the start. The trail now climbs relatively steeply for a short distance, the sound of the falls growing, and a picnic table on your left overlooks the entrance to the gorge. You are facing an exposed rock face, a massive barrier

Hunting Season

In the fall, hikers share the woods with hunters. To reduce the chance of meeting one during your walk, restrict your excursions to national parks, provincial parks, and similarly protected areas. Even there, proudly wear your orange jacket and/or toque. Always stay on posted trails, and avoid hiking at dawn and dusk, when visibility is limited.

rising directly across your path: the Cobequid–Chedabucto fault.

For most, this is where the walk ends, at the pool of water at the bottom of Wards Falls. The more adventurous may try to climb the rope (there was a ladder in 2001, much easier) from the bottom of the falls to the entrance of the gorge, where they will be rewarded with a fascinating view of the cavelike ravine. From there, ropes secured by pitons permit the agile and confident to scramble into the gap, where they may walk a few metres/yards further until blocked by deeper basins. These pools, though cold, may even invite spontaneous skinny-dipping.

Whether you venture into the gorge, or just enjoy a few minutes admiring the view and resting, when you are ready retrace the same path to return.

34. Gaff Point

Osprey

Look closely at that crow-sized bird circling lazily nearby. If the wings are heavily banded with white, it is likely that it is an osprey, the official bird of Nova Scotia. Once almost extirpated from the East Coast by the effects of insecticide pollution, the osprey has made a remarkable comeback and now is a common sight in shallow bays, estuaries, and lakes.

The diet of these beautiful summer residents is almost exclusively fish. Anyone who has ever seen one hovering 30 m/yd above the water before plunging straight in with an explosion of spray — only to emerge a few seconds later with a victim firmly grasped in its talons — will probably want to throw away their own fishing rod.

Look for their large stick nests at the top of tall trees or on electrical towers.

31. Bay to Bay Trail

◄---► 21.5 km (13.4 mi) return

🕐: 5+hrs

🏃: 4 [distance]

Type of Trail: crushed stone, compacted earth

Uses: walking, biking, horseback riding*, ATVing*, snowshoeing, cross-country skiing, snowmobiling*

⚠: Animals. Ticks. Road crossings. Motorized vehicles. Hunting is permitted in season.

🔖: Adequate throughout.

Facilities: none

Gov't Topo Map: 21A08 (Lunenburg)

Trailhead GPS: N 44° 22' 46.5" W 64° 19' 05.1"

Access: Take Exit 11 off Highway 103, turning onto Highway 324 in the direction of Lunenburg. Follow for 10.2 km (6.4 mi) to the junction with Highway 332. Keep straight, then left onto Highway 324/Dufferin Street for 500 m/yd. Continue on Dufferin Street for a further 1.2 km (0.75 mi), turning left into the parking are by a former train station.

Introduction: The South Shore does not contain two more iconic communities than Lunenburg, home of the *Bluenose*, and Mahone Bay, with its three churches side by side facing the ocean. This former rail corridor connects these two popular destinations.

If you plan to walk this all in one day, walk in the direction I suggest. If you wish to walk one way and overnight, I recommend starting the walk in Mahone Bay. Dogs are to be on leash on the Bay to Bay Trail.

Route Description: Starting from the former train station in Lunenburg, the path at first is part of the Back Harbour Trail. There is a gate partially blocking the path and both regulatory signage and a map. On the Back Harbour portion of the route only walking and biking are permitted.

Continue along the smooth, crushed stone surface for 600 m/yd before you reach the junction that connects to the Bay to Bay Trail. Turn left, and continue through the enshrouding vegetation (I was here in late August) for 350 m/yd until you reach a wooden staircase, which you climb. The path then traverses a grassy field for 50 m/yd to a crosswalk over Maple Avenue. Once across, turn right and immediately cross Sandy Hollow Road; when you reach the guardrail, you will see a path — indicated by a regulatory sign and a wooden railed fence. All this takes place in 100 m/yd.

You are now on the Bay to Bay Trail, where the crushed stone gives way to a more natural compacted earth surface. This is still in excellent condition, however, without ruts or rocks, and even includes a thin centre strip of grass.

The path initially is quite a bit lower than the roads on both sides, and 300 m/yd later you pass underneath a large road bridge. Once beneath, the trail enters forest, in a long curving arch to the right, which ends passing right beside Highway 3 at 2 km (1.25 mi) from the start. Still curving left, the path parallels the highway, moving slightly farther away as it does. About 350 m/yd later, the trail runs behind a number of houses, almost in the swimming pool of one.

For the next 1.5 km (0.9 mi), with the exception of a few driveway crossings, you are mostly in forest, though quite near — within hearing distance — of Highway 3. At 3.75 km (2.3 mi) you cross Schnares Road (paved). Highway 3 is less than 50 m/yd to your right.

The path continues through the forest, passing through an open area

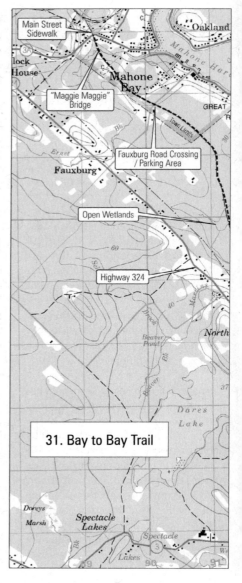

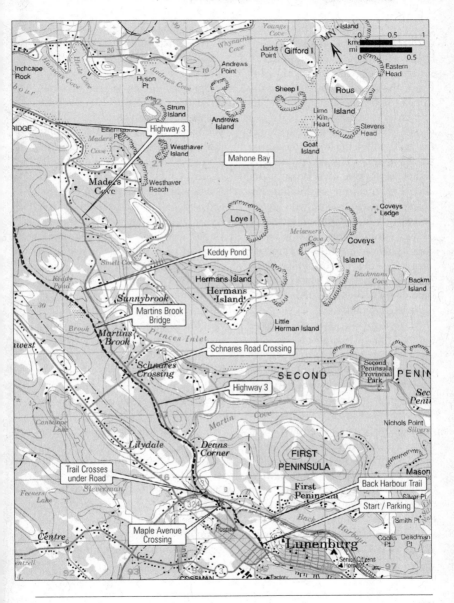

250 m/yd later, and the first bridge, over Martins Brook, about 300 m/yd beyond that. And then, at 5 km (3.1 mi), the large open expanse of Keddy Pond, ahead and to the right, finally forces the trail to separate from its proximity to Highway 3.

This is the most remote section of the walk, where the trail enters an extended area of thick vegetation with no houses or driveways. However, for almost the first time, as the route noticeably begins to climb, you have a canopy of leaves overhead, including a large number of old white pine. To your right is a large hill. You proceed almost 1.6 km (1 mi) before emerging into a large open area where the trail is bordered by wetlands on both sides for more than 300 m/yd.

You might notice some beaver lodges in the wetlands, and the fact that there are wet spots in the treadway for the first time. This is the site of an ongoing contest between hyperactive rodents (a.k.a. beavers) who want to raise the water level and flood the track and trail builders who wish to maintain it.

The trail then returns to thick forest and begins to descend slightly, the woods uninterrupted by anything other than occasional ATV side paths for the next 2.5 km (1.6 mi), when you reach the Fauxburg Road (paved), at 9.2 km (5.75 mi).

Across Fauxburg Road is more thick vegetation, although after 500 m/yd a power line cuts a wide swath through the forest. The land here slopes lower to your right quite a bit, and the trail curves right as well. After the power-line cut, the path passes through an attractive stand of young white birch, which on a windy day sway quite soothingly. There are also stands of pine on small knolls nearby.

Hawthorn Hills Road (paved) is crossed 250 m/yd after the power line, and shortly after that the gravel Cemetery Road. There is one last section of woods, then the path drops slightly to cross the "Maggie Maggie" Bridge over Ernst Brook, constructed through the Canadian Military Engineers' Bridges for Canada Program, 10.5 km (6.6 mi) from your start.

You are now in the village of Mahone Bay, where the trail crosses Kinburn Avenue 100 m/yd later, then passes between houses to reach the sidewalk on Main Street, Highway 325, at 10.7 km (6.7 mi) from the Lunenburg Trail Station.

The trail continues further, all the way to Halifax if you wish. However, the restaurants and shops of Mahone Bay are to the right, if you want a snack before your return walk, as are its famous churches. When you are ready to return to Lunenburg, retrace your route.

32. Chebogue Meadows Wildlife Interpretive Trail

◀ - - - ▶ 5.5 km (3.4 mi) return

🕐: 1+hr

🏃🏃: 1

Type of Trail: natural surface, boardwalks

Uses: walking, snowshoeing

⚠: Animals. Ticks. Hunting is permitted in season.

🍂: Good throughout.

Facilities: benches, lookoff towers, washrooms

Gov't Topo Map: 20016 (Yarmouth)

Trailhead GPS: N 43° 53′ 28.2″ W 66° 03′ 15.7″

Access: From Exit 34 off Highway 101, turn onto Highway 340 north. Just past the interchange, turn right onto Tinkham Road. Follow for 2.5 km (1.6 mi) to the junction with Hardscratch Road, turning left. The parking area is on the right, 400 m/yd further.

From the end of Highway 103 near Yarmouth, turn right onto Hardscratch Road (towards Brooklyn). Continue for 5.9 km (3.7 mi); Chebogue Meadows parking is on the right.

Introduction: While this trail is worthwhile for the walk itself and the scenery of the meadows, a number of interpretive panels have been erected at different locations in the park where various habitats are found. The panels describe the characteristics of each habitat type, and go on to explain its value to different species of wildlife. This is particularly helpful for people who want to know more about the woods in which they walk.

Chebogue Meadows is a good introductory hike, one that should be possible for almost the entire family. However, the high grasses are a perfect breeding ground for ticks. Make sure everyone receives a thorough inspection after your walk, especially the dog.

Route Description: There is a large sign in the parking lot confirming that you have reached the Chebogue Meadows Wildlife Interpretive Trail. Next to it is a sign advising wearing hunter orange from September 15 to February 15. The path starts in the clearing under the power lines, grass covered and surrounded by thick underbrush. About 75 m/yd from the parking area you will find a large map showing an (outdated) route of the trail and the location (also outdated) of the interpretive stations.

Immediately after the sign, the trail turns right, leaving the power

Bunchberry

Barrens and meadows are ideal habitats for a common Nova Scotia herb, the bunchberry. Bunchberries also thrive in heath, the edge of thickets, and bogs and often grow in thick carpets beneath softwoods.

In the fall, when the bright red berries are clustered together in the centre of each plant, it is easy to understand how these plants received their name. In June, small, greenish-white flowers adorn the plants, providing a welcome splash of colour to the stark landscape.

The berries are edible, although the hard seed at the centre makes them difficult for humans to eat. Some bird species enjoy them much more.

line and entering the mostly spruce forest. This first section of the path is excellent. It has some gravel over the natural surface and is distinct. Signage is limited, but there are occasional rectangular red metal markers affixed to the trees. (Yellow is used for the return trip.)

Only 150 m/yd from the map you find the first discrepancy with it; interpretive panel alternate 1A, "Merchantable Thinning" — it does not show on the map — is on your left. This is an attractive spot; in the spaces between the uniformly aged spruce there is a dense carpet of spreading ferns.

About 60 m/yd later you cross the first of what will be many boardwalks — this is a very wet area — and 400 m/yd beyond that, on the right, interpretive panel alternate 1B, "Remnant Removal." After this the trail becomes more challenging walking, with numerous small rocks intruding and jutting roots.

The walking remains trickier, with larger, moss-covered rocks scattered throughout the path. Any crushed stone in the treadway has long since disappeared. There are also larger wet areas as well, including one, about 750 m/yd from the start, which requires a 100 m/yd boardwalk to cross. You continue through the forest until you come upon a completely unsigned, but quite distinct, junction at 1.25 km (0.8 mi).

I chose to continue straight, or right. For another 300 m/yd the path continues through forest, then it emerges into a meadow area. A few metres/yards to the right is a raised platform, providing views over the

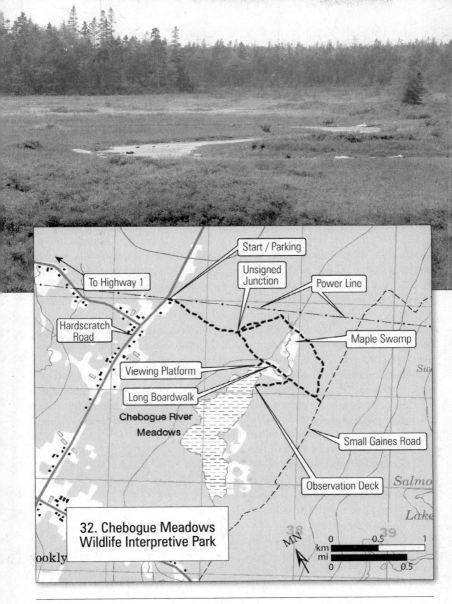

Start / Parking

Unsigned Junction

Power Line

To Highway 1

Hardscratch Road

Maple Swamp

Viewing Platform

Long Boardwalk

Chebogue River Meadows

Small Gaines Road

Observation Deck

Salmo

Lake

32. Chebogue Meadows Wildlife Interpretive Park

MN

38

39

0   0.5   1
km
mi
0   0.5

ookly

meadow, which also is home to Interpretive Panel 12.

The main trail continues over the spongy meadow, once again on a boardwalk, this one being quite long. There is even a small open stream, the Chebogue River, at one point, and Interpretive Panel 5, "Waterside Community," has been moved to the bridge here. After about 250 m/yd in the open, the path returns to the forest, starting to climb a small hill.

Just across the river you reach a junction, one not on the map near the trailhead. Turn right and follow this path, which meanders over a ridge for about 450 m/yd before dropping down the hill to another observation deck. This is located right at the edge of the forest, and overlooks a larger expanse of meadow. The impressively bullet-riddled map — oddly, more recent than the one at the trailhead — states that this is a watercourse managed by Ducks Unlimited. The riverbank is only a few metres/yards from the platform and is easily reached, especially in summer when water levels are lower. Some of the best viewing is found here.

Returning to the main trail, turn right, and continue up the hill. In only 250 m/yd you will reach panel 11 and an unsigned junction. The straight-ahead route leads in less than 100 m/yd to Small Gaines Road; turn left, more than 90°, to follow the main trail. This heads into an area of thick, dark forest. Within 100 m/yd you reach interpretive panel 10A, followed within 250 m/yd by panels 10 and 9. You are now in an area of wonderful hardwoods, and there is a bench situated on the hillside to permit you to enjoy the fragrant forest.

You quickly drop down to an area known as the Maple Swamp. More long boardwalks assist you through this soggy section, where you will find interpretive panels 8 and 7 — just before you leave the forest and return to the meadow. For about 350 m/yd you follow a boardwalk across the open landscape, passing panels 6 (on ticks), 4, and 3.

Back in the woods, you reach another unsigned junction in about 100 m/yd. Keep right. In little more than 150 m/yd you reach panel 2, where there is also a bench. The trail has only another 150 m/yd before you return to that first unsigned junction. Just keep right, and return the 1.25 km (0.8 mi) to the trailhead.

33. Chester Connector

◄ - - - ► 23 km (14.4 mi) return

🕐 : 6+ hrs

🏃 : 5 [distance]

Type of Trail: crushed stone, compacted earth

Uses: walking, biking, horseback riding, ATVing, snowshoeing, cross-country skiing, snowmobiling

⚠ : Animals. Ticks. Road crossings. Motorized vehicles. Hunting is permitted in season.

🚻 : Adequate throughout.

Facilities: benches, garbage cans, interpretive panels, picnic tables

Gov't Topo Map: 21A09 (Chester)

Trailhead GPS: N 44° 32' 50.4" W 64° 14' 38.3"

Access: Take Exit 8 off Highway 103 onto Highway 14 in the direction of Chester. Follow for 3.1 km (1.9 mi) to the junction with Highway 3. Turn left, and follow for 1.9 km (1.2 mi), turning left onto Smith Road. Park by the former train station; there is a trailhead pavilion, #30 Smith Road.

Introduction: The Chester Connector Trail runs for 35 km (21.9 mi) between the communities of East River and Western Shore and connects to other trails, extending, in 2011, all the way from the Halifax peninsula to the village of Lunenburg. The section profiled begins in the village of Chester and continues to the 112 m/yd long Gold River Bridge, which is not only the longest bridge between Halifax and Bridgewater but is also the highest.

Rail trails are not noted for their scenic aspects, because their original design intent was to remain as near level as possible to reduce wear on trains' brakes and engines, but this route provides several fine views of the ocean. In the fall, the maples in particular display fiery reds and orange hues.

Dogs must be on leash between Chester and Marriotts Cove.

Route Description: Start at the trailhead pavilion at the far end of the parking area, where there is a map of the entire route. Then return down Smith Road and cautiously cross very busy Highway 3. The path climbs the bank on the far side — the rail bridge over Highway 3 was removed — and you begin your walk along an attractive section surfaced in crushed stone. Mill Cove is to your left and the path is sandwiched on the steep bank

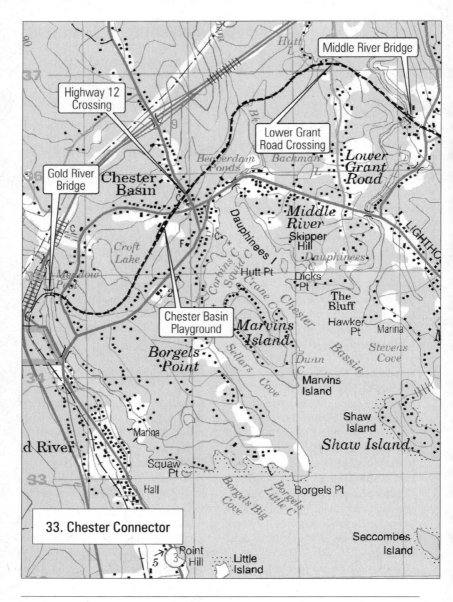

Middle River Bridge

Highway 12 Crossing

Lower Grant Road Crossing

Lower Grant Road

Gold River Bridge

Chester Basin

Beaverdam Ponds

Backman

Middle River

Skipper Hill

Dauphinees

Croft Lake

Dauphinees I

Corbins C

Squid C

Crane C

Chester

Hutt Pt

Dicks Pt

The Bluff

Hawker Pt

Marina

Meadow Pool

Chester Basin Playground

Marvins Island

Dunn C

Stevens Cove

Borgels Point

Sellars Cove

Marvins Island

Marina

Shaw Island

Shaw Island

d River

Squaw Pt

Hall

Borgels Big Cove

Borgels Little C

Borgels Pt

LIGHTHO

Bassin

33. Chester Connector

Point Hill

5 3

Little Island

Seccombes Island

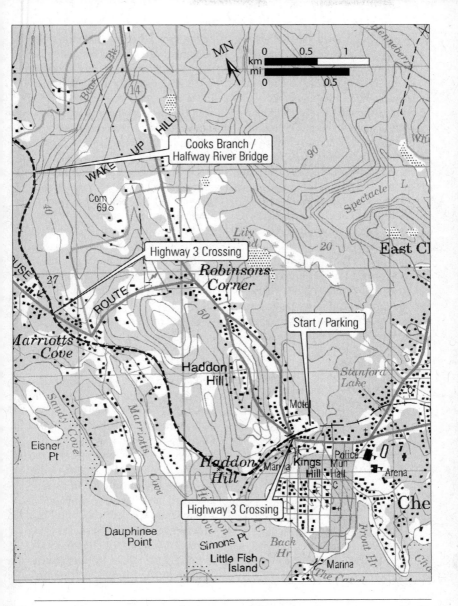

Cooks Branch /
Halfway River Bridge

Highway 3 Crossing

Start / Parking

Highway 3 Crossing

between Walker Road, left and below, and Walker Cut Road, to your right. Large houses are everywhere.

After about 750 m/yd the path curves right, and you leave Chester behind, although there are still many houses scattered about. There is one more view of the ocean before the trail heads between two drumlins. It stays here, sheltered by forest, although passing one huge house on top of the left drumlin, until arriving at the road crossing at Marriotts Cove, about 3 km (1.9 mi) from the start.

When you reach this road, there is a metal post in the middle of the trail, both to prevent cars from accessing the trail and to slow ATVs. There is also a garbage can and plastic bags for dog waste. To the left you gain a long view up the length of the narrow

Drumlin

Drumlins are low, sloping, rounded hills made up of glacial deposits. As the glaciers advanced, they ground slate and shale bedrock into clay deposits, which they left behind as whaleback ovals pointed in the direction of the glacier's flow.

In Lunenburg County, which is the drumlin capital of Nova Scotia, the soils on the drumlins were virtually the only arable lands, so that is where all the farms were located. Even today, most of the cleared fields in the area angle up the gentle slopes of drumlins.

ocean arm. The crushed stone also ends, with the surface becoming the compacted surface of the rail bed.

There are many houses nearby in the next 300 m/yd to the crossing with Highway 3, which is particularly dangerous as the road speed is 70 kph (45 mph) and drivers have no sign warning of the trail.

Once safely across, you rapidly move into a seemingly remote area. To your left is a large dome used to store road salt, then after only trees. For the next 1.5 km (0.9 mi) there is nothing but forest, although there has been a substantial amount of cutting. At least a fringe of young white pine has been left between trail and the clear-cut.

Slightly more than 5 km (3.1 mi) from Chester you reach the small Cooks Branch/Halfway River Bridge, which is fairly high above the water, and an attractive spot. Beyond this, only 400 m/yd will bring you to the crossing of McInnis Road (dirt). Only 150 m/yd beyond that you cross Middle River Road (paved).

There are some houses close to the road, and a few fields, at least until you cross the Middle River Bridge, 200 m/yd later. This is a much wider stream than Cooks Brook, and the water's edge is easier to access from the trail if you wish to dip your toes.

Beyond the bridge, the trail returns to undisturbed forest for the next kilometre (0.6 mi) to the Lower Grant Road, although one house is visible from the trail for in the final 400 m/yd straightaway before the crossing. Once across Middle River, the path has been noticeably, but very gently, climbing, and is often raised a little higher than the surrounding land.

After crossing Lower Grant Road (paved), you should be able to see small Hutt Lake on the right within 100 m/yd. After that, there is more forest for the next 2 km (1.25 mi) to Chester Basin. However, through here you will notice numerous ATV tracks veering off the trail. These are unsigned and should pose no navigational confusion.

You emerge from the forest at a crossing on Highway 12, directly across from the Aenon Baptist Church, 9.5 km (5.9 mi) from the start. On the opposite side of the road, there is also a trail parking area. For the next few hundred metres/yards you pass through this small village, crossing Croft Road (paved) 150 m/yd later then passing next to the Chester Basin Playground, where there are benches if you want to rest, or a basketball court if you happened to have brought a ball with you.

Back into the forest, the trail works its gradually curving way the final 2 km (1.25 mi) to the Gold River Bridge. This is a heavily populated area, and the trail is squeezed between busy

Highways 3 and 103, so you will probably hear automobile noise.

When you reach and cross Croft Road (paved), barely 10 m/yd remain before you find yourself on the bridge and high above the river. The trail continues as far as you care to walk, but at this point, I suggest you retrace your route back to Chester.

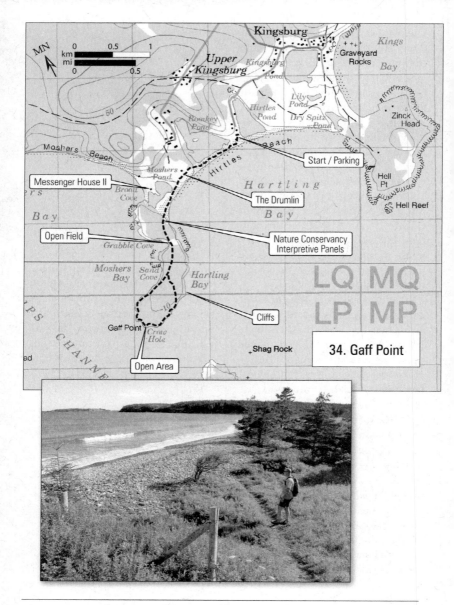

Kingsburg

Upper Kingsburg

Kings Bay

Graveyard Rocks

Kingsburg Pond

Hirtles Pond

Lily Pond

Dry Spitz Pond

Zinck Head

Moshers Beach

Romkey Pond

Hirtles Beach

Start / Parking

Hell Pt

Messenger House II

Moshers Pond

Hartling

The Drumlin

Bay

Broad Cove

Hell Reef

Open Field

Grabble Cove

Nature Conservancy
Interpretive Panels

Moshers Bay

Sand Cove

Hartling Bay

LQ MQ

LP MP

Cliffs

Gaff Point

Crow Hole

Shag Rock

34. Gaff Point

Open Area

34. Gaff Point

◄╌╌► 6.5 km (4.1 mi) return

⏱ : 2 + hrs

🏃 : 2

Type of Trail: natural surface

Uses: walking, snowshoeing

⚠ : Animals. Ticks. Cliffs. Exposed coastline. High winds and waves.

🌧 : Adequate throughout.

Facilities: benches, interpretive panels, outhouses, picnic tables

Gov't Topo Map: 21A01 (LaHave Islands), 21A08 (Lunenburg)

Trailhead GPS: N 44° 15′ 56.0″ W 64° 16′ 23.2″

Access: Take Exit 11 off Highway 103, turning onto Highway 324 in the direction of Lunenburg. Follow for 10.2 km (6.4 mi) to the junction with Highway 332. Turn right and continue for 12.8 km (8 mi), turning left onto Kingsburg Road. Follow for 4.3 km (2.7 mi), turning right onto Hirtle Beach Road. Drive to the parking lot at the end of the road, 1.6 km (1 mi).

Introduction: Because of the scenic beauty of the South Shore coastline, it is in high demand for homes and cottages, especially in Lunenburg County. As a result, very little remains undeveloped. One area is Gaff Point, where groups such as the Kingsburg Coastal Conservancy, the Nova Scotia Nature Trust, and the Nature Conservancy of Canada have joined forces to preserve a small, but oh so beautiful headland that projects into Ships Channel at the mouth of the LaHave River.

This is a wonderful walk at any time of the year, but I cannot imagine a more splendid experience than what I enjoyed hiking it in late afternoon on a sunny August day.

Route Description: Your route begins at busy Hirtles Beach, where there are outhouses, picnic tables, and garbage cans — and maybe even an ice cream truck on hot summer weekends. There are also a number of interpretive panels that describe the walk, including one by the Nature Conservancy that features a map.

Follow a boardwalk to the white sand of the beach, and turn right. Gaff Point dominates the skyline ahead. After about 750 m/yd you come to the base of a drumlin, and a distinct footpath runs to its top. Climb the grassy 150 m/yd to its top, where there are

wonderful views of both Gaff Point and Hirtles Bay. When you reach the bottom of its far side, about 1.1 km (0.7 mi) from the trailhead, you continue your walk along a rocky cobble beach.

As you walk along this low area, to your right you can see an area known as Upper Kingsburg. On the open land bordering it is a cluster of distinctive buildings, including the award-winning Messenger House II created by Nova Scotia architect Brian MacKay-Lyons.

Traversing the shifting stones can be challenging, so depending upon the tide state either walk below them on exposed sand or up above the crest. To your right are several barachois

ponds, quite active with waterfowl. The cobble gives way to sand just before you reach the approaching forest. Here you will find another interpretive panel, including a map, 1.5 km (0.9 mi) from the trailhead.

From water level, the path ascends the rocky headland along a former road, climbing through a thick spruce thicket draped with old man's beard. The former road becomes a footpath, the only signage being a warning of undercut cliffs, and after 350 m/yd you emerge onto a grassy shelf high above the ocean. This is a narrow ledge, so you will be able to see the ocean quite close on both sides.

The trail continues across this field, with low posts topped by yellow metal markers and yellow paint on stones, providing signage. After 100 m/yd in the open the path re-enters the woods and begins to climb again. Here all the old spruce have died (in 2011), and the only living trees seem to be quite young. As a result, it seems as if you are passing through the skeleton of a forest.

The trail surface is interesting. With so many dead trees, a layer of smaller trunks has been laid horizontally over the path and covered by wood chips. As a result, when you pass over a wet area — this happens quite frequently — the path appears to be almost floating on its surface.

You reach an unsigned junction 300 m/yd from the clearing. Keep right; within 400 m/yd the path works back towards the edge of Gaff Point, and you gain views of Ships Channel. Your ground cover is either bright green sphagnum moss or a carpet of ferns; the path is often quite soggy.

About 650 m/yd from the junction you come out of the trees and onto a narrow grass-covered border between forest and ocean. On a clear day, the LaHave Islands may be seen to the right, and directly ahead you can begin to see West Ironbound Island.

The next 425 m/yd are probably everybody's favourite, because the path stays in the open next to the water, curving left around the tip of Gaff Point before returning to the forest. Along the way you come the closest you will to West Ironbound Island, pass a collection of inukshuks on one of the rocky ridges angling into the water, and enjoy expansive views of the ocean. It is usually very windy here.

When you turn back in the direction of Hirtles Beach there is one interesting section where the trail continues on the beach for a further 350 m/yd. The so-called beach is all rocky ridges, and you might need to depend upon yellow paint markers to distinguish the path. When the trail turns back into the forest, it is because the shoreline soon becomes a vertical cliff.

Only 300 m/yd remains before you return to the unsigned junction. Keep straight/right, and retrace your route back to Hirtles Beach and the trailhead.

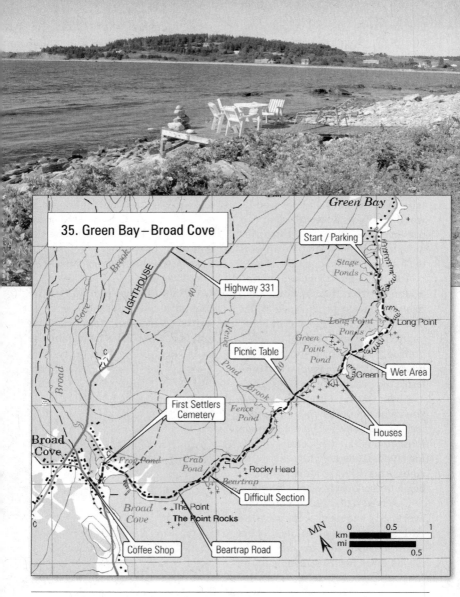

35. Green Bay – Broad Cove

Green Bay

Start / Parking

Stage Ponds

Highway 331

LIGHTHOUSE

Long Point Ponds

Long Point

Picnic Table

Green Point Pond

Wet Area

Green

First Settlers Cemetery

Fence Pond

Brook

Fence Pond

Houses

Broad Cove

Frog Pond

Crab Pond

Rocky Head

Beartrap

Difficult Section

Broad Cove

The Point

The Point Rocks

MN

Coffee Shop

Beartrap Road

km
mi

0   0.5   1

0   0.5

35. Green Bay – Broad Cove

◄ - - - ► 12 km (7.5 mi) return

🕐: 4+hrs

🏃: 4 [rugged terrain]

Type of Trail: compacted earth, natural surface

Uses: walking, snowshoeing

⚠: Animals. Ticks. Exposed coastline. Motorized vehicles.

👜: Good throughout.

Facilities: picnic tables, stores at either end

Gov't Topo Map: 20A01 (LaHave Island)

Trailhead GPS: N 44° 12' 17.3" W 64° 26' 21.5"

Access: Take Exit 15 off Highway 103 onto Italy Crossing Road in the direction of Petite Rivière. Continue for 8.4 km (5.25 mi), keeping left on Petite Rivière Road. Follow for 2.3 km (1.4 mi) to the junction with Highway 331. Continue straight on Green Bay Road, following for 3.7 km (2.3 mi); park on the left of the "Last Turning Area" sign.

Alternatively, park near #392 Green Bay Road (there is a large inukshuk), and add an easy 1.7 km (1.1 mi) (each way) stroll alongside the ocean through the cottages of Green Bay.

Introduction: If you enjoy ocean, waves, sandy beaches, and seabirds, you will love this walk. An old cart track follows the coastline for its entire length, and, although it is no longer maintained by the Department of Highways, this is an old road. (You will even find some signage.)

One of the few coastal hikes avail-

able in Lunenburg County, this was once a much easier amble. Rising ocean levels have washed away sections of the old road, forcing diversions through rougher terrain. This is no longer suitable for families or casual walking.

However, if you like things a little on the rugged side, this is a fairly enjoyable hike. Every little cove has its family of eider ducks, which travel in groups of several females and all their chicks. They are very shy, and will head out to sea as soon as they detect your approach. If you have binoculars, scan the waters not far offshore. A little investigation will probably reveal large rafts of eiders, often hidden by the swell, their numbers disclosed only to patient watchers.

Route Description: From the sandy parking area, continue along the road, the barachois Stage Ponds on your right. This continues to the last

---

cluster of cottages on the rocky promontory of Long Point 500 m/yd later, where you will encounter a barricade of rocks, with a sign that informs you that pedestrian traffic only is permitted beyond this point.

Beyond here, your route starts by following a beach out to the actual tip of Long Point, 325 m/yd later. From here you can look back into Green Bay. Rissers Beach and the provincial campground are easily visible, as is the long, flat line of dunes of Crescent Beach.

A distinct footpath heads to the right, through a thicket of white spruce. The ocean is to your left; to your right are a series of small barachois ponds. Within 150 m/yd you are out in the open, your route a footpath along sandy dunes through thick grasses. To your left now are uninterrupted views over the ocean.

You trace the edge of the shoreline, curving right to reconnect with the old road 550 m/yd after you left the thicket. Turn left on the distinct track, and — probably — wade across a short section flooded by Green Point Pond. Or return to the beach and try your luck that way. That minor inconvenience passed, the old road, mostly sand surfaced, works around small Green Point.

About 30 m/yd from the pond you will pass a newer house, just off the ocean, to your right sheltered by some trees. Once beyond this the route becomes rougher, mostly following the coastline, encountering numerous small sandy beaches. The old track heads through sand, and your feet sink deep into the soft footing.

After 450 m/yd you reach another house, and this time you must walk practically underneath its window. I think you are assured of a welcome, however, as there is a highway sign, "Roadside Table," positioned next to two picnic tables.

The track becomes rougher again, with the old road buried under deadfall and your route a footpath over rocky cobble. But when it cuts behind a small headland, the road appears in excellent condition, at least until the next cove, 175 m/yd past the house. Once again, the road disappears, and your path is the rocky cobble beach to the next headland, where you will find the road again.

The trail continues in this way for the remainder of the walk, alternating between a distinct track and sections of beach where the road has been washed away. One particularly bad section occurs near the 3 km (1.9 mi) mark, where large rocks have been thrown by the ocean into the road, turning it into an obstacle course for more than 50 m/yd. Another occurs at Beartrap Cove, where the ocean at high tide covers the old road, (cont. on p. 209)

29. Victoria Park

30. Wards Falls

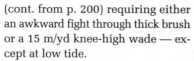

Changing Coastlines

For thousands of years, sea levels in the Atlantic Ocean have been rising. As a result, most shorelines have been retreating inland, sometimes at a rapid pace, geologically speaking. This is particularly true along the low, Atlantic shoreline.

The most dynamic shorelines are barrier beaches, which can migrate inland as much as 10 m/yd per year where they are low and composed of rocky gravel. Where they receive a fresh supply of sand from adjacent eroding coastal headlands, such as Hirtles Beach, they are more stable and may move only about 0.5 m/yd per year.

This erosion is ongoing and constant, but it can be rapidly accelerated by severe storms, which can burst through both low- and high-barrier beaches and dramatically change any particular coastline overnight.

(cont. from p. 200) requiring either an awkward fight through thick brush or a 15 m/yd knee-high wade — except at low tide.

Once across this water hazard is the most challenging walking: the old road disappears and you must pick your way along the muddy then rocky shoreline. When you see a fence, keep to the left. Barely 100 m/yd further you reach the vehicle end of Beartrap Road, with a sign for house #213 on your right, 4.2 km (2.6 mi) from the start.

Continue on this narrow gravel track as it rounds The Point and turns in Broad Cove. More and more little cabins can be glimpsed through the trees on your right, and the track begins to look like a road. Rounding The Point, marvellous views of the picturesque village of Broad Cove gradually unfold.

Beartrap Road reaches the Beach Road at the First Settlers Cemetery in 1.1 km (0.7 mi). Turn left, then right at Highway 331, and up to the Best Coast Coffee Gallery coffee shop, 500 m/yd farther, because a coffee — or an ice cream cone — might be just the thing at the halfway point of your hike. Return by the same route.

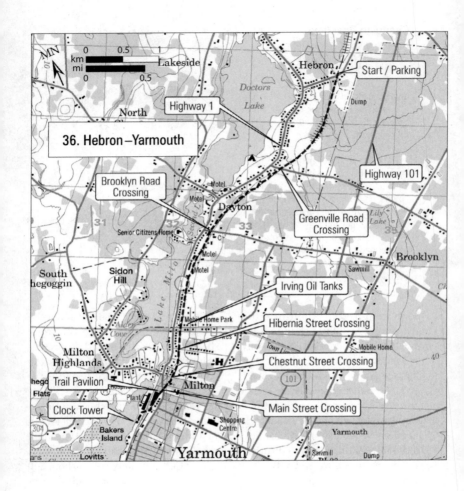

36. Hebron–Yarmouth

Start / Parking

Highway 1

Highway 101

Brooklyn Road Crossing

Greenville Road Crossing

Irving Oil Tanks

Hibernia Street Crossing

Chestnut Street Crossing

Main Street Crossing

Trail Pavilion

Clock Tower

36. Hebron–Yarmouth

◄---► 12 km (7.5 mi) return

🕐 : 3+hrs

🏃 : 3

Type of Trail: crushed stone, asphalt

Uses: walking, biking, horseback riding, ATVing, snowshoeing, cross-country skiing, snowmobiling

⚠ : Ticks. Road crossings. Motorized vehicles.

📱 : Adequate throughout.

Facilities: benches, garbage cans, interpretive panels

Gov't Topo Map: 20016 (Yarmouth)

Trailhead GPS: N 43° 53′ 21.4″ W 66° 05′ 03.5″

Access: Take Exit 34 off Highway 101, turning onto Highway 340 in the direction of Hebron/Yarmouth. Follow for 1.3 km (0.8 mi), turning right into the parking area just before crossing the trail.

Introduction: Few groups have been as successful in developing the abandoned rail lines into shared-use recreational pathways as the Yarmouth County Trail Development Association. Formed in 2003, by 2010 they had completed all 87 km (54.4 mi) of a former rail corridor as trail. This included upgrading, decking, and adding railings to the twenty-six bridges along their corridor, and adding 102 concrete benches along the route.

Personally, I am happy to hike any route that passes close to a coffee shop or restaurant, so when I discovered that the Yarmouth Trail

was just across the street from a Tim Hortons, and one in the former train station at that, then I had to include it in this book.

Dogs must be on leash on the trail within the town of Yarmouth.

Route Description: From the parking area, cross Highway 340, travelling in the direction of Yarmouth. There is no sign there, but there is a sturdy concrete bench. Metal posts sit in the middle of the trail on either side of the highway, and there are also large rocks positioned on either side of the wide, crushed-stone treadway. ATVs are permitted on the trail, but not other motorized vehicles.

The path begins in a 600 m/yd long straightaway, and in quite open terrain. Surprisingly, the houses of Hebron soon disappear from sight, although the many apple trees growing alongside the trail suggest that

Gulls

Almost anywhere in Nova Scotia you will find "sea" gulls. Their harsh, laughing call is as familiar as the sound of the waves. Did you know, however, that at least ten species of gull live in or regularly visit this province, and that "sea" gull is merely a convenient catch-all name?

The most common species are the herring gull, identified by pale grey wings with black tips, white body, and flesh-coloured legs, and the great black-backed gull, very large with dark slate-coloured back and upper surface of wings. Dirty-looking brown-and-white birds are immature gulls, which do not reach full adulthood for three or four years.

Gulls have increased dramatically in number in recent decades and are now breeding and scavenging far inland. They are valuable as aggressive scavengers, living on the remains of fish and other garbage that washes into the ocean.

more houses once existed in this small village.

As the trail curves right, it lifts above the surrounding terrain on an embankment, and at 800 m/yd you cross a small stream on a bridge with metal guardrails. The next bench, facing right overlooking a wetland, is located 200 m/yd later.

Coming into another long straight section, you will see buildings and fields ahead. The brush gives way on both sides, and you will probably notice traffic driving parallel with the trail a few hundred metres/yards to your right: Highway 1. At 1.6 km (1 mi) you cross Greenville Road (paved). Once again, there are metal posts and boundary rocks (actually, square concrete blocks). Just on the opposite side sits another concrete bench and another parking area.

About 400 m/yd from Greenville Road the trail passes through a low cut, where the bordering trees completely enclose the path. There is another bench 200 m/yd later and a crossing of a gravel driveway 300 m/yd beyond that.

You are getting close to Yarmouth now, so when you sight a new Hyundai car dealership on your right, it should not be too shocking. However, on the trail itself, if that building weren't visible it might be easy to think you were far into the interior of the province.

The trail next crosses Brooklyn (or New) Road, 2.9 km (1.8 mi) from Hebron, where there is another bench. And now you truly begin to feel you are coming into a community. There are more houses in sight and many close to the trail. The next bench and crossing, Maple Hill Lane, can be found less than 150 m/ yd further.

For the next 750 m/yd, until it crosses Churchill Street, the trail passes close to houses, mostly on your right, where you should be able to see Lake Milo. Interestingly, most adjacent homeowners appear to mow the lawn from their own doorstep right up to the edge of the crushed-stone treadway.

Just 200 m/yd after this you reach the town limits of Yarmouth, indicated by two metal gates creating a chicane in the path. Beyond this point the trail looks increasingly urban. Long lawns run down to the treadway, and benches become too frequent to mention.

Prospect Street, with its Irving storage tanks, is crossed 300 m/yd later, 4.3 km (2.7 mi) from Hebron. For the next 900 m/yd the trail continues through Yarmouth, with houses on either side, although there is often a pleasant fringe of trees alongside the path. You cross Hibernia and Chestnut streets normally, but at Elm, where the path has started to curve to the right, things are a little unusual. The trail does not connect directly to the other side at Elm Street. A guardrail on the right directs you onto the asphalt. Cross Elm Street and turn right. However, rather than follow the trail, which must now cross busy Main Street but has no formal crossing, continue on the sidewalk on Elm Street to Main Street, only 25 m/yd away. Cross Main Street at the crosswalk, then turn left and walk the 25 m/yd on the sidewalk to the trail pavilion. (This will be clearer when you are standing at Elm Street!)

The trail now makes an amazing run behind and between buildings to emerge on and cross Water Street, where you find yourself on the paved surface of the Waterfront Trail, where there are numerous interpretive panels, benches, and garbage cans. Continue 200 m/yd further to a clock tower — directly across the street from the old train station, which is now a Tim Hortons and a Wendy's — and end your walk here, 6 km (3.75 mi) from Hebron.

When ready, retrace your route.

Red Pine

Also known as the Norway pine, this tree is favoured for use as wharf and bridge pilings, power poles, and other purposes requiring a sturdy wood that is easily rot-proofed. Red pine was also used for ships' masts, and its heartwood was popular for ships' decks. Because of its commercial value, almost all the old-growth trees in the province have been harvested.

Red pine adds one row of spreading branches each year up to 350 years, and grows to heights of 24 m (80 ft). Its bark is reddish-brown with broad, flat, scaly plates. The needles come in bundles of two that are slender, whorled, and dark green year-round. Red pines prefer well-drained soils, particularly sand plains, and usually grow in mixed forests rather than pure stands.

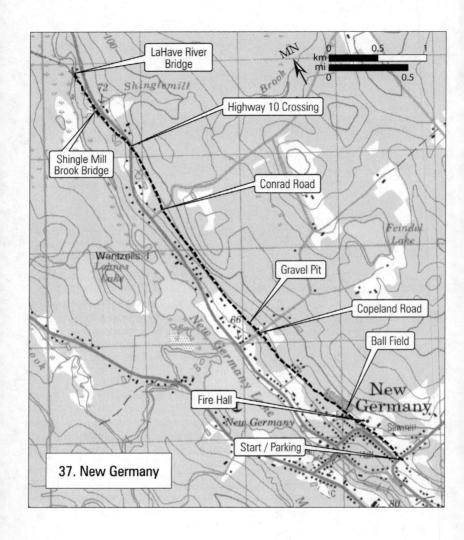

LaHave River Bridge

MN

Highway 10 Crossing

Shingle Mill Brook Bridge

Conrad Road

Gravel Pit

Copeland Road

Ball Field

Fire Hall

Start / Parking

New Germany

37. New Germany

37. New Germany

◄---► 11 km (6.9 mi) return

🕐 : 2+hrs

🏃 : 3

Type of Trail: crushed stone, compacted earth

Uses: walking, biking, horseback riding, ATVing, snowshoeing, cross-country skiing, snowmobiling

⚠ : Animals. Ticks. Road crossings. Motorized vehicles.

📱 : Adequate throughout.

Facilities: none

Gov't Topo Map: 21A10 (New Germany)

Trailhead GPS: N 44° 32' 38.0" W 64° 43' 01.8"

Access: Take Exit 12 off Highway 103, turning onto Highway 10 in the direction of New Germany. Follow for 23.4 km (14.6 mi), turning right onto Delong Lane. Park by the side of the road or in the restaurant parking lot; access to the trail (unsigned) is at the north corner of the restaurant parking lot.

Introduction: The South Shore Annapolis Valley Recreational Trail extends 65 km (40.1 mi) between Middleton in the Annapolis Valley and New Germany, about as far away from the ocean as you can get in Nova Scotia, and only opened in 2010. There are not many managed hiking opportunities in the province's interior, except for Kejimkujik National Park, so I thought this might make an interesting variation. I would recommend it mostly for fall walking.

There are two spots where you might start, either in the parking lot of Delong's Restaurant or near the fire hall. I chose the former because of the lovely maples in the first few hundred metres/yards in New Germany. However, if you wish to head right into the woods, the fire hall is a better place to start and shortens the distance by 1.2 km (0.75 mi).

Route Description: A small path connects the Delong's Restaurant parking lot to the trail. I do not think they will mind you parking there, especially if you buy an ice cream cone or lunch. The trail crosses Barss Corner Road immediately and heads parallel to Highway 10.

I find this first section to be almost the most attractive part of the route. For the next 600 m/yd you pass beneath a magnificent canopy of mature

Don't Leave the Trail
A number of trails pass through private property; respect that and do not leave the public pathway. Even in parks you should stay on the defined track, because the surrounding woods may be environmentally sensitive. In addition, once off the trail it is remarkably easy to become lost. Off-trail travel is more hazardous than walking along a maintained path, and it also requires advanced navigation skills.

maples that tower overhead, providing a thick, green shield from direct sunlight. To your left are homes and businesses of New Germany (including the dubiously named Critter Burger). You only cross one driveway, about 200 m/yd from the start, then mosey down this attractive lane of hardwoods.

When you reach the fire hall, you must cross a dirt road, and the path has been rerouted to the right around the fairly new emergency service building. Rows of rocks signpost your path. A little farther, at 850 m/yd, you cross a gravel track, which provides access to the community ball field on your right.

This is a long, straight, and very wide part of the trail. The vegetation bordering it is quite young, so there is no overhead cover. About 200 m/yd later there is a house and field on the left, and 150 m/yd beyond that a dirt track crosses the trail. This looks rather too much like a road through here, although the horse droppings might suggest some recreational use.

A little more than 200 m/yd farther the trail crosses Lakeview Terrace (gravel), where there are houses on both sides. And, as the name suggests, you should be able to sight New Germany Lake to your left. For the next 600 m/yd, to the crossing of Copeland Road (paved), you are walking through an older, taller, and more attractive forest.

However, on the opposite side of Copeland Road there is a sign, "Trucks on Trail," and for the next 300 m/yd, until you reach and pass the gravel pit on the right, the trail really is a road. Fortunately, the view

to the left, of fields and farms and with a border of old, healthy maples and oak, is far more attractive.

When you move back into young, thick brush, you have been walking for about 2.5 km (1.6 mi). For the next 1.2 km (0.75 mi) the trail remains in thick forest, although you might see houses occasionally through the trees to your left. Multiple ATV or old woods road tracks cross the trail, especially near these houses.

At 3.7 km (2.3 mi) you cross Conrad Road (dirt), where there is a house and large field. You can see Highway 10, just 150 m/yd to the left. But you are soon back beneath the trees, which are mostly hardwoods. You might notice, about 300 m/yd past

Conrad Road, a gazebo on the edge of a field off to the left.

Some 500 m/yd from Conrad Road the path curves distinctly left, and also appears to descend slightly. Only 150 m/yd later you reach the crossing with Highway 10, where the speed limit is 80 kph (50 mph). For the next 350 m/yd the trail is in the open, with grassy fields on both sides. There are even small ponds to the left, and Highway 10 is to the right and a little higher.

The trail then returns to the woods, but it and Highway 10 keep converging until, at 5 km (3.1 mi), the trail crosses the small Shingle Mill Brook Bridge. Highway 10 is so close to the right that the path is nearly its

sidewalk. To your left, however, there are large fields, and you can see the LaHave River.

Trail and road remain close. About 250 m/yd past the bridge the trail appears to become a driveway again, and there are some houses very close to the path on the right. These homeowners have planted flowers on both sides of the trail, and I was tickled to see an old "White Rose" sign hanging on the wall of one of these cottages.

The final 250 m/yd are quite attractive, as you move out of the trees, past the houses, and onto the large bridge crossing the LaHave River. This is a lovely spot, the lush meadows bordering the placidly flowing river, with occasional grand trees, many of them willows, spreading huge canopies of leaves.

This trail continues all the way to Middleton, but I recommend that you turn back here and retrace your route to New Germany — and maybe try one of those "Critter" burgers!

38. Shelburne Trail

◄ ---- ► 8.5 km (5.3 mi) return

⏱ : 2+hrs

🚶 : 2

Type of Trail: natural surface, compacted earth, asphalt

Uses: walking, biking, snowshoeing, cross-country skiing

⚠ : Ticks. Road crossings. Poison ivy. Hunting is permitted in season.

🌲 : Adequate throughout.

Facilities: benches, campsites, garbage cans, outhouses, picnic tables

Gov't Topo Map: 20P14 (Shelburne)

Trailhead GPS: N 43° 45' 53.7" W 65° 19' 04.0"

Access: Take Exit 25 off Highway 103, turning right onto Highway 3/ Woodlawn Drive in the direction of Shelburne. Continue 4.2 km (2.6 mi), merging into King Street, turning left into the parking area just past the fire department. The trail begins on the opposite side of King Street (unsigned).

Introduction: The Halifax and Southwestern Railway — known, not always affectionately, as the Hellish Slow & Wobbly — operated between Yarmouth and Halifax from 1907 to 1984. After the tracks were taken up, residents used the line as an unofficial walking trail, and in 1998 the town decided to develop a 2.4 km (1.5 mi) section as a linear park.

Shelburne was once the third largest settlement in North America, with a population of sixteen thousand in the late 1780s. It was settled in 1783 by Loyalists to the British Crown after the American Revolution, and it became a transshipment point for those evacuated from the rebellious colonies. However, settlers were required in Upper Canada (Ontario) to secure it for the Crown, so in a few decades Shelburne lost its brief pre-eminence.

Route Description: The section inside the town is lovely, with a grassy surface and sufficient foliage overhead to provide some shade even at midday. At the start on King Street, there is no sign, but there is a garbage can. Wooden posts narrow the passage to walkers and bikers, and there is a sign prohibiting horseback riding as soon as you begin.

Immediately you recognize the potential of how attractive rail trails could become, given sufficient time for the vegetation bordering them to regenerate. The section in the town is marvellous, mostly deciduous trees providing a border between trail and neighbouring houses, but also thick with late-summer (September when I hiked) bushes.

The first road crossing, 150 m/yd from the start, is Bulkley Street. Neither it nor any of the first few are very busy, but still be attentive as there are no crosswalks. About 350 m/yd later you cross Transvaal Street, which you might notice is indicated on a small sign on one of the wooden posts. The route is quite straight, so if you turn around you can see all the way back to King Street.

At 800 m/yd you cross Minto Street, and 250 m/yd later cross the bridge over shallow, but attractive, Black Brook. The path begins to curve now to the left, in a long, gradual arc. Many of the trees are mature, towering high overhead, and there are a good number of pines near the path. Except for a central strip of compacted earth, the treadway is grass covered.

When you cross underneath a power line, still curving left, you are 1.5 km (0.9 mi) from the start, and 200 m/yd past that the trail crosses Wrights Road. The path straightens, and you begin to see houses and clearings again to the left. At 2.3 km (1.4 mi) you reach the very busy, and very awkward, crossing of Highway 3.

This crossing is unusually dangerous because it occurs in a curve at the intersection with the Ohio Road, which is also an access point to Highway 103, and there is again no crosswalk. Fortunately, there are many houses and businesses around here, so visibility is good, and motorists have a warning sign.

Once safely across, you are now on the Roseway River Trail, which starts by paralleling Highway 3 with only a grassy strip separating them. Then, 200 m/yd later, or 2.5 km (1.6 mi) from the start, you cross two bridges over the Roseway River, where there is an attractive view of Shelburne Harbour to your left. There is even a bench if you want to sit and enjoy the view and a picnic table after the second bridge.

On the far side of the Roseway, the trail surface becomes a little rougher, more of a natural surface. But it is an excellent walking path, wide enough for two and dry throughout the year. Many houses are close to the path here, and 800 m/yd beyond the river the road leads into The Islands Provincial Park.

Turn left, and follow the paved road the 200 m/yd to the park administration building. Before you reach it there are picnic tables in the fields lining the road, should this be as far as you wish to walk. Turn right when the road splits, once back under

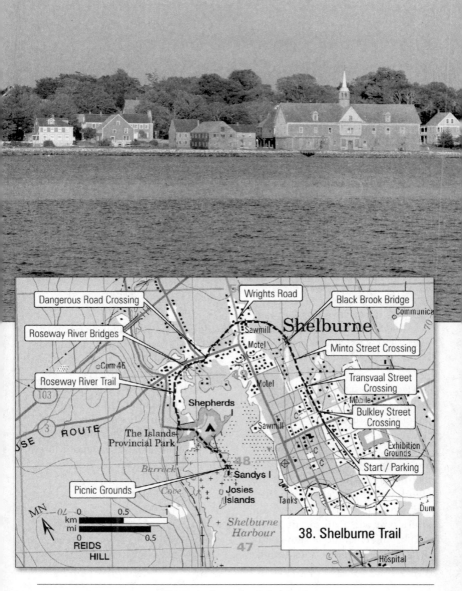

Dangerous Road Crossing

Roseway River Bridges

Roseway River Trail

Picnic Grounds

Wrights Road

Black Brook Bridge

Communica

Shelburne

Sawmill

Motel

Minto Street Crossing

Transvaal Street Crossing

Mobile

Bulkley Street Crossing

Motel

Shepherds I

Sawmill

Exhibition Grounds

Start / Parking

The Islands Provincial Park

Com 46

103

3 ROUTE
SE ROUTE

Barrack

Cove

Sandys I

Josies Islands

Tanks

Dum

MN
70

km
0   0.5   1
mi
0   0.5
REIDS HILL

Shelburne Harbour

47

38. Shelburne Trail

Hospital

Food

I always carry something to snack on, even for short hikes. Although many people enjoy a picnic, I prefer to nibble, so I carry nuts, dried fruits, and hearty breads. Anything is better than nothing, but try to stay away from chips, chocolate bars, and snack foods with a high glycemic index.

the tall trees, and continue along the gravel track, keeping always to the right.

After a little more than 200 m/yd you will reach the causeway connecting the main park, Shepherds Island, with Sandys Island, which is ahead. Continue to the very tip, where you will find picnic tables and absolutely fabulous views of the town of Shelburne and its heritage buildings across Shelburne Harbour, 4.25 km (2.7 mi) from the trailhead on King Street. This is an exceptional location for a lunch break.

The Islands Provincial Park, open between June and October, contains seventy campsites on Shepherds Island, should you decide to overnight. Otherwise, retrace your route when you are ready.

39. Thomas Raddall Provincial Park

◄---► 8 km (5 mi) return

🕐 : 2+hrs

📶 : 3 [navigation]

Type of Trail: crushed stone, natural surface, compacted earth

Uses: walking, biking*, snowshoeing, cross-country skiing

⚠ : Animals. Ticks. Poison ivy. Road crossings.

📱 : Adequate reception on both trails.

Facilities: benches, camping, garbage cans, outhouses, pay phone, picnic tables, , playground, pop machine, showers

Gov't Topo Map: 20P15 (Port Mouton)

Trailhead GPS: N 43° 49' 49.8" W 64° 53' 05.6"

Access: From the junction of Highway 8 and Highway 103 (Exit 19) at Liverpool, continue on Highway 103 west for 27.1 km (16.9 mi). Turn left onto Port L'Hebert Road, and follow for 4.1 km (2.6 mi), turning left in Thomas Raddall Park (signed). Follow the gravel road for 2.8 km (1.75 mi), turning right onto Day Use Road. Continue to its end, 800 m/yd further.

Introduction: I first walked through the proposed Thomas Raddall Park in August 1994, when it was uncertain whether it might ever open because of budget concerns. However, a community association formed to operate the campground with assistance from the Department of Natural Resources, and in 1997 this 678 ha (1,675 ac) site opened.

Thomas Raddall features a variety of natural habitats including tremendous coastal scenery and excellent white sand beaches. The park has day-use picnic facilities, including three unsupervised beaches and also features eighty-two campsites. More importantly, from our perspective, the park contains more than 11 km (6.9 mi) of trails.

Route Description: There is an excellent trailhead map at the parking area, where there are also picnic tables, garbage cans, and outhouses. You begin on the wide multi-use trail, Sandy Cove Road. A different sign says that it is 600 m/yd to reach the beach.

Right away you reach the first interpretive panel, explaining who Thomas Raddall was and what he did to get a park named after him. At 150 m/yd you reach historic MacDonald House, where there are more interpretive panels. Just past is a trail junction; continue right towards Sandy Beach, where you will find a

Thomas Raddall

Three-time recipient of the Governor General's Award for Literature, Thomas Raddall was born in 1903 in Hythe, Kent, England. He moved to Nova Scotia with his parents in 1913, served in the Canadian Merchant Marine from 1919 until 1921, and then went to Sable Island as a wireless operator from 1921 until 1922. In 1923 he came to Liverpool to serve as the accountant for pulp and paper mills on the Mersey River. In 1927 he married Edith Margaret Freeman, and in 1938 he became a full-time writer.

For distinguished service to Canadian literature, he was made an Officer of the Order of Canada and a Fellow of the Royal Society of Canada. In addition, he received the Gold Medal of the Royal Society of Canada and the Gold Medal from the University of Alberta. Dalhousie University, the University of King's College, Saint Mary's University, and Saint Francis Xavier University presented him honorary degrees.

Thomas Raddall had a life-long affection for this region of Nova Scotia. He died here in 1994.

picnic area, outhouses, interpretive panels, and an extensive boardwalk crossing the dunes to the water's edge. Before reaching it you will pass the MacDonald Family Cemetery.

Your route is left, initially along the beach, where at the end of the sand you will find a sign marking the Sandy Bay Trail. This narrow footpath works around a spruce-covered headland for 700 m/yd, before reaching Cove Beach. Turn right again and walk across your second gleaming white sand beach, this one at the base of a tiny granite rock-studded cove.

Once again, watch for a tiny blue sign, your signal to leave the water and follow another rough footpath,

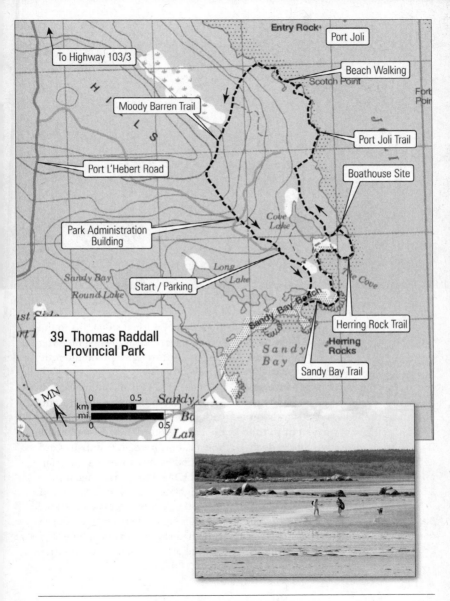

Entry Rock⁺

Port Joli

To Highway 103/3

Beach Walking

Scotch Point

Fort Poin

Moody Barren Trail

Port Joli Trail

Port L'Hebert Road

Boathouse Site

Cove Lake

Park Administration Building

Long Lake

The Cove

Start / Parking

Sandy Bay Round Lake

Sandy Bay Beach

st Side
ort L

Herring Rock Trail

39. Thomas Raddall Provincial Park

Herring Rocks

Sandy Bay

Sandy Bay Trail

MN

km   0   0.5

mi   0   0.5

Sandy
Ba
Lan

the Herring Rock Trail. This also traces the perimeter of a headland, providing wonderful views of the waters of Port Joli and, incidentally, the Kejimkujik Seaside Adjunct across the bay. Follow the tiny footpath through the many dead trees festooned with old man's beard, until it ends on a broad pathway; turn right to the Boathouse Interpretive Site, a dead end, but a scenic picnic site with more interpretive panels. You have walked 2.5 km (1.6 mi) so far.

Retrace your steps from the Boathouse site, continuing until you reach the historic Port Joli Road, in 200 m/yd, where you turn right. As you follow this, you should be able

to see Cove Lake to your left. There are several informal side trails to the water's edge, and for the first time you are passing through a predominantly hardwood forest.

The Port Joli Road continues a full 1.2 km (0.75 mi), over rolling terrain with little view, before emerging into the campground, beside some outhouses, on the road. Campsites are all around us, and there is a water tap as well. One thing is missing: a sign. Turn right, and continue on the road only 50 m/yd, when on your right, just after campsite #69, you will see a crushed-stone path and a blue sign for the Port Joli Trail. It says it is 1.1 km (0.7 mi) long.

This footpath reaches the ocean within 100 m/yd and then follows the magnificent coastline, sometimes on sand, sometimes on rocky cobble, and other times just inside the thick coastal forest, for the remaining 900 m/yd to Scotch Point. It can be a little confusing at times, although there are numerous signs posted, but as long as you remain close to the water you cannot get lost. Watch for other signs warning about poison ivy.

The footpath rejoins a wide multi-use trail, where you turn right and in 100 m/yd reach a large deck overlooking Port Joli with several interpretive panels. This is Scotch Point. There are also picnic tables and benches both here and nearby.

From here, follow the beach northwest. At low tide there is exposed a broad strip of glaringly white sand, ideal for slow, purposeless walking. If you choose, you can continue following the sandy shoreline for several kilometres/miles, all the way into the Port Joli Migratory Bird Sanctuary at the head of the bay.

However, a footpath exits into the woods on your left near a small stream about 600 m/yd from Scotch Point. When I was there in August 2011 there was no sign, and the footpath was almost completely obscured by high, thick grasses. I was not even certain at first that I was on a park trail.

The trail heads into a hardwood forest, meandering across the uneven, very rocky, and hilly terrain, although with no view, until you reach a junction about 650 m/yd from the ocean. This section is far more demanding than any of the previous routes and is not well signed.

At the junction a sign states that to the right is the Moody Barren Trail, 2 km (1.25 mi) long, which will take sixty minutes to complete! It does not say what is to the left, but it is the Coastal Hardwood Ridge Trail.

The Moody Barren continues its meandering, and although there are no great views of the barrens, this is an attractive woodland saunter nonetheless. And sure enough, in almost exactly 2 km (1.25 mi), but only twenty-five minutes, I stepped out of the woods less than 100 m/yd from the park administration centre.

Turn left, and just across from that building, with its water fountain, pop machine, and map, a sign directs you into the forest again on the Semi Barren Trail. Follow this for its 800 m/yd length; it will conduct you back to the day-use trailhead and your car.

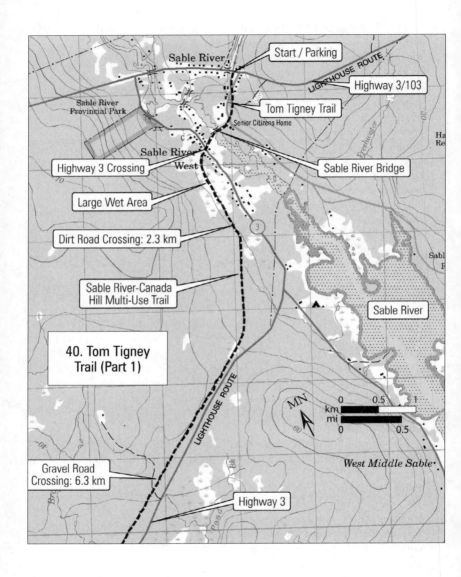

Sable River

Start / Parking

Highway 3/103

LIGHTHOUSE ROUTE

Sable River Provincial Park

Tom Tigney Trail

Senior Citizens Home

Sable River West

Highway 3 Crossing

Sable River Bridge

Freshwater

Large Wet Area

Dirt Road Crossing: 2.3 km

3

Sable River-Canada Hill Multi-Use Trail

40. Tom Tigney Trail (Part 1)

Sable River

LIGHTHOUSE ROUTE

MN

km
mi

0   0.5   1

0   0.5

60

Gravel Road Crossing: 6.3 km

West Middle Sable

Highway 3

40. Tom Tigney Trail

◄----► 23 km (14.4 mi) return

🕐: 6+hrs

🏃: 5 [distance, remote location]

Type of Trail: crushed stone, natural surface, compacted earth

Uses: walking, biking, horseback riding*, ATVing*, snowshoeing, cross-country skiing, snowmobiling*

⚠: Animals. Ticks. Road crossings. Motorized vehicles.

🚰: Adequate throughout.

Facilities: benches, garbage cans, picnic tables

Gov't Topo Map: 20P14 (Shelburne)

Trailhead GPS: N 43° 50′ 28.8″ W 65° 03′ 07.2″

Access: The trailhead for Sable River is on Highway 3/103, in the community of Sable River approximately 178 km (111 mi) from Halifax. Parking area is on the right, opposite the East Sable Road, before crossing the Tom Tigney River.

Introduction: How could I pass up a trail with such a charming name? Actually, the majority of the route follows the Woodland Multi-Use Trail. I think we can all agree that "Tom Tigney" is a much better name.

The South Shore has seen a considerable amount of trail development in the past decade, and most of it has been on the abandoned rail lines. With their long straight sections and wide corridors, they are not usually well regarded as hiking paths. However, these routes often pass through quite interesting natural areas. The Woodland Trail takes you quite literally through the middle of a beaver-impounded marshland. You could not access it any other way.

Dogs must be leashed on the Tom Tigney section.

Route Description: Cross Highway 3/103. On the other side, there is a picnic table, garbage can, and a sign for the Tom Tigney Trail. They sit just behind several wooden posts that feature a "No ATV" notice.

Your path is an abandoned rail line, but what a difference from so many on which you may have walked. This one is almost completely surfaced in grass, with trees — many tall pines — growing up thickly beside it, narrowing the treadway and providing a cosy closeness. For the next 900 m/yd you follow this charming track as it crosses the East

a spot where painted boulders narrow the trail.

Just beyond this it becomes very interesting. For the next 700 m/yd the trail is a narrow causeway running through the middle of a large wetland. The trees that bordered the former railway have died, drowned by the rising waters, but their leafless (needle-less, mostly) trunks remain standing in rows on both sides of the trail. The pond is quite large, and the sight of beaver lodges explains how this unusual situation has occurred. You might wonder how long before the trail is flooded.

At 2.3 km (1.4 mi) from the start you reach a driveway, where rocks have again been positioned to narrow the entrance to the trail. Casual walkers should turn back now, because for the remainder of this trek you will be in a remote area with no sight of habitation until the very end.

The improvements to the treadway end, and even the trees become rougher-looking, with more spruce and tamarack. The path begins a long, very gradual curve to the right, and is distinctly climbing as well. About 500 m/yd past this driveway you pass underneath a power line, where there are large bogs to the left.

The curve ends, and a straightaway begins that stretches seemingly forever. In fact, it continues straight, and climbing, for 1 km (0.6 mi)

Sable Road twice and passes another bench, before arriving at the very large bridge across the Sable River.

There are long views available here, although you are far from the river's mouth. On the far side of the bridge is another picnic table, perched high on an embankment. The trail curves slowly left, passing a recreation area to your left, and reaches Highway 3 at 1.2 km (0.75 mi).

On the opposite side of Highway 3 are signs that tell you that are entering the Sable River–Canada Hill Multi-Use Trail — which means motorized vehicles. This path looks much different, wider with crushed stone or sand. You will notice that there appears to be a large pond on the right, and 300 m/yd later you pass

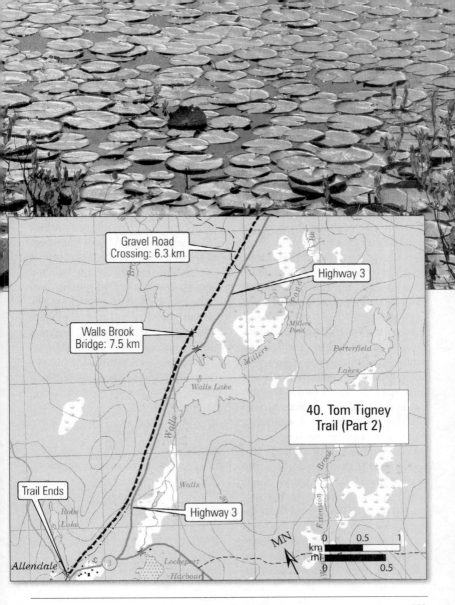

Gravel Road
Crossing: 6.3 km

Highway 3

Walls Brook
Bridge: 7.5 km

40. Tom Tigney
Trail (Part 2)

Trail Ends

Highway 3

Allendale

MN

km
mi

0   0.5   1

0   0.5

from the power line before making a 200 m/yd curve to the right. Then it settles into another straight line, but at least the climb ends 400 m/yd later. The condition of the trail is quite good, with no ruts or wet areas.

At about 4.5 km (2.8 mi) you might hear traffic on Highway 3, which is actually quite close, though you probably will not see it. There does not appear to be much traffic on this trail, even ATVs, because it has a good grass-covered surface. Almost 1.5 km (0.9 mi) into the straightaway, you finally enter an area where there is bog on either side of the path, and you can see Highway 3, perhaps 100 m/yd to your left. The power line is somewhat further to the right.

At 6.3 km (3.9 mi) from the trailhead at Sable River, a gravel road cuts across the trail, the first road crossing in 4 km (2.5 mi). The straightaway continues, now slightly downhill.

You can see you are approaching a bridge from quite far away, and you reach it, crossing Walls Brook, 1.2 km (0.75 mi) from the gravel road.

Shortly after this the trail makes a little shimmy to the left, before becoming straight again. However, it moves quite close to the road, and you even have more hardwoods and pine in the forest, meaning you can sometimes see Highway 3.

Essentially, the path remains straight, with one more curve to the right, passing through featureless forest until, at 11 km (6.9 mi), there is a gated road on the right, and it is clear the owners use the trail for access. Only 250 m/yd remains before you reach the trail's end at the Canada Hill Road (dirt), only about 100 m/yd from Highway 3 and the tiny community of Allendale.

There are no services here. Simply turn around and head back to Sable River.

Abandoned Railroads

Railroads were the superhighways of the late nineteenth and early twentieth centuries, the only practical method to move goods and people over land before the invention of the automobile. Every community vied for a railway connection: having a rail station meant prosperity and growth; being passed by meant decline and economic stagnation.

By the end of World War II, however, railroads were unmistakably in decline, and most of the province's branch lines, and even a few main routes, were abandoned. Yet their role in transportation is not over, for in the past two decades hundreds of kilometres of rail lines have been converted to recreational trails, such as the section between Yarmouth and Digby or between Halifax and Lunenburg.

SUNRISE SCENIC TRAVELWAY

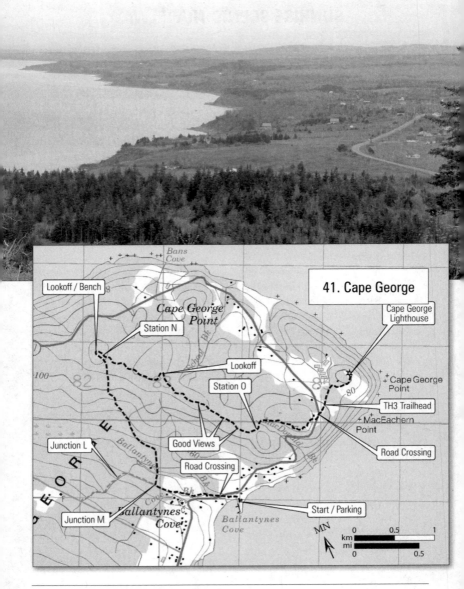

41. Cape George

Lookoff / Bench

Cape George Point

Station N

Cape George Lighthouse

Lookoff

Station O

Cape George Point

TH3 Trailhead

MacEachern Point

Good Views

Road Crossing

Junction L

Road Crossing

Ballantyne

Junction M

Ballantynes Cove

Start / Parking

MN

| km | 0 | 0.5 | 1 |
| mi | 0 | | 0.5 |

41. Cape George

◄----► 18.5 km (11.6 mi) return

⏱: 5+hrs

🚶: 4 [distance]

Type of Trail: compacted earth, natural surface, asphalt

Uses: walking, snowshoeing

⚠: Animals. Hunting is permitted in season. Road crossings. Motorized vehicles.

📱: Good reception throughout.

Facilities: benches, garbage cans, interpretive panels, outhouses, picnic tables

Gov't Topo Map: 11F13 (Cape George)

Trailhead GPS: N 45° 51' 32.7" W 61° 55' 04.0"

Access: Take Exit 32 off Highway 104, turning onto West Street in the direction of Antigonish. Follow West Street for 700 m/yd, turning right onto Main Street/Highway 4. Continue for 1.2 km (0.75 mi), keeping straight on Main Street/Highway 337 when Highway 4 turns right. Follow Highway 337 for 31.5 km (19.7 mi); turn right onto Ballantynes Cove Wharf Road. Continue 300 m/yd; the trailhead is on the left (signed).

Introduction: Cape George was originally named Cape St. Louis, probably by Nicolas Denys, the noted diarist who was the French governor of this area in the middle of the sixteenth century. Denys resided for many years in Nova Scotia. In the late 1700s, Scottish settlers from the Pictou area moved into the Antigonish Highlands, which they found reminiscent of the old country. During the American Revolution, United Empire Loyalists also settled here. The Cape George region is made up of picturesque farming and fishing communities, crystal cliffs, and beautiful sandy beaches.

The tip of Cape George consists of 100 m (330 ft) cliffs, scoured by strong ocean currents. The first lighthouse was built in 1861 and is still an important navigational aid. There are tremendous views of the Northumberland Strait, with Prince Edward Island visible to the west and Cape Breton Island to the east.

The hiking trail system opened in September 2000. Designed as a maze system with interconnecting paths, a wide variety of options of varying length can be selected. I have profiled a full-day hike that takes you to the lighthouse.

Spruce

Three native species of spruce and one European introduction, the Norway spruce, make up more than 50% of the boreal forest of Nova Scotia and are the primary source of pulp for the paper industry.

White spruce, often found in pure stands reclaiming abandoned farmland, is also the dominant tree on the Atlantic coastline because of its tolerance of high salt concentrations. Mi'kmaq used its roots for sewing birchbark on canoes.

Black, or bog, spruce grows in poorly drained areas. Children used to chew its hardened resin as gum, and spruce beer once was a remedy for scurvy. Fishers prefer its wood for lobster traps.

The red spruce, Nova Scotia's most common softwood used extensively for pulpwood and boat building, is the provincial tree. It frequently hybridizes with black spruce.

stockxchng.com

on a small bridge and passes through a yard. On the far side there is a sign, including a map, and a bridge over Cove Brook with a bench on the opposite bank.

Turn left and follow the slender footpath alongside this tiny creek at the bottom of a narrow ravine. After only a few hundred metres/yards you reach Bills Road. The path flirts with it for a while, passing a few houses, but for the final 200 m/yd to junction "M" you follow the dirt road.

Here we find a bench, another map, and a bold red arrow pointing down the right, gravel-surfaced track. Head in the direction of "N," 2.8 km (1.75 mi) from the start. The road drops to cross Ballantynes Brook, 200 m/yd from the junction, then begins to climb. For the next 750 m/yd your route is a distinct road, ascending the hillside. Although there are some junctions, there is clear directional signage at each.

The trail splits left from the road onto a grass-covered track that does not appear to have been used by

Route Description: This route begins at the Tuna Interpretive Centre, trailhead TH2. There is a sign there with an excellent map — it tells us to walk back out to Highway 337, and that it is 1.2 km (0.75 mi) to junction "N." (Every junction or major route change is identified by a letter code.)

The path heads the 300 m/yd back to the highway and crosses it, heading into the forest on the far side. Follow the dirt track for about 100 m/yd, when it crosses Ballantynes Brook

motorized vehicles for some time. Not much more than 100 m/yd further, the trail splits right at a junction. The only marking is orange paint flashes. The forest through here is very young birch, with only occasional dabs of paint. About 250 m/yd later, at the well-signed next junction, you leave the old track for a footpath.

This next section is quite wet, especially alongside the little brook you are following. There are plenty of paint markings, and you are still climbing. When you leave the little streams behind, you have the sense that you are close to the crest. In fact, you leave the solid forest for an area where the softwoods are quite scattered, and the ground around then is grass surfaced. There is one final climb to the top of a grassy knoll, and you reach a bench with quite a view in every direction.

The trail turns almost 180°, and just a few steps away from the bench, in a small copse, is the "N" sign and map. The distance from here to "O" is 2.9 km (1.8 mi). From here the path is quite indistinct, with fewer paint markings than I would have preferred. The route undulates, and with the thick vegetation there are few views, other than of the occasional pile of rocks. This is a reminder that, although the land appears deserted, it was once cleared as pasture and for homesteads. About 1.2 km (0.75

mi) from "N" you emerge onto a knoll with views that include Cape Breton Island. According to the map there should be a bench here, but in May 2011, when I hiked, there was not.

Turning sharply again, the path begins a stretch where it follows the ridgeline, crossing a number of knolls where the trees are frequently somewhat scattered, allowing good views back towards Ballantynes Cove. The trail is not very distinct, so paint-topped posts have been placed to guide you.

You reach "O" just after the trail turns sharply left, away from perhaps the best lookoff thus far. (There are a number that do not show on the map, each better than the last.) The trail passes through a wet area and climbs another knoll to another lookoff in 400 m/yd, then crosses through some dense spruce and boardwalked bogs — and a cellphone tower — to emerge onto Highway 337.

Turn left, following Highway 337 for 100 m/yd to the turnoff to the Cape George Lighthouse. At the day park, 150 m/yd later on the right, there are picnic tables and outhouses, and TH3, the trailhead sign. Continue down the road for another 500 m/yd to reach the lighthouse.

To return to your car, retrace your route.

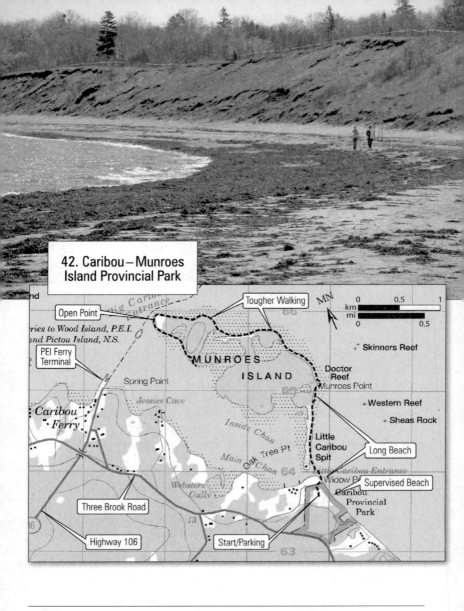

42. Caribou–Munroes Island Provincial Park

Open Point

Tougher Walking

MN

km
mi

0   0.5   1

0   0.5

Skinners Reef

ries to Wood Island, P.E.I.
and Pictou Island, N.S.

PEI Ferry Terminal

MUNROES

ISLAND

Doctor Reef

Munroes Point

Spring Point

Jessies Cove

Caribou Ferry

Inside Chan

Western Reef

Sheas Rock

Oak Tree Pt

Little Caribou Spit

Long Beach

Main Chan

Little Caribou Entrance

Webster's Gully

Widow P

Supervised Beach

Three Brook Road

Caribou Provincial Park

13

Highway 106

Start/Parking

63

42. Caribou – Munroes Island Provincial Park

◄ - - - ► 10 km (6.25 mi) return

🕐 : 2+hrs

🏃 : 2

Type of Trail: natural surface

Uses: walking, snowshoeing

⚠ : Animals. Exposed coastline.

🧭 : Good throughout.

Facilities: firewood, garbage cans, outhouses, picnic tables, supervised beach, washrooms, water

Gov't Topo Map: 11E10 (New Glasgow)

Trailhead GPS: N 45° 43′ 34.2″ W 62° 39′ 17.8″

Access: Turn off Exit 22 on Highway 104, onto Highway 106. Continue through Pictou Rotary towards Caribou Ferry. After 7 km (4.5 mi), take the last exit before PEI Ferry east: Ferry Road. Turn left in 550 m/yd onto Three Brook Road. Follow it for 2.6 km (1.6 mi); the park entrance is on the left. Continue 500 m/yd straight to the last parking area.

Introduction: The coastline bordering the Northumberland Strait between the New Brunswick border and New Glasgow is some of the most sought-after real estate in Nova Scotia. Ideal as summer cottage country, the gentle sandstone, siltstone, and shale of this district sharply contrast with the rugged granites of the Atlantic coastal region. The shallow channel separating the mainland from Prince Edward Island offers the warmest salt water north of the Carolinas, and its long sandy beaches ensure easy access to it. This is one of only three true lowland areas in the province, with the topography ranging from flat to undulating. It is also a submerged coastline, the land link with Prince Edward Island having been severed by the rising ocean between five thousand and seven thousand years ago. Pictou Island is a remnant of a ridge that ran through the centre of what is now the Northumberland Strait. Caribou–Munroes Island represents one of the few natural settings remaining along this beautiful coast.

This is a wonderful stroll for a lazy Sunday. The flat, wide beaches encourage dawdling, and I find it difficult to resist the urge to build a sandcastle (too much sharing?). Except for its occasional rocky sections, this is a walk for everybody. Those not interested in exertion may always remain on the supervised beach or the picnic area on the high ground overlooking it.

It the park is closed and you start from the road, this adds another kilometre (0.6 mi).

Route Description: This trail requires little elaboration. In essence, you just follow the shoreline. From the parking lot, a wooden stairway leads to the beach. If the park is closed, it is a 700 m/yd walk from the road to the stairs, keeping to the left track throughout. Pictou Island and Prince Edward Island should be visible to the north and Merigomish to the south.

In the summer, lifeguards supervise a clearly marked section of the beach, and you might feel overdressed in your hiking gear as you walk past. Munroes Island, or Little Caribou as it was once called, is no longer separated from the mainland. As recently as the early 1980s, a narrow channel of water cut it off from Widows Point, where the picnic area is located.

For nearly 1 km (0.6 mi) you tramp a beautiful exposed sandspit populated only by low grasses. Stay on the right side of the beach. As you near the point at the far end, the sand gives way to rocks, especially in areas exposed at low tide. There is a small impounded salt marsh on your left worth examining, home to ducks and sandpipers.

By now you have reached the forested area, and as you do you will notice how wave action has chewed into the soft soils and knocked over many of the trees at the edge. Your route works left now, after 1.4 km (0.9 mi) of walking, following the curve of the island. Actually, it is several small islands, connected like a string of pearls by thin strands of sand.

Continuing along, whimbrels, yellowlegs, spotted sandpipers, and other shorebirds will probably be combing the exposed shore for dinner, and you may spot terns and gulls sitting on the rocks offshore. At 2.1 km (1.3 mi), another pond appears on your left, and at high tide you might get wet feet crossing its channel to the ocean. At low tide, however, this is only a shallow indentation through the sand.

The next point beyond the pond contains the rough walking. Practically no sand fringe exists, and the shore is small, rocky cobble between forest edge and water level. The footing is difficult, and if there is any spot that will be exposed to waves, it will be here. Fortunately, only about 400 m/yd of careful walking are required before you reach another section of beach. Look on your left again, and you will gain a view of the other end of the second pond.

This might be the most attractive beach you will see, about 500 m/yd long and also quite broad. Walk to the grass fringe on top, and you will look into a lagoon open to the ocean at the far end. I have sighted as many as ten herons here. This beach ends at another wood-covered point, with the highest exposed slopes yet seen. Rounding this is also the most challenging walking, requiring picking your way across a field of large rocks.

You reach the sand again at 3.5 km (2.2 mi). From here, only 500 m/yd remains to the very tip of the island, where you have an excellent view of the ferry terminal beneath the automated light. The ferries connecting Wood Island, PEI, and Caribou pass very close. This is a good place to sit on the sandy beach and enjoy a lunch or snack.

The last kilometre (0.6 mi) follows the beach until it ends, providing more views of Caribou Island, Caribou Harbour, and the ferry terminal. Although you might be able to venture a little further, I recommend that you turn around and retrace your steps.

Bald Eagle

Almost anywhere along the coastline of Nova Scotia you may sight a bald eagle gliding past or perched high in a tree scanning for prey. Their numbers have increased rapidly in recent years and at times more than two hundred have been sighted in one tree (in winter in Kings County outside a chicken farm).

These massive birds are enormously popular with visitors. With a wingspan reaching 2-2.5 m (7-8 ft) and its distinctive white head, this majestic bird is unmistakable in flight, slowly riding the air currents with as little wing movement as possible. Once killed indiscriminately as a pest, it is now illegal to kill or injure an eagle in Nova Scotia.

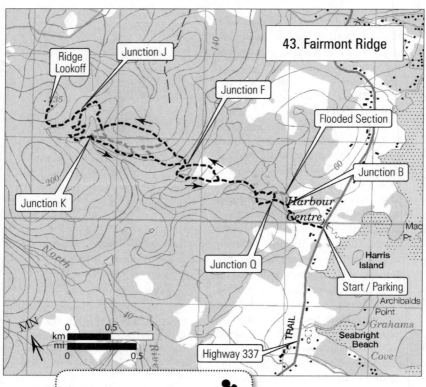

43. Fairmont Ridge

Ridge Lookoff

Junction J

Junction F

Flooded Section

Junction B

Junction K

Harbour Centre

Mac Pt

Junction Q

Harris Island

Start / Parking

Archibalds Point

Grahams

North

MN

0   0.5   1
km
mi
0   0.5

TRAIL

Seabright Beach

Cove

Highway 337

Rain Gear

Choose fabrics that are highly breathable. Completely water-proof clothing traps perspiration, making you wet from the inside out. If possible, obtain two sets of rain gear, one for summer and something heavier for spring/fall. Always carry wet weather clothing in the spring and fall, when the weather is notoriously fickle, and year-round when hiking Nova Scotia's coastlines.

43. Fairmont Ridge

◄----► 12 km (7.5 mi) return

⏱: 3+hrs

🚶: 4 [rugged terrain]

Type of Trail: natural surface

Uses: walking, snowshoeing, cross-country skiing

⚠: Animals. Hunting is permitted in season.

📱: Good reception on most of route; none in the ravine.

Facilities: benches, garbage can, parking lot

Gov't Topo Map: 11F12 (Antigonish)

Trailhead GPS: N 45° 41' 15.6" W 61° 54' 58.6"

Access: Take Exit 32 off Highway 104, turning onto West Street in the direction of Antigonish. Follow West Street for 700 m/yd, turning right onto Main Street/Highway 4. Continue for 1.2 km (0.75 mi), keeping straight on Main Street/Highway 337 when Highway 4 turns right. Follow Highway 337 for 9.5 km (5.9 mi); the parking area is on the left (signed).

Introduction: The Fairmont Ridge Hiking Trail System, constructed by the Antigonish Hiking and Biking Trails Association, will appeal to either experienced hikers or a family of novices. Within its compact boundaries can be found lakes, fields, beaver dams, eagle nests, steep climbs, deep ravines, and mature woods. Those desiring a good trek will "enjoy" the 370 m (1,200 ft) of climb over the full hike. Less experienced outdoors people will appreciate that there is a map sign found at nearly every trail junction.

Rising from the peaceful waters of Antigonish Harbour, Fairmont Ridge offers scenic vistas of Antigonish Harbour, St. Georges Bay, and Cape Breton from numerous locations along the route. Many options are available with this maze design of trail network. The hike I outline is created by taking the right-hand path at every trail intersection.

Route Description: From the parking area, where there is a large trailhead sign, including a map, the path crosses a grassy field. At 300 m/yd you reach point "A," where an arrow directs you into the forest. The trail descends a wooden staircase and crosses a small stream.

On a narrow footpath close to the brook, the trail meanders to intersection "B," 400 m/yd further. Here you must turn left, towards "Q," because

---

beaver activity has flooded the section to "C." So the path crosses the small bridge and heads the 400 m/yd to junction "Q." Occasional red paint blazes mark the route, and you pass a small pond about 300 m/yd along.

From "Q," turn right and follow the rerouted trail 100 m/yd as it skirts the large beaver pond to "C," where there is a map. The 200 m/yd to "D" climbs over a small, softwood-covered ridge with good views of several small ponds and the large wet areas created by beaver activity. Sinkholes, eroded into the soft gypsum underlying this area, are everywhere,

At "D," head straight/right for the 400 m/yd to "E." The path soon crosses the brook and heads onto drier ground, quickly turning away from the water and climbing the hillside into a regenerating field growing over in white spruce and white birch.

The 600 m/yd from "E" to "F" are quite pleasant, climbing moderately on a hillside populated with white pine, your path on a soft grass treadway. You will need to skirt around more sinkholes, some very large. If you look back, after about 350 m/yd, you will have a good view of Antigonish Harbour. And perhaps 100 m/yd later, on your left, you will find a wooden platform and bench lookoff.

But it is after "F" that your work begins, the trail climbing more than 100 m (325 ft) in the next 500 m/yd to "G." Your calves will be burning as you follow the old road through the thick hardwood, reaching the junction after 2.9 km (1.8 mi) of walking. Several ATV tracks separate from or cut across the trail route; keep more or less straight.

Continue towards "H," a 900 m/yd trek through an upland hardwood grove. Most of the climb is complete, with the trail working back and forth over low ridges. In the last few hundred metres/yards, it begins a steep descent into a deep ravine forested in old-growth red spruce and hemlock. To reach "I," keep going down the near vertical slope 300 m/yd, to the bank of a small brook in a deep ravine.

Turn right yet again, and head upstream towards "J." Hardwoods dominate this lovely trek up a narrow gully choked by deadfall. Steep-sided slopes line both sides, extremely attractive and very demanding. The path crosses over an unbridged brook and struggles up the steep hillside to "J" some 500 m/yd later — the most rugged section of the trail.

At "J" you encounter a surprise, something not on any of the posted maps: a sign directing you onto a side trail to the "Ridge Lookoff." This unexpected bonus 750 m/yd footpath continues up the hillside, working its way to another ravine, then as-

Acadian Forest

When you hike in Nova Scotia, you are passing through the distinctive foliage of the Acadian Forest, which began developing more than ten thousand years ago when the glaciers began retreating north after the last ice age. At first made up of species adapted to colder conditions, such as spruce, white birch, and poplar, increasingly warm summers have permitted southern species to establish a foothold. As of 2012, at least thirty-two varieties of tree are native to the region, including many that are either at the extreme northern, or southern, limits of their range. Our forest remains a diverse mix of both northern and southern species. The mature Acadian forest can grow to be very old. Sugar maple, ash, cedar, and yellow birch can reach ages of over two hundred years, while red spruce and white pine can attain four hundred. Our oldest living species, eastern hemlock, sometimes lives to the age of eight hundred years.

cending to reach a grassy lookoff, where there is a bench and the best view of the hike.

Returning to "J," follow the main trail the 900 m/yd to intersection "K." This follows the ridgeline initially, then switches back while descending and returning to the hemlock-shrouded creek bed and the junction. The 200 m/yd to "L'" first follows the creek, crossing twice, before climbing sharply. Keep right towards "N," a 600 m/yd narrow footpath hugging the hillside. This is a lovely walk with views through the hemlocks of the deep canyon to your right. The route to "O," a further 400 m/yd, is similar, though the ridge is less steep.

From "O" the path drops rapidly to "F," where we have been before. This time, however, turn right towards "P," where the path works around a beautiful small pond formed in a gypsum sinkhole, hugging the hillsides and climbing sharply for short distances.

From "P," head the 800 m/yd through the forest to "E," then along the 400 m/yd path you have walked before to "D." Keep right at this intersection, working around another small pond and granite outcroppings the 400 m/yd to "Q," briefly walking on a woods road. Watch closely for directional signs. From "Q" the 700 m/yd remaining back to the trailhead follows the path you walked initially.

Cape to Cape Trail

One of the most exciting new trail development projects in Nova Scotia is the Cape to Cape Trail. This envisions the creation of a 400 km (250 mi) long footpath traversing the rugged ground of the Cobequid Mountains from Cape Chignecto in Cumberland County to Cape George in Antigonish County.

Community trail groups, mostly volunteers, have completed several new sections of the route, with more planned for upcoming years. You can learn more at www.capetocapetrail.ca.

44. Gully Lake

◄╴╴╴► 17.5 km (10.9 mi) return

⏱: 5+hrs

🔋: 4 [distance]

Type of Trail: natural surface

Uses: walking, snowshoeing, cross-country skiing

⚠: Animals. Hunting is permitted in season.

📶: None at trailhead, near Salmon River, Gully Lake Brook, or Gully Lake. Reception about 600 m/yd from trailhead and on the east slopes of hills.

Facilities: none

Gov't Topo Map: 11E11 (Tatamagouche)

Trailhead GPS: N 45° 33′ 03.8″ W 63° 00′ 15.9″

Access: Take Exit 18A off Highway 104, turning onto Highway 4 in the direction of Mt. Thom. Drive 5.3 km (3.3 mi), turning left onto Glen Road (dirt). Follow for 3.6 km (2.25 mi); the parking area is on the left (signed, but not prominently).

Introduction: It is always exciting when new wilderness trails are developed. By their nature, these are paths that head away from human habitation and are developed to minimalist standards, and for the first-time walker, there is always a frisson of discovery and adventure. When I hiked this route on the afternoon of May 13, 2011, I was surprised to discover that the bridge over Juniper Brook had posts but no railing. I learned later that the crew had only built it that morning, and had I been there

twenty-four hours earlier I would have had to wade across.

The volunteers of the Cobequid Eco-Trails Society have developed these and many other trails in the northern mainland of Nova Scotia, eventually to become sections of the 400 km (250 mi) long Cape to Cape Trail. We all benefit from their vision and dedication.

Newer maps (2012) have shortened this distance to 16.5 km (10.3 mi). I have chosen to keep it longer rather than possibly understate the effort required.

Route Description: The full name of this hike is the Gully Lake–Nuttby Hiking Trail System, and we are beginning on the 3.2 km (2 mi) Juniper Head Trail. Once you find the trailhead, there is good signage, including a map. You receive a number of warnings that this is a wilderness experience — one for which you should be prepared.

The path starts by crossing a wet area before climbing onto a recently cleared hillside. You might gain views of the startlingly huge wind turbines on hills to your east. You will probably hear them. After about 400 m/yd you head into a hardwood forest, where there is a sign informing you that you are heading into a wilderness protected area.

There are no particular features to mention: no large rocks, no views, and no clearings. You will notice that stones have been placed to assist over wet areas, and that any forestry roads that you cross are signed. Red metal markers are affixed to trees at regular intervals. These are attractive woods, seeming almost exclusively hardwoods and of a similar age. Even the slopes are gentle and featureless. You do not even spend a long time following the tiny brook that you must cross.

You encounter Snowmobile Route 104 quite suddenly, crossing it. There is a map here as well. Less than 100 m/yd later you reach bubbling Juniper Brook, where there is a sturdy bridge (now with railings!) and another map.

Once across, turn left. The path is instantly rougher, with many more

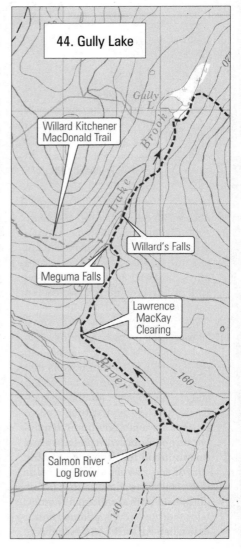

44. Gully Lake

Willard Kitchener MacDonald Trail

Willard's Falls

Meguma Falls

Lawrence MacKay Clearing

Salmon River Log Brow

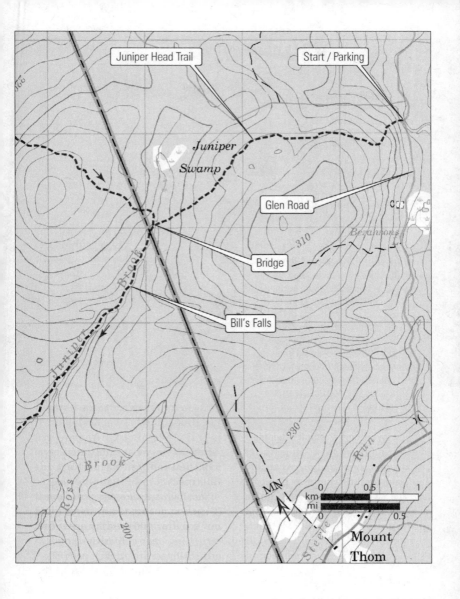

Juniper Head Trail

Start / Parking

Juniper Swamp

Glen Road

Bridge

Bill's Falls

Brook

Juniper

Bezansons

310

230

200

Ross Brook

MN

Steele Run

Mount Thom

0   0.5   1
km
mi
0   0.5

Wilderness Protected Areas

In 1998, Nova Scotia declared thirty-one parcels of Crown land to be Wilderness Protected Areas. This partially met a commitment of the federal government and all provincial governments to complete Canada's network of protected areas by the year 2000. Subsequently, a number of other areas have received similar protection.

The lands selected as Wilderness Protected Areas are representative examples of Nova Scotia's typical landscapes and ecosystems, so designated in order to protect their rare or outstanding natural features or processes and to provide recreational opportunities.

The 3,810 ha (9,414 ac) Gully Lake Wilderness Area, a forest of mature sugar maple, yellow birch, and spruce and containing a network of cart tracks and old woods roads, was designated in March 2005.

rocks in the treadway, following Juniper Brook downstream. The forest is still predominantly hardwoods. After 800 m/yd, a sign indicates a lookoff, where you can see the Bill's Falls cascade in Juniper Brook.

As you continue, the trail climbs to more than 10 m (33 ft) above water level, before descending steeply, switching back across the slope, to cross a small brook. The path here, perhaps 1.5 km (0.9 mi) from the bridge, has been grubbed deeply into the spruce-covered hillside. It continues to climb and descend, several times, before finally returning to stream level to make a 90° turn and head into thick softwoods, so densely packed that they swallow all sound.

Shortly afterward, a boardwalk assists across a wet area, and a few hundred metres/yards later, now on an old woods road, you reach a junction with a map. Turn left for the less than 300 m/yd side path to the Salmon River. Then return to the main trail and follow the woods road until you reach Gully Lake Brook at Lawrence MacKay Clearing.

Gully Lake Brook is now on your left, and the trail follows it upstream, although not always very close. The path is often very wet, but there are many excellent stone bridges built into the treadway. Less than 1 km (0.6 mi) from the clearing, the trail returns to Gully Lake Brook by small Meguma Falls and the junction with the Willard Kitchener MacDonald Trail. You have walked almost 10 km (6.25 mi).

Keep right, and following Gully Lake Brook, passing tiny Avalon Pool and Willard's Falls. Just after this, the path works onto the hardwood hillside away from the water. You spend more than 1 km (0.6 mi) working along this hillside before the route turns slightly downhill and arrives,

quite suddenly I thought, at the edge of Gully Lake. Actually, not quite the edge, because there is a considerable distance of swampy land between the forest edge and open water, but from where the map has been placed you can see the lake clearly.

For a few hundred metres/yards the trail works around the lake, before turning right and climbing steadily up another hardwood hill. The climb is not particularly challenging, but steady, and for almost 1 km (0.6 mi). After that there is a further considerable distance where it appears almost level, although as you progress the downward tendency becomes more pronounced.

I found this section to be the most featureless of the entire walk, with every tree being a similar size and even shape. Worse, when I walked their leaves were not out, and a heavy fog blanketed the hillside. Without the metal markers, I question whether I could have recognized the pathway.

With your route quite distinctly downhill, you hear Juniper Brook well before you sight it. When the path intersects the stream, it turns right, and follows it no more than 150 m/yd downstream before reaching the bridge. Turn left and retrace your initial 3.2 km (2 mi) back to the Glen Road trailhead.

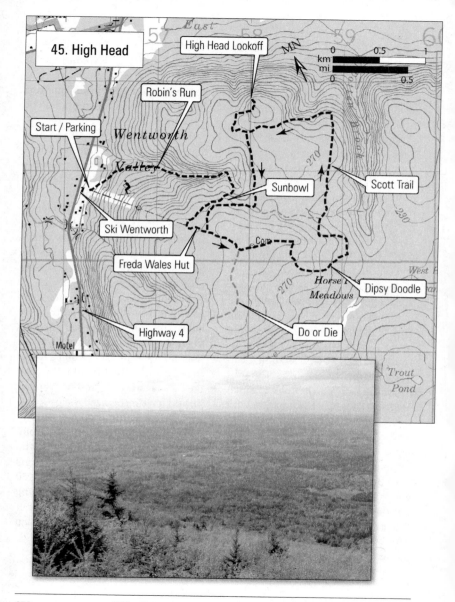

45. High Head

High Head Lookoff

Robin's Run

Start / Parking

Wentworth

Valley

Ski Wentworth

Freda Wales Hut

Sunbowl

Scott Trail

Dipsy Doodle

Highway 4

Do or Die

Horse Meadows

Motel

Trout Pond

West

MN

km
mi

0   0.5   1

0   0.5

45. High Head

◄---► 12 km (7.5 mi) return

⏱: 4+hrs

👟: 4 [steep climbs]

Type of Trail: natural surface

Uses: walking, biking, ATVing*, cross-country skiing

⚠: Animals. Motorized vehicles. Hunting is permitted in season.

📶: Good reception throughout.

Facilities: benches, outhouse

Gov't Topo Map: 11E12 (Oxford)

Trailhead GPS: N 45° 36′ 36.9″ W 63° 33′ 39.5″

Access: Take Exit 11 off Highway 104 onto Highway 4 in the direction of Folly Lake. Drive 22.8 km (14.25 mi). Wentworth Ski Hill is on the right with the parking area past the main buildings.

Introduction: For me, one of the great places to hike in the fall on mainland Nova Scotia is the ski hill at Wentworth, which boasts one of the best lookoffs in the province, High Head — and it can only be reached by foot.

On a clear day the view can be quite astonishing. Wentworth Valley is spread out beneath you. The brightly painted houses peek through the trees like out-of-place plants. Trains, using the main line halfway up the hillside across the valley, can be heard approaching from far away, and they look like little toys as they pass through. A considerable expanse of the Carboniferous lowlands — that part of the province on the other side of the Cobequid Mountains — is spread out and visible. Pugwash, Oxford, and maybe even Amherst can be seen through binoculars, and the Northumberland Strait and PEI can be sighted.

The owners of Ski Wentworth are very accommodating to requests to use the trail network. Orienteering meets are often held on the hill's front and back slopes, and Volksmarch clubs also take advantage of the scenic views. Just remember, you are on private property. Take special care to pack out your garbage and leave undisturbed any equipment left by the staff.

Route Description: From the parking area, take the left-most ski trail, grassy and wide Robin's Run, up the hill. Within a few hundred metres/ yards you have climbed high enough to gain views of the Wentworth

---

Valley, and at 600 m/yd you reach the first junction with another run on the right. Continue holding to the left trail as more paths connect on your right. Tiny Henderson Brook bubbles downstream on your left as you climb. At 1.2 km (0.75 mi) you reach the base of the Explosion run. Keeping left will be an easy decision facing this almost vertical wall!

The path narrows somewhat now as you ascend the gentler Chickadee Trail, with a fantastic hardwood slope on your right. The path turns broadly right, widening again, with a large cleared area appearing on the left. At 2.6 km (1.6 mi) from the parking lot, near the top of the hill, you reach the start of Explosion, to your right. You can see the top of the chairlift ahead; walk towards it. The view is magnificent.

From here, you should notice signs on your left giving distances for hiking trails and for the cross-country trails entrance. Just beyond that is a small cabin, the Freda Wales warming hut, where there is an outhouse.

Continue past the hut, with the large ponds on your right. After about 200 m/yd you reach a junction. Scott Trail heads left; continue on Dipsy Doodle. (There are big signs; I am not making this up!) These are primarily cross-country ski trails, so they are wide like roads but mostly grass covered. The forest is mostly hardwoods, and very attractive.

After another 500 m/yd, Do or Die splits to the right. Happily, you continue straight/left on Dipsy Doodle, which lives up to its name with constant undulations. That is, until after 400 m/yd when it makes a sharp turn right and descends in a sweeping turn left for almost 400 m/yd. At that point it enters into a confusing succession of steep ups and downs, culminating in a 90° right turn and a 300 m/yd descent to another junction, with Scott and Katimavik.

Follow Scott, to the right. You immediately cross a little brook, where there are far more softwoods evident. After working past this wet area, Scott begins a long gradual climb, with a few little twists and turns, for about 400 m/yd before it more or less levels. There is no signage along the path, but its width makes it unmistakable. After another 600 m/yd of level walking, on a hill almost completely covered in hardwoods, Scott drops steadily.

After about 300 m/yd of descent you encounter an unsigned junction, on the right. Keep straight, because Scott quickly turns sharp left and embarks on a solid 300 m/yd ascent. After another 300 m/yd, roughly level, there is a roped-off path on the right. Continue past, and in less than

100 m/yd you reach another junction where there is a sign indicating the route to High Head.

Turn right, and again at the next junction 100 m/yd later. ATV use is evident in the treadway. After about 200 m/yd level, the path turns right again and climbs the final short distance (150 m/yd) through thick softwoods to the open spot on the hillside that is High Head. One of the most extensive views on mainland Nova Scotia extends before you. A considerable amount of vegetation has been cleared from around the rock, and a cairn of rocks has been built to mark the spot.

Return the 450 m/yd to Scott Trail, turning right. The route is undulating, with small inclines and repeated descents — quite enjoyable hiking. Keep right at the next junction, 700 m/yd later, with Katimavik, and ignore the temptation to take a shortcut across Sunbowl when you pass beside it. About 600 m/yd after the junction with Katimavik you reach the first junction with Dipsy Doodle.

Turn right, and when you reach the top of the ski lift, 200 m/yd later, either turn right to retrace your route back, or consider descending the ski hill by another route. After all, from here all trails lead to the bottom!

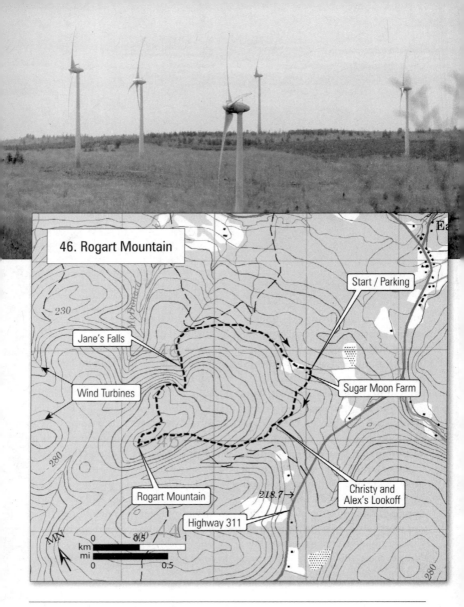

46. Rogart Mountain

Start / Parking

Jane's Falls

Wind Turbines

Sugar Moon Farm

Rogart Mountain

Christy and Alex's Lookoff

Highway 311

218.7 →

230

280

45

MN

km
mi

0   0.5   1

0   0.5

46. Rogart Mountain

◀ - - - ▶ 6.5 km (4.1 mi) return

🕐: 2+hrs

🚶: 2

Type of Trail: natural surface, compacted earth

Uses: walking, snowshoeing

⚠️: Animals. Hunting is permitted in season.

💧: None at trailhead or lower slopes. Only available on hilltops, about km 2 (mi 1.25) to km 4 (mi 2.5).

Facilities: interpretive panels, restaurant at trailhead

Gov't Topo Map: 11E11 (Tatamagouche)

Trailhead GPS: N 45° 33' 53.7" W 63° 09' 12.1"

Access: Take Exit 17 off Highway 104, turning onto Brookside Road in the direction of Tatamagouche. Follow Brookside/Mountain Lee for 4.8 km (3 mi) to the junction with Highway 311. Turn right, and follow for 23.8 km (14.9 mi), turning left onto Alex MacDonald Road (dirt). Continue for 1.1 km (0.7 mi), turning left into Sugar Moon Farm parking area (signed). The trailhead is on the far left of the lot.

Introduction: The Rogart Mountain Trail is a fine footpath exploring one of the higher points of land on the Cobequid Mountains. By itself it would be a worthy addition to this book. But what makes this special, almost unique in Nova Scotia, is its relationship with the Sugar Moon Farm restaurant, a maple syrup and pancake house. The community group that developed and maintained the trail, the Cobequid Eco-Trails Society, and the business work together. The restaurant provided access to its land for the trail to be built and promotes its use; the trail group returns that bounty by keeping the path in excellent condition, year-round.

This is an excellent woodland hike that should be within the range of effort for the entire family. It is defined as a wilderness trail, and there are significant climbs required, but it is only 6.2 km (3.9 mi) in length. (I have said that it is 6.5 km, but I always prefer to round up to the nearest half kilometre.)

Of course, Rogart Mountain's inclusion in the book has nothing to do at all with the great breakfasts/ brunches I have — I mean, COULD have — every time I hike it. Pure coincidence.

Route Description: The trailhead is well marked; indeed, it is almost garish with a large pavilion standing in the southwest corner of Sugar Moon Farm's parking lot. There is a map of the route, and the first of many interpretive panels. An obvious footpath leads into the forest, paralleling an old stone wall to its left.

At 200 m/yd you cross a tiny brook over a small bridge. The path curves right and begins to noticeably climb. Within 100 m/yd you reach another stone wall, first following it up the maple-covered hillside, then crossing it. A small woods road is crossed 100 m/yd later, by which time your cellphone should be working again. You should also have noticed by now that the route is signed with yellow metal markers nailed to trees.

Once across the road, the path route is not all uphill but occasionally level or even, briefly, down — at least for 200 m/yd, then it turns sharply right and begins a fairly steep climb. About 900 m/yd from the start, you reach Christy and Alex's Lookoff, Interpretive Site 3, where there is a map. There are also more softwoods on this slope than there were at the start of the walk.

About 100 m/yd past site 3, the path cuts sharply left and drops quite steeply down to New Portugal Brook. Turning right again, the trail follows the brook upstream for several hundred metres/yards before gradually turning to the right and climbing the steep hillside. About 200 m/yd after leaving the brook, you emerge into a large cleared area, Andrew's Plateau. The path hugs the forest edge at the left for a short distance, then cuts across the field, still climbing. Through here there are wooden poles topped with yellow paint to mark the route; one of these is signed "2 km" (1.25 mi).

Back in the forest, and still climbing, you reach Interpretive Site 6, Catherine's Lookoff, about 200 m/yd after the end of the clear patch. There is a map here as well. After this you enjoy a brief level stretch, passing now through fantastic maple-covered ridges. But one more short, moderate climb remains. This places you on the top of Rogart Mountain, which the trail curves around, passing the north, south, and west lookoffs. (When the maples are fully leafed, you might not have much of a view; early spring and fall might be the best times for this hike.)

Curving right almost 180°, the trail finally begins to descend. From site 10, you should be able to view the massive wind turbines that rise so startlingly from the otherwise unbroken forested landscape. It is about 400 m/yd to site 12, a hardwood ridge, after which the descent becomes steep, with the path wrap-

GPS/Compass

Nothing has revolutionized wilderness travel recently as much as Global Positioning System satellite navigation. With a GPS unit, you can travel directly to any location for which you have the coordinates. I use one, but I also carry a compass as a backup — it requires no batteries, which might inconveniently die on you.

ping itself right around the hillside.

After 300 m/yd, you cross a tiny stream, Leattie Brook. The trail turns left and follows the brook down the hillside, into a deepening ravine. You reach Jane's Falls, which is on your left, perhaps 400 m/yd downhill. It is only usually a tiny trickle of water, but it falls over a wide, moss-covered rock wall.

The trail runs alongside Leattie Brook for another 350 m/yd, then turns right and leaves the forest. You emerge onto an area that appears to be regenerating woodland, but your route follows a woods road, though this is mostly a grass surface. About 400 m/yd after you leave the trees, you reach a post labelled "5 km" (3.1 mi).

The remaining 1.2 km (0.75 mi) follows old roads. After 800 m/yd you reach a gravel road; turn right. In the final 400 m/yd the route passes a farm, where there should be horses in the fields. The trailhead is to your right, as is the wonderful Sugar Moon Farm restaurant.

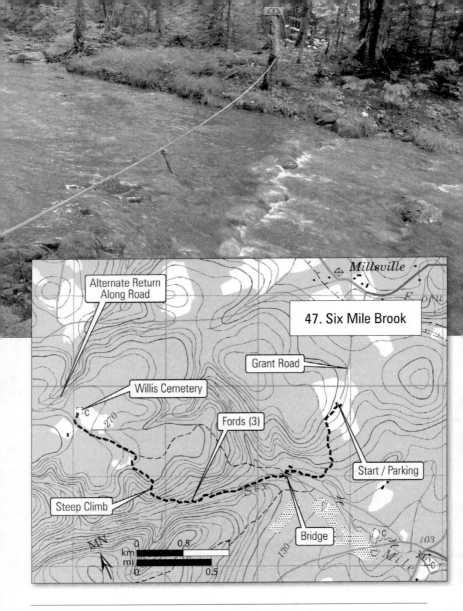

47. Six Mile Brook

Alternate Return Along Road

Willis Cemetery

Grant Road

Fords (3)

Start / Parking

Steep Climb

Bridge

Millsville

47. Six Mile Brook

◄ - - - ► 10 km (6.25 mi) return

⏱: 3+hrs

👣: 4 [rugged terrain, steep climbs]

Type of Trail: natural surface, compacted earth

Uses: walking, ATVing*, snowshoeing, cross-country skiing*

⚠: Animals. Motorized vehicles. Rugged terrain. Steep climbs.

💧: None near the brook or lower slopes; good at the trailhead and around fields.

Facilities: none

Gov't Topo Map: 11E10 (New Glasgow)

Trailhead GPS: N 45° 36' 07.3" W 62° 54' 43.1"

Access: Take Exit 19 off Highway 104, driving in the direction of Highway 4. Turn right onto Highway 4 east, continuing 650 m/yd then turning left onto Stillman Road. Follow Stillman Road for 5.4 km (3.4 mi), turning right onto Four Mile Brook Road. After 5 km (3.1 mi), turn left onto Millsville Road. Follow for 3.5 km (2.2 mi), turning left onto New Road (dirt), then right in 150 m/yd onto Grant Road (dirt). Follow to the end, 1.1 km (0.7 mi) further, parking just after the last house, near a collapsing barn.

Introduction: I enjoyed this route, which has been unabashedly developed as a backcountry standard footpath and a section of the Cape to Cape Trail. It is rough, requiring you to ford the brook not once but three times and demanding that you undertake several steep climbs. This is not a route for the casual walker, but if your tastes run to something a little demanding, I strongly recommend it.

Route Description: The route starts as a continuation of the old road, although it is no longer used for automobiles. Walk past the collapsing barn; you should find one of the "Cape to Cape Trail" markers on a post. You start walking through a grassy hillside, the land to your left sloping gently lower, and there is actually a fairly extensive view.

You go only 250 m/yd, then turn left off the road and follow a path along the edge of a wooded strip. Again, there should be a sign indicating the route. At the bottom of the field you turn right, into the vegetation, and cross a tiny brook. Staying in the woods, you work down the indented hillside, sometimes following the brook, sometimes working around

or even into a small gully. There is good directional signage, as the trail several times makes sharp turns.

About 700 m/yd from the start you encounter a rough-hewn bench, located on top of a small knoll in the woods. After this, the narrow footpath fights through the encroaching vegetation and continues downhill, not too aggressively, until, after crossing a woods road, it reaches Six Mile Brook, 400 m/yd from the bench. Although most of the forest through here is quite young, you might notice a few mature hemlocks on the slope.

The trail continues alongside the water, heading upstream. Six Mile Brook is shallow and maybe 5 m/yd wide. Its banks are low, and you can tell that your path probably floods every spring. As you walk along, you pass a couple of small fields, aban-

doned homesteads, now populated only by apple trees. And after about 600 m/yd with Six Mile Brook on your left, you cross it on a questionable-looking bridge.

Once across, the path continues upstream, the brook now on your right. In summer (I hiked in July), the vegetation in the brook ravine is lush and fully shrouds the route; the air is heavy and humid.

Barely 150 m/yd from the bridge you get your first shock: a short, steep climb, the trail grubbed into the earthen bank. The hillside slopes almost vertically into the brook, now 10+ m (33+ ft) below, and there is no railing on the narrow footpath perched precariously above: this is a wilderness standard path.

The trees in this narrow ravine are now mostly softwoods, hemlock, spruce, and fir, and they are high enough that you can see along the hillside. The path continues fairly high above Six Mile Brook, undulating over small ridges/gullies. About 300 m/yd past where you first climbed, you will see that the entire hillside to your right has slumped into the ravine, carrying away large amounts of earth and all the trees.

You return to water level 500 m/yd after you left it, right at a very wet spot but connecting up with an old woods road. Watch carefully for the white-coloured Cape to Cape markers. There is also quite a bit of orange flagging tape hung around, but this is often used by hunters as well, so do not depend upon it.

For the next 600 m/yd you follow the former road upstream, watching the ravine narrow with each metre/yard. There are a few places where the road has been washed away and usually that means a very wet few metres/yards to get past it. At 475 m/yd, Six Mile Brook has washed up to the foot of the cliff, and the narrow shelf remaining for the path is, well, really, really narrow.

If you have managed to keep your feet dry so far . . . too bad, because the trail now crosses Six Mile Brook — but not with a bridge. Instead, there is a single rope strung between trees on each bank, and some larger stones arrayed in a line, more or less beneath it. Even in July the water covered the rocks. Moreover, in the next 200 m/yd you cross Six Mile Brook three times by the same method.

After the third crossing, you should find yourself on the right bank, and close to a cairn of rocks topped with a red painted post. You have been walking for slightly more than 3 km (1.9 mi). From here, the path begins to climb the hillside, leaving the brook behind. And for the next 750 m/yd you climb steeply — trudge, really — following an old forestry road through the thick vegetation before emerging onto a large field.

You walk along the edge of the field for only 75 m/yd before turning back into the woods, where in another 100 m/yd you reach a dirt road next to a house. Turn left and follow this road, past blueberry fields, for about 800 m/yd to a junction, where a sign directs you right to the Willis Cemetery.

Continue uphill another 100 m/yd, where you arrive at the settlement graveyard, dated 1827. Just off to the right is a new memorial for a 1942 bomber crash. There is a good view from here, a scenic site for lunch. Retrace your route to return.

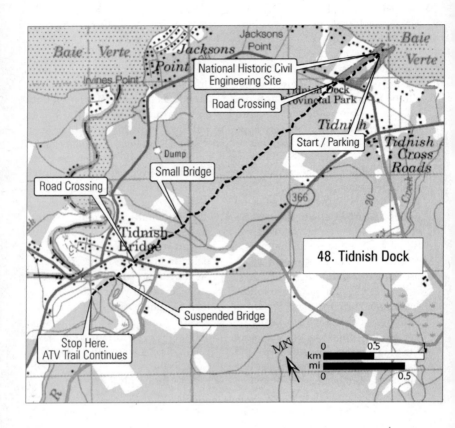

Baie Verte

Jacksons Point

Jacksons Point

Jacksons Point

Baie Verte

Irvines Point

National Historic Civil Engineering Site

Road Crossing

Tidnish Dock Provincial Park

Tidnish

Tidnish Cross Roads

Start / Parking

Dump

Small Bridge

Road Crossing

Tidnish Bridge

366

20

48. Tidnish Dock

Suspended Bridge

Stop Here.
ATV Trail Continues

MN

0   0.5   1
km
mi
0   0.5

48. Tidnish Dock

◄----► 8 km (5 mi) return

⏱: 2+hrs

🚶: 2

Type of Trail: natural surface

Uses: walking, biking, ATVing*, snowshoeing, cross-country skiing

⚠: Animals. No signage. Road crossings.

🧭: Adequate throughout.

Facilities: beach, benches, covered tables, garbage cans, outhouses, picnic tables, water

Gov't Topo Map: 21H16 (Amherst)

Trailhead GPS: N 45° 59′ 47.9″ W 64° 00′ 33.0″

Access: Take Exit 4 off Highway 104, turning onto Highway 2 into Amherst. Follow Highway 2 (Albion Street) for 2.7 km (1.7 mi) to Church Street, turning left and following for 350 m/yd to Victoria Road. Turn right and follow Victoria Road, then Highway 6, for 3.8 km (2.4 mi) to the junction with Highway 366. Turn left, continuing on Highway 366 for 21.9 km (13.7 mi). Turn left onto Tidnish Head Road; the park entrance is on the right in 550 m/yd. Drive to the end of the parking lot, about 350 m/yd.

Introduction: This is a walk along a former rail line that has been abandoned for more than one hundred years. It starts from an attractive picnic ground on the shores of the Northumberland Strait, and passes through quite thick forest to end in one of the few suspended footbridges in the province.

This was once a good walk for families, but the lack of brush clearing between the park and the community of Tidnish Bridge makes it more suitable for adults. The suspended bridge can be accessed easily from the community, and young people love how it sways deliciously when you bounce up and down on it.

Dogs must be on leash inside Tidnish Dock Provincial Park, but they are then permitted off leash on the remainder of the route.

Route Description: You begin at the marker commemorating the location as a National Historic Civil Engineering Site (1989), the eastern terminus of the historic Chignecto Marine Transport Railway. The path of the former railroad is clear, heading southwest across a lush, grassy field. Soon the footpath leaves the old rail bed, which becomes very wet and choked with alders. There are several signs to indicate the trail's route, and the track cleared through the forest is well marked with red, and occasionally yellow, metal markers affixed to trees.

The trail parallels the former railway track, winding through thick spruce and firs and over a small bridge until it reaches the road and leaves the provincial park, approximately 500 m/yd later. From here turn right on the highway and cross the bridge; just over it, on the left, there should be a sign and a small boardwalk crossing the ditch, indicating where the trail re-enters the woods.

You pass very close to a house as you walk along a grass-covered ridge. To your left, the rail bed is now a pond, impounded by beaver activity and flooded. Within 300 m/yd you enter an area of thick white spruce, where you will spend most of the walk. The treadway becomes an ATV track, wide enough for two to walk side by side as it winds between the large trees. This can be a good walk for a summer day, as most of the route is sheltered from the sun by a dense overhead canopy of trees boughs.

Unfortunately, the rotting remains of numerous benches can be found overlooking the rail bed pond, and occasional steps and bridges are too often in a similar state. As a result, when I hiked it in May 2011, it had the feel of being long neglected.

For the next nearly 2.5 km (1.6 mi) your path is through thick forest, with heavy brush that hangs into the track at many places. There are even quite a few deadfalls that nearly block your passage. ATV trails join and split off from the trail at several places, but keep on the straight path. For most of the route, the former rail line is a water-filled gully on your left, providing a navigational beacon; there is no signage of any kind through this section.

Occasionally the path is surprisingly good, a broad track on a spruce-covered ridge, but there are few of these spots, and they usually last only a couple of hundred metres/yards. You cross a small bridge over a creek after nearly 1.6 km (1 mi) into the forest, where there is a bench just on the far side, and 400 m/yd beyond that point you will be able to see fields through the trees on your right. The path continues quite straight through the woods for a further 500 m/yd before emerging on paved Highway 366, which can be quite busy, so be cautious crossing.

On the far side, there is a sign that says "Walking Trail Bridge" and another with the number "366." There are no trail signs on your side. The path continues another 200 m/yd until it reaches a magnificent suspension bridge spanning the river. A sign at the start says that people use the

Stranger than Fiction

The Chignecto Marine Transport Railway was planned to be a method of reducing the sailing distance between ports on the Atlantic coastline and those on the St. Lawrence River. In 1875, Henry Ketchum, a New Brunswick engineer, proposed to construct a 28 km (17 mi) double-tracked railway between Fort Lawrence, on the Bay of Fundy, and Tidnish Dock, on the Northumberland Strait. Ships would be transported by rail between the two locations, providing reduced sailing time and also a much safer route than around the length of Nova Scotia.

The project ran into difficulties almost immediately. The Isthmus of Chignecto is a flat area covered by marsh and bog and was not a suitable place to build a railroad. It kept sinking into the swamp! One boggy area had to be filled with rocks 18 m (60 ft) deep to provide a solid foundation. Even so, by 1891 the route was nearly completed. Financial difficulties led to its charter being revoked by Parliament and the project died.

Several legacies remain: the rail bed, a stone culvert on the Tidnish River that has been designated a provincial heritage site, and the remains of the docks near Tidnish, which were established as a provincial park in 1982.

bridge at their own risk, no motorized vehicles are permitted (although you will notice a broad ATV track leading up to, and presumably over, it), you must walk your bicycles, and there is no jumping!

This is highlight of the scenic walks, the bridge high over the Tidnish River, a narrow wooden pathway hanging from steel cables. The trail continues a further 300 m/yd,

crossing over the stone culvert, which is marked by a provincial heritage site marker, and ends on a dirt road by several houses.

To complete the walk, retrace your route back to the park.

49. Trenton Park

Little Egypt Road

MN

km
mi

0   0.5   1

0   0.5

Optional Footpath

Morash Trail

Hillside

Park Road

Power Line

Louden

Logan
Subdivision

Start / Parking

Druhan Trail

Tree O Trail

Trenton

49. Trenton Park

◄--► 4.5 km (2.8 mi) return

🕐: 1+hr

👥: 1

Type of Trail: asphalt, crushed stone, compacted earth, natural surface

Uses: walking, biking, snowshoeing, cross-country skiing

⚠: Ticks.

🔖: Adequate throughout.

Facilities: benches, outhouses, picnic tables

Gov't Topo Map: 11E10 (New Glasgow)

Trailhead GPS: N 45° 37' 18.5" W 62° 37' 36.9"

Access: Take Exit 22 off Highway 104 onto Highway 106. After 1.1 km (0.7 mi), turn right onto Mt. William Road in the direction of Trenton. Continue on Trenton Connector for 6.4 km (4 mi). Continue straight as it turns into Bruce Street, then 250 m/yd later into Park Road. Drive 600 m/yd; the park entrance is on the left, 119 Park Road.

Introduction: Once known as the Trenton Steeltown Centennial Park, this 228 ha (565 ac) park was also one of the largest in Atlantic Canada for many years. Although camping is no longer available, it still boasts a picnic area, a large outdoor amphitheatre, a swimming pool, and several man-made ponds stocked with fish.

The park always seems busy, but I have noticed that the majority of local walkers restrict themselves to a loop around the ponds. While this might be the easiest walking, it neglects the most natural surfaced trails that take you into stands of stately, mature hemlocks, reputed to be among the oldest surviving trees in Nova Scotia.

The route described on the main trails is 4.5 km (2.8 mi). Adding the footpath I describe adds 1.3 km (.8 mi) — 900 m/yd of footpath plus 400 m/yd additional on the main trail — for a total walk of 5.8 km (3.6 mi).

Route Description: Start at the gate near the park administration building. Once past it, you are on a paved surface. To your left is a fenced field, and directly ahead is an area with several monuments, including an old navy gun. Keep straight, with the field on your left, and at the corner of the fence, 75 m/yd later, turn left, passing around another gate.

On your right there is a pond, with picnic tables and benches all around it. The main route, however,

and with roots and rocks in the path. It follows the creek uphill slightly more than 300 m/yd to a series of large wetlands expanded by beavers, then works back over a number of small hills to emerge back on the gravel path by the observation deck. It is well signed with white metal markers on trees, and the total distance is 900 m/yd.

Back at the creek crossing on the main trail, continue straight. The path curves to the right and passes under a large power line. An ATV track follows under the wires; continue straight to the next junction, were there is a "Trenton Park Trails" sign, including a map, 125 m/yd later.

Turn left, crossing a rope over the wide track. You are on the Founder's Trail, which is still wide, but nearly grass covered and with tall trees bordering it. There are many mature hemlocks. After 400 m/yd, turn left at the next junction, onto the Morash Trail (no sign), and cross under the power line again less than 100 m/yd later.

You continue to gradually climb, turning sharply right 100 m/yd later. You might notice some of the mountain bike trails off to the left. Your broad walking track continues through the mature forest, a very attractive walk through magnificent forest. Curving right again, the path wiggles its way to the top of the hill

continues alongside the fenced field, on crushed stone now. This is a very busy park, so there are benches, picnic tables, a bandshell, and oodles of side paths. Continue around the pond, on a wide path with a broad, grassy border. The route curves right around the pond, and 850 m/yd from the start you are on the opposite side of the pond and at an observation deck.

The broad crushed-stone track continues up a small rise, bordered now by mature pine, and begins to move away from the water. About 300 m/yd from the deck you reach a junction; keep left. Not quite 100 m/yd later you reach a small creek, which you cross.

You might also notice a signed footpath on your left. If you are adventurous, follow it. This is a much different proposition from the main trail, as it is a windy footpath, narrow

Black-Capped Chickadee
If you see tiny, energetic birds flitting among the trees, chances are you will soon hear their easily identifiable call: *chik-a-dee-dee*. Black-capped chickadees are found throughout the province, and they are quite comfortable around people. They are curious as well, and a slow, steady *pish-pish-pish*, repeated while standing motionless, can soon result in several of the little birds landing in nearby trees to get a closer look. If you put seeds in your hand and sit very still, they may land momentarily on your fingertips.

stockchng.com

and back to the power line, 900 m/yd later.

There are many informal trails that connect, but when you reach the next major junction, 200 m/yd later, there will be no mistake, even though this is unsigned. Turn left; you are now on the Tree O Trail, another broad track. This works gradually to the right, and in here the forest completely changes to mostly hardwoods. After 325 m/yd you come to a major junction; keep right. The junction with the Druhan Trail is almost another 100 m/yd.

Turn left here, onto a very soggy pathway. It is wide and grass covered, but in much poorer condition than the other paths. It continues in a straight line, descending back into the former camping area, reaching a gate after 500 m/yd. (On the way you cross over a fairly deep ravine.)

Once past the gate you are in the middle of campsites, now unused, and your route appears to be a gravel road. Follow this, continuing in a straight line. After 400 m/yd you reach the pool, on the right, and a children's play area. Continue along and in 150 m/yd you return to the gate at the park administration building.

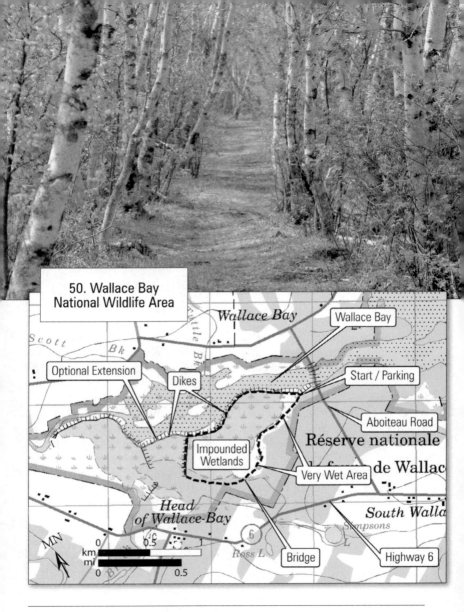

50. Wallace Bay National Wildlife Area

Wallace Bay

Wallace Bay

Scott Bk

Cattle Bk

Optional Extension

Dikes

Start / Parking

Aboiteau Road

Réserve nationale

de Wallac

Impounded Wetlands

Very Wet Area

Head of Wallace-Bay

South Walla

Simpsons

MN

km
mi

0   0.5

0   0.5

6

Ross L

Bridge

Highway 6

50. Wallace Bay National Wildlife Area

◄---► 4 km (2.5 mi) return
🕐: 1+hr
🐾: 1
Type of Trail: natural surface
Uses: walking, snowshoeing

⚠: Hunting is permitted in season. Poison ivy.

👃: Good throughout.
Facilities: none
Gov't Topo Map: 11E13 (Pugwash)

Trailhead GPS: N 45° 49' 42.7" W 63° 34' 01.5"

Access: From Exit 11 on Highway 104, turn onto Highway 4 in the direction of Wentworth. Drive 36 km (22.5 mi) to the junction with Highway 368. Turn right, and follow for 17.5 km (10.9 mi) to the junction with Highway 6. Turn right, and follow for 2.1 km (1.3 mi) to Aboiteau Road, turning left. There is a parking lot on your left 1.2 km (0.75 mi) further, just before bridge over Wallace Bay.

Introduction: Situated at the upper limit of Wallace Bay on the Northumberland Strait, this area has long been an important migration and breeding habitat for waterfowl. Since the habitat management work initiated by Ducks Unlimited, and the protective status afforded by the establishment of a National Wildlife Area, there have been significant increases in both the numbers of waterfowl born here and the varieties of species inhabiting the area.

Other marsh birds, birds nesting in the surrounding uplands, and even bald eagles have moved into the territory since its creation.

The protected area includes more than the original wetlands, although they make up more than 75% of the total area. Of the 585 ha (1,445 ac) incorporated, 17% is forest and the remainder abandoned farmland.

What this all means is, if you like birds, this is a good place to find them. But this is also a pleasant little walk for the entire family. The trail is easy walking with practically no elevation change, particularly on the dike, and the distance is within most people's comfort level. One word of caution: the final 2 km (1.25 mi) are usually wet and especially mosquito infested. Be prepared!

Route Description: Start your stroll along the dikes next to Wallace Bay. Not only is the viewing better, but the walking is easier. Your first 2 km (1.25 mi) follows the flat, unobstructed, hard-earth surface of the dike. Young white birches predominate, creating a fairly low, but relatively thick, screen of leaves for most of this section of the hike. On your left are freshwater wetlands, the protected area created by the dike, on your right tidal channels and salt marsh.

Birding opportunities are everywhere, so remember your binoculars. Soon after your start you will notice an elevated nesting box to your left. Originally intended for wood ducks, these boxes have proven equally beneficial to the hooded merganser population. In addition to the ducks in the water on both sides of you, the trees are likely to be home to warblers and vireos, and the grasses and rushes populated with several species of sparrow and the raucous red-winged blackbird.

Throughout the entire length of the dike you are walking along a slender finger of land separating the waters of the bay from the impoundments. You will pass some of the water flow control devices, built by Ducks Unlimited and managed now by the Canadian Wildlife Service. From the dike you can observe both fresh and salt wetlands, although I found the viewing best on the river side, especially at low tide. Across Wallace Bay the land is cleared and is treeless for a considerable distance. Various hawk species patrol there regularly.

After about 1.5 km (0.9 mi), the dike forks. Continuing directly ahead, you will eventually come to a dead end, but you may walk in that direction for more than 1 km (0.6 mi). To continue on the loop, turn left and head towards the forest. You still have water on both sides, but the vegetation is sparser and you have a wider view. Watch around this area in particular for beaver and muskrat. In late spring and summer, especially towards dusk, you will be serenaded by a chorus of frogs.

At the end of the dike the trail enters a hardwood stand. From this point on, brightly painted blue jay figures affixed to trees will mark your path, although there are fewer now than when I walked this in 2001. As the foliage changes, so do the birds (the real ones, not the painted ones),

photo: Paul Lavoy

with warblers, thrushes, and wood-peckers much in evidence.

Turning back towards the parking lot, the trail leads you through over-grown fields, an alder swamp (always wet despite the bridges), and finally into dense softwoods. Boreal and black-capped chickadees, nuthatches, and kinglets will be found among the spruce. The wetlands are now out of sight on your left, but not far away, as the occasional loud quacking will re-mind you. After nearly 2 km (1.25 mi) among the widely different groves, the trail returns to the parking lot.

Poison Ivy

This nasty little bush is increasing found throughout Nova Scotia, and if you brush against it you might end up in the emergency room. Despite its typical three-leafed appearance, poison ivy can be difficult to recognize, as it can creep along the ground, grow as a bush, or even climb like a vine. Usually found near the edges of fields and forests, if you come into contact with it, you have less than thirty minutes to thoroughly (and I do mean "thoroughly") wash the affected skin with cold water.

59. Seaside Adjunct

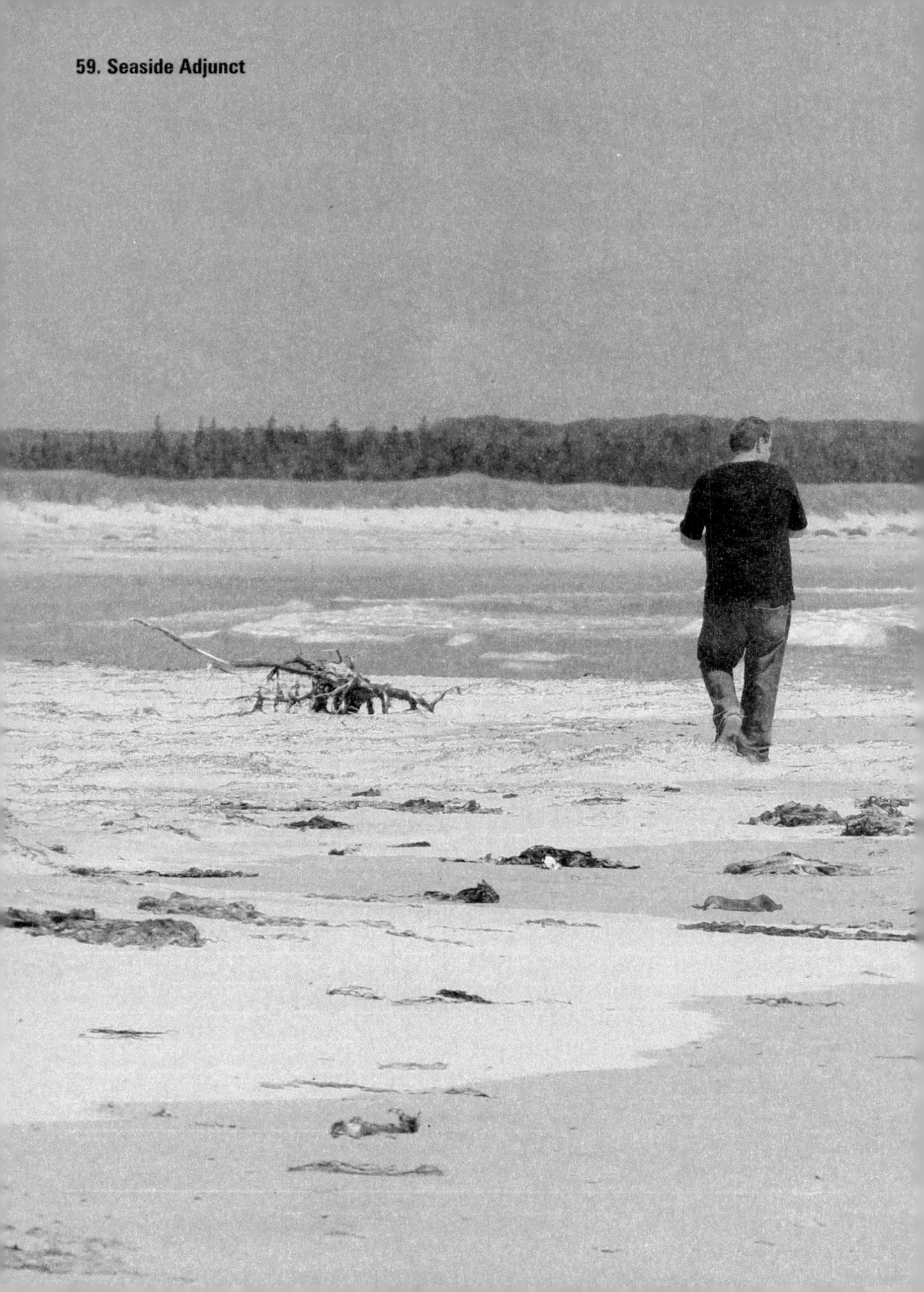

51. Channel Lake

◀ ---▶ 24 km (15 mi) return

⏱: 7+hrs

🏃: 5 [distance]

Type of Trail: natural surface, compacted earth, crushed stone

Uses: walking, snowshoeing, cross-country skiing

⚠: Animals. Ticks. Poison ivy.

🐾: Good throughout.

Facilities: campsites, firepits, garbage cans, outhouses, picnic tables

Gov't Topo Map: 21A06 (Kejimkujik)

Trailhead GPS: N 44° 26′ 32.4″ W 65° 15′ 12.5″

Access: From the Kejimkujik National Park entrance, drive 5.1 km (3.2 mi) to the turnoff for Jeremys Bay Campground. Turn right and drive about 700 m/yd; on the far side of the bridge over the Mersey River, the road divides, with a dirt road going right. Follow this 2.5 km (1.6 mi) to a parking lot. The trail starts at the far end.

Introduction: Channel Lake can be an excellent choice for a weekend hike. At 24 km (15 mi), it can be completed in one long trek or, because of the many campsites along the route, can be broken into two more relaxed strolls.

There is some disagreement over the length of this hike. Parks Canada gives it as 24 km, while the Backcountry Hiking Distance Chart developed by the Friends of Kejimkujik gives a total distance of 22 km (13.75 mi). To add to the confu-

sion, the signs along the route do not always agree with each other — or what is on Kejimkujik Park's Web site! I have chosen to use the longer figure for safety reasons: better to expect too much than prepare for too little.

Route Description: Just 15 m/yd from the trailhead, a sign directs you left, indicating "Channel Lake 4.6 km" (2.9 mi). The trail is a narrow, winding footpath that works its way through a solid forest: beautiful mature hardwoods, with large numbers of young pine shooting up everywhere and a forest carpet of ferns. There are markers attached to trees, yellow and red, which are also reflective.

There is little remarkable for this first section. There are several small wet areas (in Nova Scotia, what a surprise!), although one requires a lengthy puncheon (a kind of boardwalk). There are also a few gentle

---

hills, but it is generally easy walking. It seems as if the trail turns more than indicated in the park's Backcountry Guide, but there is never any doubt about the route, so no harm is done.

So it should take not much more than one hour before you arrive at the signed junction to the turnoff for campsite #17, which is signed at 500 m/yd (I measured it at 675 m/yd). Channel Lake, when I visited in July, is shallow with many exposed rocks near its shoreline. If you are lucky, you may see a family of loons or sight the barn swallows that nest on one of the small rocky islands. At the campsite, there is a picnic table, a firepit, and an outhouse.

Back at the main trail, head in the direction of Frozen Ocean Lake, which the sign says is 9 km (5.6 mi). From the turnoff, the main trail takes a wide, curving route for the next several kilometres/miles, as the ground near Channel Lake is boggy and prone to flooding, and a detour is required to ensure reasonably dry feet.

Conditions on the trail can vary depending where it is in the maintenance schedule. When I was there in July 2011 the brush had been freshly cleared from Big Dam Lake to 1.7 km (1.1 mi) past the campsite #17 junction. It was easy walking and very relaxing. But then I reached where work had stopped, and I found myself

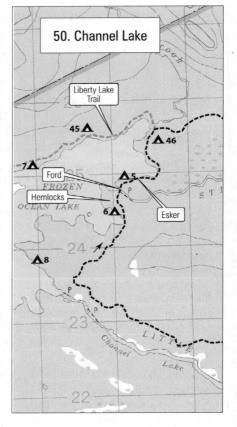

in an overgrown tangle of deadfall and rotted boardwalks. The yellow/red markers had not been placed either, so the route was not always clear. Ask about trail conditions before you undertake any of the backcountry trails.

After 1.4 km (0.9 mi) the trail makes a 90° turn to the right, and an older

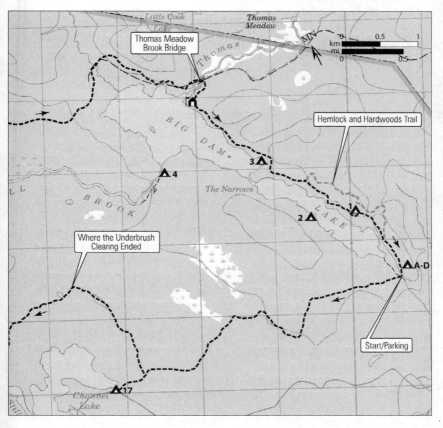

style sign confirms your route. Now the trail parallels Channel Lake Stillwater, for 1.8 km (1.1 mi), although on a ridge well away from it. Only when you approach portage T, and come within 100 m/yd, are you certain to sight the river.

Turning right almost 90°, the trail follows high ground for 1.6 km (1 mi) until it reaches the shore of Frozen Ocean Lake and campsite #6, situated in a magnificent hemlock stand. Some 500 m/yd beyond that is unbridged Still Brook, which is easily waded. However, during spring flood or after heavy rain, it may be impassable.

About 100 m/yd later you reach

campsite #5, attractively positioned on the shore of Frozen Ocean at the base of an esker. It is 1.2 km (0.75 mi) to campsite #46, including 400 m/yd following the top of the esker, and nearly 200 m/yd on a boardwalk through an open meadow.

At 75 m/yd beyond campsite #46 you reach the junction with the Liberty Lake Trail, where there is a large shed for firewood. Turn right; the sign says it is 10 km (6.25 mi) to Big Dam Lake, along an old — very rocky — former road. Note the large piles of granite boulders scattered throughout the forest by glaciers.

For the next 4.8 km (3 mi), until you cross the bridge over Thomas Meadow Brook, you follow the old road through the forest, towards the end passing close to Big Dam Lake. A sign directs you right, where, on top of the next hill, you merge with another road for 100 m/yd before branching left. (At the end of the road is a warden's cabin.) Continue through magnificent conifers, paralleling Big Dam Lake, to campsite #3, 1.5 km (0.9 mi) later.

You reach the signed junction with the Hemlock and Hardwoods Trail in a further 1.1 km (0.7 mi). Continue straight; the remaining section is wide with some crushed stone lightly topping the treadway. Little more than 2 km (1.25 mi) remains; keep straight as you pass campsite #1, the first junction with Hemlock and Hardwoods, and the turnoff to group campsite D. Finally, just before the parking lot, you will encounter your starting point, completing the loop.

52. Gold Mines

◄---► 3 km (1.9 mi) return

🕐: 1+hr

🏃: 1

Type of Trail: natural surface

Uses: walking, snowshoeing, cross-country skiing

⚠: Animals. Ticks.

🎒: Good throughout.

Facilities: benches, garbage can, outhouse, picnic table

Gov't Topo Map: 21A06 (Kejimkujik)

Trailhead GPS: N 44° 21′ 50.9″ W 65° 11′ 00.1″

Access: From the Kejimkujik National Park entrance, drive 11.4 km (7.1 mi) to the fish hatchery on Grafton Lake. Continue on the gravel road an additional 3.3 km (2.1 mi). The parking area and trailhead are on your left and are well signed. The road along Grafton Lake is gated in winter.

Introduction: Abandoned mine shafts, long narrow trenches from "snake diggin'," and remains of mining equipment can be found along the self-interpretive trail. This is a pleasant walk accessible to almost any fitness level. Interpretive panels, railings, and benches make this an excellent choice for a short, interesting walk.

This is the shortest route found in this book, but Gold Mines is such a popular trail, and the interpretive work is so well done, that I consider it a worthwhile addition. Gold Mines is ideal for families, and in the fall

and winter, when there is almost no traffic on the road from Grafton Lake, it can be made part of a solid 10 km (6.25 mi) hike starting from the end of pavement.

Route Description: A garbage can, picnic table, and outhouse are found by the parking area, as well as a few very interesting looking painted wooden representations of gold miners. The path begins by passing through a gate, over the top of which is the name "Gold Mine D'Or." There is also an interpretive panel here.

It begins comfortably wide, passing underneath a splendid canopy of white pine. The first interpretive panel, looking uncomfortably like a tall gravestone, is reached almost immediately. It tells the story about the discovery of gold in the area by Jim McGuire in the 1880s.

The path resembles an old road, and although I have said that it is a

natural surface treadway, I could just as easily have said it was compacted earth. In addition, there appears to have been some crushed stone spread on the path some time before, but that has largely disappeared.

A second sign, 100 m/yd later, explains geographical features of the landscape, particularly its slate composition. There is no view available, as the woods grow thickly in every direction. A significant number of young pine, about head high, are growing all throughout the forest.

The walking is very easy, with virtually no roots or rocks intruding into your path. Although the vegetation on both sides is fairly thick, the trail

Gold Mining

In 1884, Jim McQuire, hiding in the woods to evade the law, discovered gold 9 km (5.6 mi) east of this spot. Soon gold fever spread, and mines were opened throughout south-central Nova Scotia. A Caledonia businessman, Nelson Douglas, was the first to work this area, claiming the land from 1888 to 1890. However, he soon sold his interests to Charles Ford, a Maitland Bridge lumberman, whose family went on to work this claim for thirty years, even though very little gold was found.

In 1922, John McClare, a former prospector who had worked for Nelson Douglas, found a 6 cm (2.5 in) vein of gold in the quartzite rock. Named "Blue Lead," this thin vein was not large enough to be profitable, but too enticing to abandon. McClare died in 1932, never having found the motherlode he expected, and until 1939 his son Horace continued to work the claim. But heavy rains that spring flooded the most promising sites, and the outbreak of World War II finally forced an end to the exploration. The claims lapsed, and the "big gold," if present, is still undiscovered.

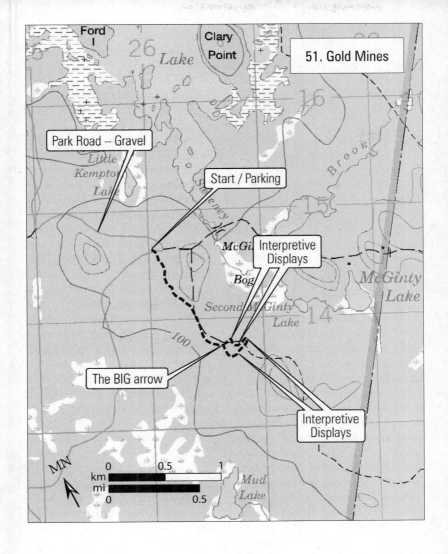

51. Gold Mines

Ford

Clary Point

26 Lake

16

Park Road – Gravel

Little Kempton Lake

Start / Parking

Brook

15

McGi...

Interpretive Displays

Bog

McGinty Lake

Second McGinty Lake

14

100

The BIG arrow

Interpretive Displays

MN

km
mi

0   0.5   1

0   0.5

Mud Lake

a junction, where the largest arrow I have ever seen on a trail directs you left.

You are now on the main interpretive loop. Over the next 600 m/yd you will encounter quite a few more interpretive panels, many positioned next to a piece of equipment or beside a pit or a trench — usually on the other side of fence — that describe in detail the history of the success, and failures, of gold mining in the Caledonian and Kejimkujik areas. There are also several life-sized painted caricatures of miners in these displays, as well as a few more benches.

Several of the panels tell the stories of the men who searched for gold on this spot, as well as their methods. The trail circles through the debris of their digging, eventually returning to the old road that was their supply line. The last interpretive spot, featuring a number of pieces of old equipment, I found particularly interesting.

The loop completes shortly past the old equipment, returning to the junction with the arrestingly large arrow. If you can resist the urge to follow it, continue straight and retrace your path to return to the parking lot.

is still wide enough for two to walk side by side. The next interpretive panel, about 500 m/yd from the start, talks about the value of the forests as an energy source for the miners.

The next panel, 200 m/yd later, describes the outfit used by a typical prospector in the 1860s. In case you need a rest, after 700 m/yd of walking, a bench has also been provided. About 150 m/yd after that the trail makes a noticeable descent, although fairly gently. At the bottom of this, the fifth interpretive panel, "Extraordinary Rocks," is found.

The trail now begins to curve to the left and climbs slightly. About 1.2 km (0.75 mi) from the start you reach

53. Hemlock and Hardwoods

◄---► 5 km (3.1 mi) return

⏱: 1+ hr

👥: 1

Type of Trail: crushed stone, boardwalk

Uses: walking, snowshoeing, cross-country skiing

⚠: Animals. Ticks.

📵: Good throughout.

Facilities: campsites, garbage cans, interpretive panels, outhouses, picnic tables

Gov't Topo Map: 21A06 (Kejimkujik)

Trailhead GPS: N 44° 26′ 32.4″ W 65° 15′ 12.5″

Access: From the Kejimkujik National Park entrance, drive 5.1 km (3.2 mi) to the turnoff for Jeremys Bay Campground. Turn right, driving about 700 m/yd; on the far side of the bridge over the Mersey River, the road divides, with a dirt road going right. Follow this 2.5 km (1.6 mi) to a parking lot. The trail starts at the far end.

Introduction: Very little of the original forest in Kejimkujik survived the logging boom of the 1800s, but isolated groves of old-growth eastern hemlock can still be found, some of them as old as three hundred years. A significant stand of these graceful softwoods is located along the northern edge of Big Dam Lake. A trail has been created to make these trees available to nature hikers, and it offers the most spectacular forest walk in the province. Relatively short, level, and well maintained, this trail is excellent for families and people of most fitness levels.

Route Description: This short loop begins at the Big Dam parking lot, which is also the trailhead for the Channel Lake Trail and the Liberty Lake trails as well as a popular starting point for canoe trips. Fortunately, some large new signs keep traffic directed. So keep right, on the wide, level track, following the signs. You will notice that the forest is mixed, mostly tall hardwoods with a thriving population of pine growing up in their shade.

Just past the entrance to campsite A, on your left, you encounter two large interpretive panels, which talk about fires and their place in forest life and regeneration. It is 650 m/yd from the trailhead to the junction where the sign directs you right, off the Liberty Lake Trail, which continues in the direction of Frozen

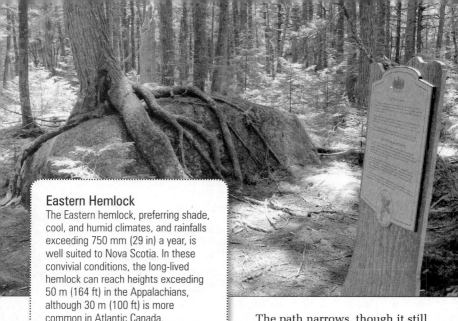

Eastern Hemlock

The Eastern hemlock, preferring shade, cool, and humid climates, and rainfalls exceeding 750 mm (29 in) a year, is well suited to Nova Scotia. In these convivial conditions, the long-lived hemlock can reach heights exceeding 50 m (164 ft) in the Appalachians, although 30 m (100 ft) is more common in Atlantic Canada.

Hemlocks can live up to six hundred years, and during that time they will create a pure stand that crowds out other species. In an old stand, such as the one in Kejimkujik, with a canopy high overhead, the ground beneath the towering trees supports no other life than mosses and lichens.

Ocean Lake. En route you pass connecting paths to campsites B-C, all on your left. As soon as you make the turn, there is an interpretive panel that outlines how rare old hemlock forests are in Nova Scotia. It also says that the loop you do will be 3.2 km (2 mi).

The path narrows, though it still contains some crushed stone on top. The trail works through the mixed forest for another 1.2 km (0.75 mi), passing interpretive panels that explain the changing forest, the tall white pines, and the importance of sunlight.

And then, as if moving from one room to another with a completely different decor, you enter into the hemlock forest. Initially you are among small, young trees, and another panel, "Keeping It Cool," explains that this is a transition zone where the towering hardwoods are protecting this young growth. Meanwhile, the young hemlocks

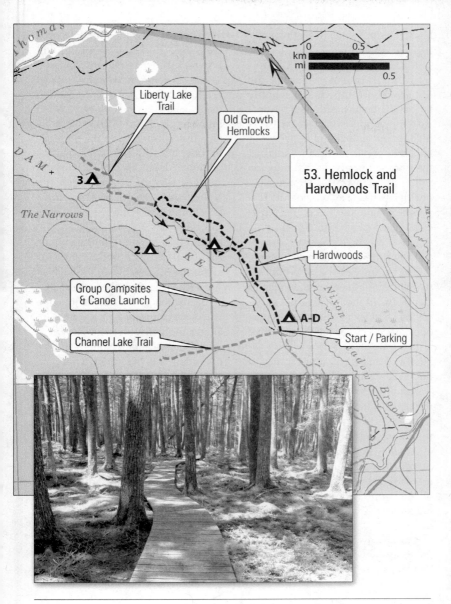

Liberty Lake Trail

Old Growth Hemlocks

53. Hemlock and Hardwoods Trail

Thomas

D A M

The Narrows

L A K E

3

2

1

A-D

Hardwoods

Group Campsites & Canoe Launch

Channel Lake Trail

Start / Parking

Nixon

Brook

block the sun so effectively that nothing else grows among them.

Little more than 2 km (1.25 mi) from the trailhead you reach the old-growth forest, where a lengthy boardwalk begins. Although the area through which you pass, with its high canopy and lack of understorey, appears open to aimless wandering, the trees are easily damaged by too much human traffic. Therefore, a boardwalk has been provided so that people may experience these towering hemlocks without destroying them.

Very little light penetrates here, giving an impression of perpetual twilight, and little other than mosses can thrive in the thick carpet of decaying hemlock needles. Only where one of the trees has fallen, admitting a shaft of light, does new growth appear, and this is either red spruce or hemlock saplings.

At the very start of the boardwalk is a panel stating that in front of you is the oldest known tree: more than four hundred years old or already alive before Europeans first settled in Nova Scotia. You are inside a massive arboreal cathedral, the huge trunks of the hemlocks the columns supporting the dome of the canopy far overhead.

The boardwalk meanders through the grove, which covers the top of a low, rounded hill for the next 600 m/

yd. There are several more interpretive panels along the way, but I will let you discover them for yourself. These are some of the painfully few remnants of the Acadian forest that many believe covered the New World of the original European explorers. I am always humbled in the presence of these magnificent giants. This is, without a doubt, a very special place.

Within sight of the end of the boardwalk is the reconnecting junction to the Liberty Lake Trail. A sign indicates that Big Dam Lake is 2 km (1.25 mi) to the left. Continue along the excellent footpath as it heads alongside Big Dam Lake, although always well back from the water's edge.

About 900 m/yd from the junction you reach campsite #1, on your right. Take a moment to venture down to the lakeshore and explore — unless, of course, it is occupied. There are tent pads, a picnic table, a firepit, an outhouse, and a large supply of firewood, and you can walk right to the lake and dip your toes, or even go for a swim on a hot day.

From campsite #1, only 800 m/yd of easy walking remains before you reach the entrance junction to the Hemlock and Hardwoods Trail. Retrace the first 650 m/yd back to the trailhead.

54. Liberty Lake

◄ - - - ► 61 km (38.1 mi) one way

⏱: 3 days

🏃: 5 [distance]

Type of Trail: natural surface, compacted earth

Uses: walking, biking*, snowshoeing, cross-country skiing*

⚠: Animals. Ticks. Remote location.

📵: Adequate through most of Day 1 and Day 3 routes, but mostly no reception between Frozen Ocean Lake and Mason's Cabin.

Facilities: campsites, firewood, garbage cans, outhouses, shelter with stove, water

Gov't Topo Map: 21A06 (Kejimkujik)

Trailhead GPS: N 44° 26′ 32.4″ W 65° 15′ 12.5″

Access: From the Kejimkujik National Park entrance, drive 5.1 km (3.2 mi) to the turnoff for Jeremys Bay Campground. Turn right, driving about 700 m/yd; on the far side of the bridge over the Mersey River, the road divides, with a dirt road going right. Follow this 2.5 km (1.6 mi) to a parking lot. The trail starts at the far end.

Introduction: There are few official overnight backpacking experiences available in Nova Scotia; the Liberty Lake Loop is the longest wilderness footpath system so far developed. The Kejimkujik backcountry is filled with lakes, interesting vegetation, and abundant wildlife. Between Frozen Ocean and Peskawa lakes, you will be in an area rarely travelled. Most years fewer than one hundred people register for the trip round the backcountry.

This trip can be undertaken either as part of a multi-day excursion around the entire park, with several side-trip possibilities, or as an overnight out and back hike. I have suggested camping at site #43, but this requires a full day of walking to reach from Big Dam Lake. Sites #44 and #45 are common alternatives, especially just to overnight.

Unfortunately, Liberty Lake is not a loop. You will need a car at both ends, as it is more than 20 km (12.5 mi) from the Eel Weir finish to the Big Dam Lake trailhead.

Route Description:

Day 1: Several trails begin from the trailhead at Big Dam Lake, including Channel Lake, and about 500 m/yd into the walk the junction to the Hemlock and Hardwoods Trail. There is also a canoe launch and a

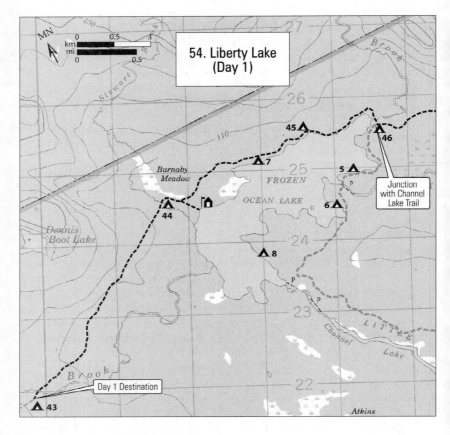

54. Liberty Lake (Day 1)

number of campsites, each with its own path. But the signage is new, and good, and the trail is well maintained and quite distinct. Keep Big Dam Lake on your left; it is usually visible through the forest, and you should be fine. Continue straight through the next junction, also with Hemlock and Hardwoods, and about

900 m/yd later you reach campsite #3. Like all the prepared sites, there is an outhouse there.

After nearly 4 km (2.5 mi), the footpath connects to a former woods road. Turn right; left leads to a warden's cabin and a dead end. Almost immediately a sign directs you sharply left again, where you cross a

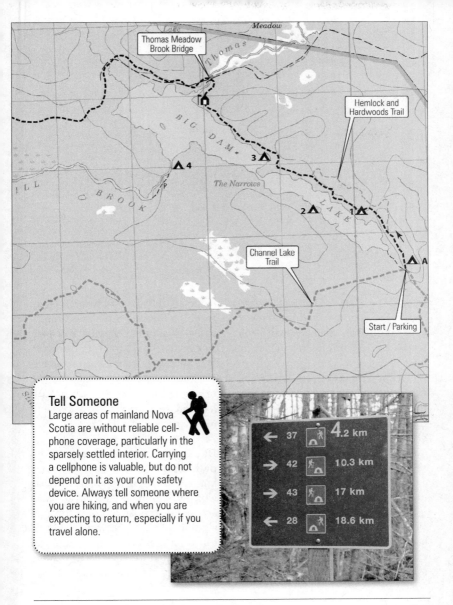

Thomas Meadow Brook Bridge

Hemlock and Hardwoods Trail

4

3

The Narrows

2

1

A

Channel Lake Trail

Start / Parking

Tell Someone

Large areas of mainland Nova Scotia are without reliable cellphone coverage, particularly in the sparsely settled interior. Carrying a cellphone is valuable, but do not depend on it as your only safety device. Always tell someone where you are hiking, and when you are expecting to return, especially if you travel alone.

← 37		4.2 km
→ 42		10.3 km
→ 43		17 km
← 28		18.6 km

bridge over sluggish Thomas Meadow Brook. You continue on this old road, used now by park maintenance, for at least 4 km (2.5 mi) to Frozen Ocean Lake.

This is a junction with the Channel Lake Trail, and a major firewood depot. Immediately to the left is campsite #46; straight ahead is a clearing and the lake. To continue on the Liberty Lake loop, turn right, crossing over lively Torment Brook on a small footbridge. The trail narrows to a footpath once again.

The path works around the north side of Frozen Ocean Lake, passing campsites #45, beyond which the trail gets rockier and narrower, and #7. After this it moves back onto a

ridge away from the water's edge, reaching Stewart Brook, and campsite #44, about 1.5 km (0.9 mi) later. The next 4 km (2.5 mi) to campsite #43 are through attractive mixed forest. You find it just after crossing the bridge at Inness Brook, a beautiful location beside the brook, a good end for the first day's hike.

Day 2: Leaving campsite #43, the path climbs gently for the next 3 km (1.9 mi), then descends towards Northwest Branch West River. Once across this brook, you pass through significant pine and spruce stands, but then continue on through the usual mixed forest. The trail stays reasonably level for the next several

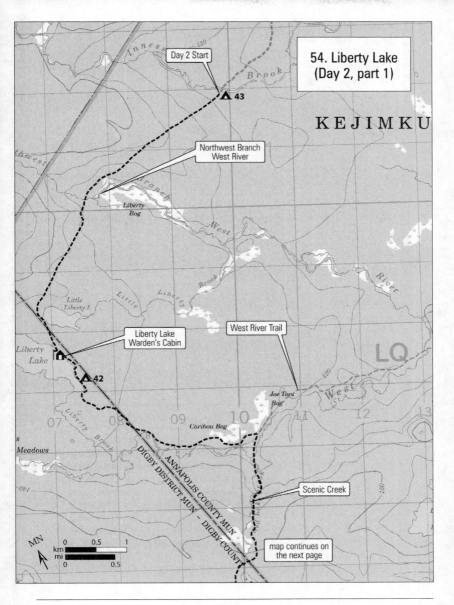

54. Liberty Lake
(Day 2, part 1)

Day 2 Start

▲ 43

KEJIMKU

Innes... Brook

Northwest Branch
West River

Liberty Bog

Northwest

Branch

West

Liberty

Brook

River

Little Liberty L.

Little

Liberty Lake
Warden's Cabin

West River Trail

LQ

Liberty Lake

▲ 42

Joe Tont Bog

120

West

Liberty Brook

07

08

09

10

11

12

13

Caribou Bog

Meadows

ANNAPOLIS COUNTY MUN

DIGBY DISTRICT MUN – DIGBY COUNT

Scenic Creek

150

MN

km 0   0.5   1
mi 0   0.5

map continues on
the next page

Kejimkujik National Park

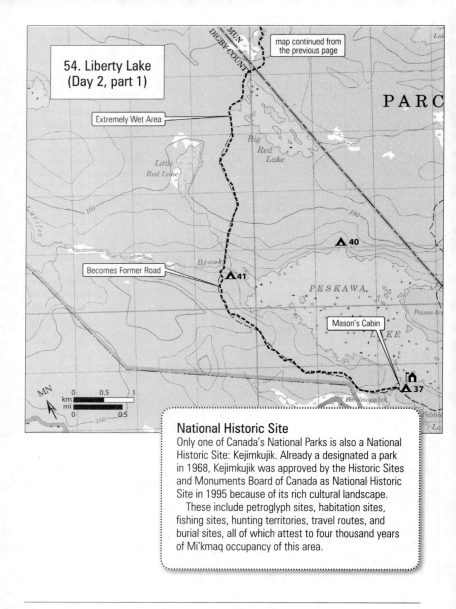

54. Liberty Lake
(Day 2, part 1)

map continued from the previous page

PARC

Extremely Wet Area

Big Red Lake

Little Red Lake

▲ 40

Becomes Former Road

▲ 41

PESKAWA

Mason's Cabin

LAKE

Poison

▲ 37

Pebbleloggitch

MN

km
0   0.5   1
mi
0   0.5

National Historic Site

Only one of Canada's National Parks is also a National Historic Site: Kejimkujik. Already a designated a park in 1968, Kejimkujik was approved by the Historic Sites and Monuments Board of Canada as National Historic Site in 1995 because of its rich cultural landscape.

These include petroglyph sites, habitation sites, fishing sites, hunting territories, travel routes, and burial sites, all of which attest to four thousand years of Mi'kmaq occupancy of this area.

kilometres/miles, gradually curving towards the south.

As you near Liberty Lake, the trail turns in a quagmire for several hundred metres/yards. By the time your feet — possibly your ankles and shins, and maybe even your knees — are thoroughly wet, Liberty Lake becomes visible to your right. The warden's cabin, though locked, is beside the trail on the lakeshore and has a well and outhouses for general use. Less than 1 km (0.6 mi) later, near the south end of Liberty Lake, is campsite #42, approximately 25.5 km (16 mi) from Big Dam.

The trail follows the lakeshore a short distance further, then turns sharply left, heading about 1.6 km (1 mi) overland before reaching the West River (at another bog, of course). For the next 2.5 km (1.6 mi), the route more or less follows the river downstream to a junction with the West River Trail. Actually, the sign simply says that campsite #22 is 9 km (5.6 mi) further; don't go that way, unless you are prepared for an extra day of hiking, as it is a dead end.

Instead, turn right. Your route descends to cross West River, another place where the trail passes through a flood zone for a good distance. Once safely across the bridge, at Red Lake Brook, you pass through one of my favourite sections of the route. The trail climbs alongside this small, lively brook for about 1 km (0.6 mi), the tea-coloured water cascading down a stream bed of moss-covered boulders, depositing huge mounds of quivering foam in every sheltered spot.

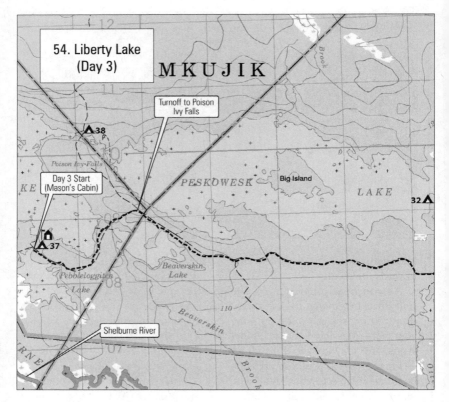

54. Liberty Lake (Day 3)

M K U J I K

Turnoff to Poison Ivy Falls

▲38
P

Poison Ivy Falls

PESKOWESK

Big Island

K E

Day 3 Start (Mason's Cabin)

LAKE

32▲

▲37

Beaverskin Lake

Pebbleloggitch Lake

110

Shelburne River

Beaverskin

Brook

After the path crosses Red Lake Brook, about 3 km (1.9 mi) from the West River Trail junction, you head into the soggiest portion of the trail. As you work around the west side of Big Red Lake, often visible on your left, it appears as if spongelike sphagnum moss has grown over the entire trail; you cannot avoid wet feet. You spend far too long picking through here before the path heaves itself over

a large hill and down the other side to reach Lucifee Brook, 7 km (4.4 mi) from the West River Trail junction. (There is another significant wet area, the brook draining Little Red Lake, just before Lucifee Brook, but since you already have wet feet . . .)

Campsite #41 is just across a respectably sturdy bridge, and about 200 m/yd farther the trail becomes a wide, dry dirt road. About 4 km

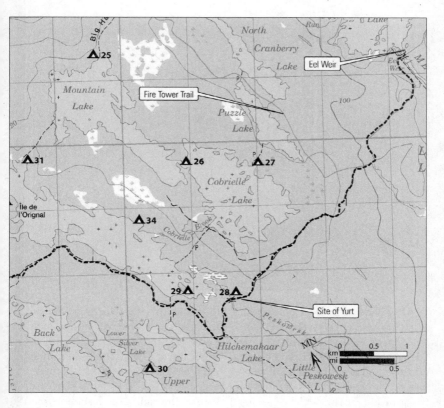

(2.5 mi) remains, very easy walking. Once across Lucifee Brook you have also moved out of the Designated Wilderness Area of the park.

Mason's Cabin, campsite #37, and the end of the day's 23 km (14.4 mi) hike, boasts a well, toilets, firewood, wood stove, indoor tables, and bunk frames. It is a wonderful spot to put up your feet.

Day 3: The final day's hike of 18.5 km (11.6 mi) is a relatively easy walk; at least it's dry. Essentially, you simply follow the road, which is mostly shaded by fine hardwoods. As you wander along, you might notice distance markers on the road — facing the other direction. The first you will see is the km 24 (mi 15) marker. Do not be too concerned; your finish at the Eel Weir is km 8 (mi 5).

After about 2.5 km (1.6 mi) you reach the junction with the side trail to campsite #38 at Poison Ivy Falls; keep right. Just before it you cross portage L, and shortly after it portage K. These are short footpaths to Peskawa and Peskowesk lakes — the trail passes next to Beaverskin Lake — and are worthwhile diversions.

A very long march follows, more than 8 km (5 mi) with few viewing opportunities, before you reach (not far after the 14 km [8.75 mi] sign) the Peskowesk River and campsite #28. In 2011, this featured a new yurt for winter camping.

The final 6 km (3.75 mi) to the Eel Weir are similar to the previous 8 km (5 mi), with a succession of ridges that need to be crossed. In the final kilometre (0.6 mi), the trail climbs to the top of a drumlinoid ridge that parallels the Mersey River, although you cannot see it. When it starts to turn to the right and descend, you have only about 200 m/yd remaining to the large, gated bridge.

The hike ends at the Eel Weir parking lot at Mersey River.

39. Thomas Raddall Provincial Park

40. Tom Tigney Trail

53. Hemlock and Hardwoods

57. Mill Falls

59. Seaside Adjunct

55. Mason's Cabin

◀╌╌▶ 37 km (23.1 mi) return

🕐 : 2 days

👣 : 4 [distance]

Type of Trail: compacted earth

Uses: walking, biking, snowshoeing, cross-country skiing

⚠ : Animals. Motorized vehicles. Road crossings. Ticks.

📱 : Good throughout, except around campsite #28.

Facilities: benches, cabin, outhouses, picnic tables

Gov't Topo Map: 21A06 (Kejimkujik)

Trailhead GPS: N 44° 20′ 00.1″ W 65° 12′ 17.1″

Access: From Kejimkujik National Park entrance, drive 11.5 km (7.2 mi) on Main Parkway to the end of the pavement. Continue 7.9 km (4.9 mi) on dirt Eel Weir Road. Park in the lot on the right; trail starts at the bridge over the Mersey River.

Introduction: There is only one cabin campsite available in Kejimkujik National Park: campsite #37, known as Mason's Cabin. This is situated in the southwest corner of the park, at the narrowest point on the slender sliver of land separating Peskawa and Pebbleloggitch lakes. Mason's is a favourite with canoeists, because less than a 1 km (0.6 mi) paddle is required through the Pebbleloggitch Stillwater to connect to the Shelburne River, which is outside of the park, a designated (1997) Canadian Heritage River and the most remote wilderness river in Nova Scotia.

For walkers, the 18.5 km (11.6 mi) route from the Eel Weir to Mason's Cabin is a relatively easy trail, a woods road in quite good condition. The cabin, with its wood stove, picnic tables, bunks, and (when I was there in November 2011) cribbage board and deck of cards, is an almost sybaritic camping destination. I strongly recommend this as a fall overnight hike.

By mid-November, the road is closed from the end of the pavement at Grafton Brook, adding 16 km (10 mi) to the trek. In the winter, Grafton Lake to campsite #28 is a groomed cross-country ski route; the remaining distance to Mason's is ungroomed.

Route Description: From the large, vehicle-capable bridge crossing the Mersey River, which is marked as "8 km" (5 mi) from Grafton Lake, the path climbs a small hill. (Canoe por-

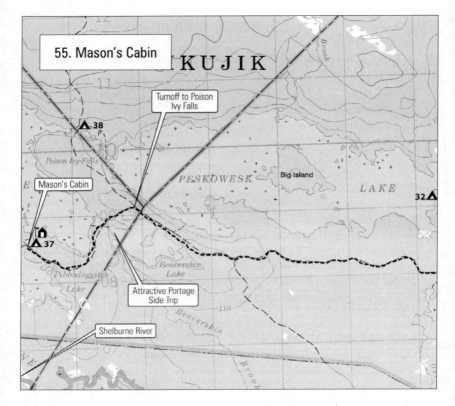

55. Mason's Cabin

KUJIK

Turnoff to Poison Ivy Falls

▲ 38

Poison Ivy Falls

PESKOWESK

Big Island

LAKE

Mason's Cabin

E

32 ▲

▲ 37

Beaverskin Lake

Tebbleloggitch Lake

Attractive Portage Side Trip

110

Beaverskin

Shelburne River

Brook

tage O follows the bank of the river on the far side.)

At the top of this hill you will find some signs that outline the fishing regulations. The road is composed of a sturdy gravel base with a centre strip of grass and healthy vegetation growing close to either side. However, it is easily wide enough for two, and there are few potholes, at least at first.

The trail does not remain on the elevated ridge for long, and soon drops lower, then turns to the right. The forest through here is thick; no views are available very far into the woods to either side, and the trail continues its pattern of ups and downs. About 1 km (0.6 mi) from the start you face the first moderately steep climb, nearly 200 m/yd long.

About 300 m/yd later you reach the first significant wet area, with the

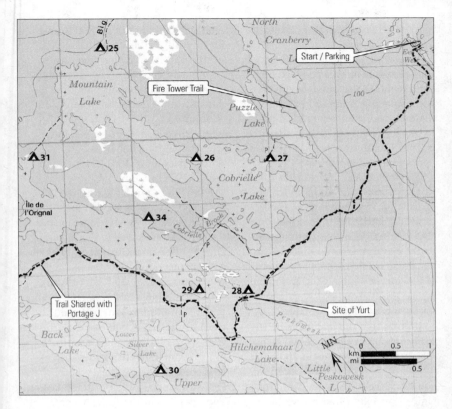

ground boggy on both sides. This is followed by another climb, at the top of which you come across the "10 km" (6 mi) sign. As the trail gradually descends again, and curves to the right, you cross tiny Square Camp Brook (unsigned) perhaps 300 m/yd later.

Only another 300 m/yd after the book, you reach the junction with the Fire Tower Trail. Keep to the left;

there is a sign that says campsite #37 is 16.4 km (10.25 mi) farther. The road becomes a little rougher now, though still excellent walking. More and larger wet areas border the path, and though no brook is marked on the map, about 800 m/yd past the junction you cross a tiny stream on a culvert. Perhaps 600 m/yd later, you pass the "12 km" (11.8 mi) road marker. (There was no marker for 11 km [6.9 mi].)

One of the enjoyable features of the Kejimkujik forest is the high number of white pines found everywhere. A considerable number are towering, mature specimens, but there appears to be a major growth of new pine taking place almost everywhere the soil conditions are appropriate.

You reach a junction that does not show on your map, about 600 m/yd later. The right fork will access Cobrielle Lake, but it does feature a "No Fishing" sign; keep straight, because in only a few hundred metres/yards you reach campsite #28, home of the yurt in winter. This is situated beside the Peskowesk River, just before you cross the bridge over it.

I found that the distances on the road signs and the hiking signs do not match. For example, about 300 m/yd after crossing the Peskowesk River, you reach the "14 km" (8.75 mi) road sign — or 6 km (3.75 mi) from the Eel Weir. However, perhaps 700 m/yd later you reach a hiking sign, facing the other direction, which states that it is 1 km (0.6 mi) back to campsite #28 but 7.9 km (4.9 mi) to the Eel Weir. I reckon that it is in fact about 5.7 km (3.6 mi) between the Eel Weir trailhead and campsite #28.

The next stretch is not especially scenic. The trail, though running alongside Peskowesk Lake for the next

nearly 9 km (5.6 mi), is sited too far for anything other than occasional glimpses through the vegetation. Fortunately, you can access the water when the trail intersects portages G (about 2 km [1.25 mi] from campsite #28) and J (around 4 km [2.5 mi]), whose route you share for 400 m/yd, with only minor side trips.

You pass a "16 km" (10 mi) sign and a "20" (12.5 mi), but there is no "18 km" (11.25 mi) sign nor a "22" (13.75 mi). You pass another junction that does not appear on your map, but the correct trail is well indicated, and shortly afterwards Beaverskin Lake appears on your left. By the time you reach portage K, at 15.5 km (9.7 mi), the trail is almost in the water.

The final 3 km (1.9 mi) are the most attractive of the walk, as the trail works its way back and forth in the comparatively narrow strip of land between Beaverskin, Peskowesk, Peskawa, and Pebbleloggitch lakes. You keep left at the junction of the side trail to campsite #38 at Poison Ivy Falls, 350 m/yd beyond portage K, and pass the "24 km" (15 mi) road sign 150 m/yd after that, then portage L.

One last hill remains, then your route turns right, descends, enters a lovely area of towering pine, and you reach Mason's Cabin. Enjoy your night; then retrace your route the next day.

56. Mersey River

Length: 9 km (5.6 mi) return

🕐: 2+hrs

🏃: 2

Type of Trail: crushed stone, natural surface

Uses: walking, biking, snowshoeing, cross-country skiing

⚠: Animals. Road crossing. Ticks. Poison ivy.

🔲: Adequate throughout.

Facilities: firepits, garbage cans, interpretive panels, outhouses, pay phone, picnic tables

Gov't Topo Map: 21A06 (Kejimkujik)

Trailhead GPS: N 44° 25' 05.6" W 65° 14' 44.7"

Access: From the Kejimkujik National Park entrance, drive 5.1 km (3.2 mi) to the turnoff for Jeremys Bay Campground. Turn right, driving about 700 m/yd. On the far side of the bridge over the Mersey River the road divides; keep left, and continue another 950 m/yd. The trailhead (signed) is on the left.

Introduction: Kejimkujik National Park does not feature dramatic scenery. There are no towering mountains or sheer cliffs. There are no deep canyons or even, except at the Seaside Adjunct, any wave-swept coastline. But Kejimkujik National Park does boast a tranquil beauty that is deeply satisfying and more so the longer you allow yourself to be exposed to it.

The Mersey River Trail, following the unhurried flow of a watercourse bordered by verdant forests, almost hidden by luxuriant green branches bending nearly into the water, is not one to be walked quickly. Rather, time should be taken to stop at every bend and watch and listen. Let the leisurely pace of the river be your guide, and allow yourself to follow nature's rhythm, at least this once.

This is an excellent walk for families and for novices, and because it is so well shaded it offers comfortable walking even on a hot summer day.

Route Description: The trailhead, sitting on the bank of the Mersey River, is home to several picnic tables, outhouses, garbage cans, firepits, and interpretive panels. There are also two signs, one of which says the trail is 3.5 km (2.2 mi), the other saying it is 5 km (3.1 mi)! Not to worry; this is an easy, wide, crushed-stone pathway that follows a languidly flowing (in July, at least) river for most of its length.

Although one of the few official bike trails in Kejimkujik, the Mersey River Trail is not very wide, so special caution must be taken by both walkers and cyclists not to become a hazard for the other. The path keeps to the bank, which is often grass covered (prime tick habitat), except to avoid little wet patches, and near the start you might even be able to see the road, to your right.

About 700 m/yd from the start you cross the first bridge, a modest affair but boasting two railings. The next one, 500 m/yd later, has none. In between there are at least two spots where the path comes right beside the water, allowing access.

About 100 m/yd later, just after passing through some large softwoods, the path enters a large open meadow, dotted with massive maples. It separates from the main branch of the river, working right around the large wetlands of the meadow. After first crossing two small bridges/boardwalks, 200 m/yd later and 50

m/yd after that, the path curves left and rejoins the main Mersey River, 125 m/yd from the second boardwalk.

Within 100 m/yd the trail encounters more wet ground, so it swings inland, to the right, heading into thick young coniferous forest. You spend the next 850 m/yd working over some small hills, gradually turning to the left and returning to the Mersey River, 2.6 km (1.6 mi) from the start.

This is a lovely spot, featuring lush grasses and shaded. The river is wider here and even appears to have a sand bottom. (Swim, anyone?) About 100 m/yd later the path makes almost a 180° round a point, then moves back into the balsam fir and spruce and away from the river. The path climbs gently, crossing under a power line — you can still see the water to your left, not too far away at first, but more the farther you walk.

You reach a junction 850 m/yd from the point or 3.5 km (2.2 mi) from the trailhead. To the right are the Jeremys Bay campground and Kedge Beach. However, you will head left towards Jakes Landing and Merrymakedge Beach.

The trail starts under a thick forest canopy, but you can see water ahead and a large, grassy meadow to the right. After 250 m/yd you emerge from the trees into this meadow, and right away start following a lengthy boardwalk, almost covered by the

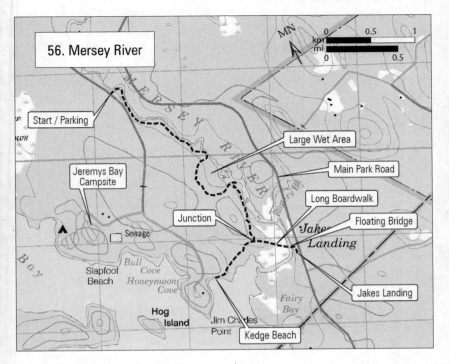

56. Mersey River

Start / Parking

Large Wet Area

Main Park Road

Jeremys Bay Campsite

Long Boardwalk

Junction

Floating Bridge

Jakes Landing

Sewage

Jakes Landing

Bull Cove

Slapfoot Beach

Honeymoon Cove

Fairy Bay

Hog Island

Jim Charles Point

Kedge Beach

long grasses on either side. Scattered stands of large hardwoods dot the expansive grassland.

The boardwalk extends for 175 m/yd to the bank of the Mersey River, where you are conducted across by a 50 m/yd long floating bridge, which features an elevated centre arch to enable canoes and kayaks to safely pass beneath. On the far bank, turn to your right and walk an additional 100 m/yd to Jakes Landing. Here you will find all manner of services, including bicycles and canoe/kayak rentals.

Situated right beside the river, it makes a good place to have lunch.

Or, if you do not mind adding a little more to the walk, once you have used Jakes Landing's facilities, return over the river and back to the last junction. Now head in the direction of Kedge Beach; in only 600 m/yd you will reach the little sandy cove on the shore of Kejimkujik Lake. You might find this a more pleasant location to relax before you retrace your route back to the trailhead.

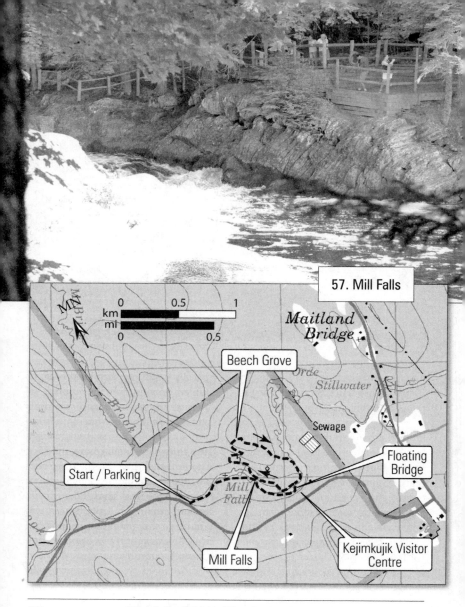

57. Mill Falls

Maitland Bridge

Beech Grove

Orde Stillwater

Sewage

Start / Parking

Floating Bridge

Mill Falls

Kejimkujik Visitor Centre

57. Mill Falls

◄---► 5 km (3.1 mi) return

⏱: 1+hrs

👣: 1

Type of Trail: crushed stone, compacted earth, natural surface

Uses: walking, snowshoeing

⚠: Animals. Ticks. Poison ivy.

🧭: Adequate throughout.

Facilities: benches, garbage cans, interpretive panels, picnic tables, shelter

Gov't Topo Map: 21A06 (Kejimkujik)

Trailhead GPS: N 44° 26′ 12.5″ W 65° 13′ 18.0″

Access: From the Kejimkujik National Park entrance, drive 2.6 km (1.6 mi) on the Main Parkway, turning right into a parking area. The path begins there.

Introduction: This is a gentle, pleasant walk alongside the Mersey River that permits you to pass through mature stands of hardwoods and hemlocks. There are numerous benches and picnic tables, and a great place to swim. What better place for an easy outdoor family activity? It is also very close to the Visitor Centre, with all its services, including flush toilets and drinkable water.

Route Description: There is little signage at this access point, only a hiker symbol. You start by descending a quite large wooden staircase that lowers you to river level and beside a picnic table.

The wide trail runs immediately alongside the tea-coloured Mersey River, heading upstream. Just after crossing a short boardwalk you come across an unusual river crossing: a cable beneath which is hanging a basket. Two interpretive panels explain that this is used for studying changes to the river over time.

The forest alongside the riverbank is mostly hemlock, so the canopy is high and there is little or no understorey. You usually can see for some distance to your right. The river is fairly wide and moves comparatively quickly along this stretch, although there are big pools where you can see the current circling.

About 200 m/yd from the start, a small gully boasts a bridge with railings; this path is designed for families and casual walkers, so there are no difficult spots. Thus, when you reach a wet area just beyond the bridge, there is a boardwalk covering its entire length.

The first bench, 175 m/yd from the bridge, is positioned looking into one of these tranquil pools, shaded by overhanging hemlocks — a lovely spot. As the path works alongside the river, climbing slightly to pass over a small rocky ridge, you notice a small unsigned path connect from the right 125 m/yd later. Keep straight.

Soon you sight Mill Falls ahead, and the path curves slightly right to approach it. From here there are many benches and picnic tables, some close to the water, and others on the hillside to the right. You can probably see a large structure that shelters a number of tables and contains a wood stove, which is useful on a winter day.

There are two cataracts, but it is the upper that is Mill Falls. When you reach it, 750 m/yd from the start, there is a long wooden rail fence along the bank. Signs warn there is to be no diving, although this is a popular swimming location, and there are rescue floats hanging on the fence. There are also two interpretive panels on the power of Mill Falls.

Above Mill Falls, the path continues along the river along the way to the Kejimkujik Visitor Centre. But just before it does, 450 m/yd above the falls, you reach a floating bridge across the Mersey River. Cross over, and on the far bank there is a sign telling you that you are now on the Beech Grove Trail, a 2.2 km (1.4 mi) loop.

Either direction will do, but I turned left, following the Mersey downstream on the opposite bank of your approach hike. This is also covered in crushed stone and provides slightly different views of the water. It is only about 350 m/yd before you are at Mill Falls, where there is a bench and some open rocks onto which you can walk.

From here, the trail continues downstream, but once past the second cataract it begins to climb and move away from the water. The hillside here is becoming increasingly steep, and the trail is soon quite high above water level — maybe 15-20 m (50-65 ft). At 400 m/yd past Mill Falls, the trail turns right nearly 90°, still climbing.

As you climb, you leave the conifers near the river and enter an area of mature hardwoods: the Beech Grove. Within another 200 m/yd the trail turns sharply left, then another right, and by now most of the climb is over.

The forest surrounding the wide path is now a thick deciduous wall, the leaves of the trees an impenetrable barrier. The trail wanders through this thicket over the top of the hill, and soon — within 400 m/yd of the sharp left turn — begins descending its far slope. This is a

much easier descent than the climb. A bench, 250 m/yd later, comes as a surprise, as there is virtually no view. (You might be able to see the river, far through the trees to your left.)

The descent is more pronounced after the bench but not severe. You cross a small boardwalk 125 m/yd later, and left you should be able to see a meadow in the direction of the river. Approaching river level, you move back into hemlocks. The path curves right, following the course of the Mersey, at first maybe 20 m/yd from its bank, but gradually moving closer.

You might be able to spot the Visitor Centre on the far bank as you pass. You should definitely see the canoe launch. The final 250 m/yd are straight along the river to the reach the floating bridge. Recross it, turn right, and retrace your route back to the trailhead.

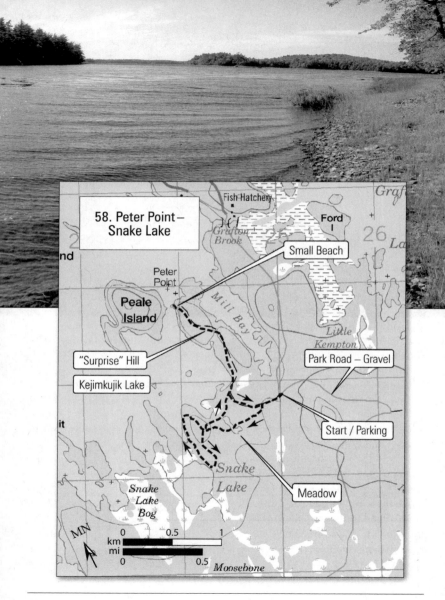

58. Peter Point –
Snake Lake

Fish Hatchery

Ford

Small Beach

Peter Point

Peale Island

Grafton Brook

Mill Bay

Little Kempton

"Surprise" Hill

Kejimkujik Lake

Park Road – Gravel

Start / Parking

Meadow

Snake Lake

Snake Lake Bog

MN

km
mi

0   0.5   1

0   0.5

Moosebone

58. Peter Point – Snake Lake

◄╍╍╍► 6 km (3.75 mi) return

⏱: 2+hrs

🏃: 2

Type of Trail: natural surface, compacted earth

Uses: walking, biking*, snowshoeing, cross-country skiing

⚠: Animals. Ticks.

📷: Good throughout.

Facilities: outhouses, picnic tables

Gov't Topo Map: 21A06 (Kejimkujik)

Trailhead GPS: N 44° 21′ 56.6″ W 65° 11′ 47.4″

Access: From the Kejimkujik National Park entrance, drive 11.4 km (7.1 mi) to the fish hatchery on Grafton Lake. Continue on the gravel road an additional 2.1 km (1.3 mi). The parking area and trailhead are on the right (signed). The road at Grafton Lake is gated in winter.

Introduction: Once the site of a lodge, Peter Point, a narrow peninsula 1.5 km (0.9 mi) long and barely 500 m/yd wide, projects into the southeastern corner of Kejimkujik Lake. The trail is the remains of the road formerly connecting the camp with the outside world, and it provides easy walking for two side by side on comfortable, dry footing. Running up the middle of the point, the path offers access to the Snake Lake Trail, a gorgeous hemlock stand, and a wonderful panorama of Kejimkujik Lake. At the very tip, a small sandy beach invites sunbathing and swimming.

Rare coastal plain plants such as bartonia and panic grass may be found in an excellent habitat between the base of Peter Point and Snake Lake, and Peale Island, just off Peter Point, contains one of the park's few stands of climax sugar maple and white ash. The rare ribbon snake has also been spotted on Peale Island and at Snake Lake.

This is a gentle, easy walk suitable for all age groups and fitness levels. Although the Snake Lake loop is restricted to walking only, cyclists may continue to the end of Peter Point.

Route Description: At the trailhead there is a bike rack for those intending to walk Snake Lake and a picnic table under the trees. A sign provides a brief description of each route, plus a map. The very wide and nearly

straight Peter Point Trail continues from the parking lot.

After only 225 m/yd you reach the first junction with the Snake Lake Trail. A look at the map there shows this to be designed in a figure-eight shape. Turn left onto the windy, undulating footpath through lovely, high hardwoods, though with a large number of head-high pines growing everywhere.

You sight an open meadow to your left 250 m/yd from the junction and cross the tall grasses on an unrailed puncheon/boardwalk 175 m/yd later. After climbing a small hill, you cross a second boardwalk over a forested boggy area 225 m/yd later. Barely 150 m/yd beyond the boardwalk, you reach the four-way junction (the trails don't actually quite all meet together). There is another map here.

Keep left; the trail works through the forest to reach the shore of small Snake Lake, 500 m/yd from the junction. There is a very short path to the left that leads to the shore; the main trail turns sharply right and passes parallel to the lakeshore but maybe 5-10 m/yd in the woods. Informal footpaths permit access to the water.

After 175 m/yd you pass the edge of Snake Lake, and there is now an area of meadow on your left. But in 200 m/yd the trail reaches the shoreline of Kejimkujik Lake. You enjoy about 325 m/yd walking with views into this large lake before the path turns right, away from the water, and climbs over a low ridge and back to the four-way intersection, 350 m/yd from Kejimkujik Lake.

When you reach the four-way junction with the map, keep left so you are not returning along the same route. This path is wider, and almost appears to be a former road. It drops a bit and comes close to the lake again, crossing a bridge over a small brook 250 m/yd from the junction. This is the same meadow you crossed earlier but nearer Kejimkujik Lake. Some 300 m/yd later you reach the Peter Point Trail, where there is another map.

Once again, turn left and follow the wide track as it heads towards the point. You can see the lake on your left, and within 60 m/yd you are practically walking in it. This section is short, however, and soon the trail is back beneath a canopy of hemlocks, the trees so thick that you lose sight of the lake — even though it is actually close on both sides.

Even more of a surprise, after having been in fairly gentle terrain, there is even a hill to climb, 750 m/yd from the junction. This is not a terribly difficult hill, but it might be somewhat unexpected. So you climb for about 225 m/yd, then begin a long descent to the end of the trail, at a small beach on the shore of Kejimkujik Lake, 300 m/yd later.

This is a very pleasant location, with the evening breezes making it an excellent end-of-day stroll. There is even an outhouse situated nearby. Relax and enjoy the views of the lake, several of the islands, and, to your right, Merrymakedge Beach. When you are ready, follow the Peter Point Trail back to the parking lot.

Snapping Turtle

You may be forgiven if you think you have encountered a small dinosaur, because with its sawtooth back ridge, armoured claws, and long tail, the snapping turtle — Nova Scotia's largest freshwater turtle — looks as if it is from a long-past age.

Snapping turtles only venture from the water in late June and early July to lay their eggs, and because they cannot run or hide they will defend themselves aggressively. Don't be fooled by the withdrawn head; this turtle's neck extends over half its body length, so if you are unwary . . . well, there's a reason it's named "snapping." Leave these turtles alone.

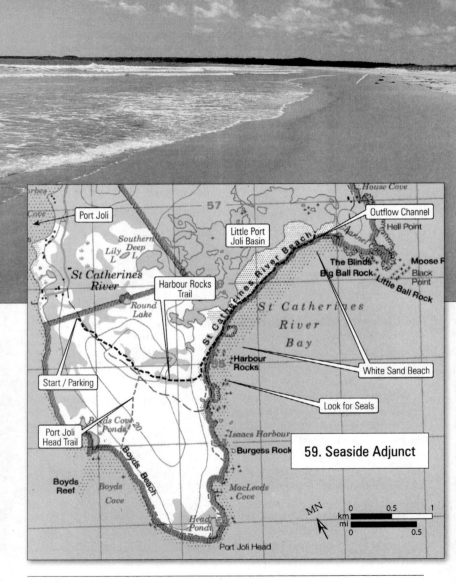

Port Joli

Little Port Joli Basin

Outflow Channel

Hell Point

The Blinds
Big Ball Rock

Moose P

Black
Point

Little Ball Rock

Southern
Lily Deep
L L

St Catherines
River

Harbour Rocks
Trail

Round
Lake

St Catherines
River
Bay

White Sand Beach

Start / Parking

Harbour
Rocks

Look for Seals

Port Joli
Head Trail

Boyds Cove
Ponds

Isaacs Harbour

59. Seaside Adjunct

Burgess Rock

Boyds
Reef

Boyds
Cove

Boyds Beach

MacLeods
Cove

Head
Ponds

Port Joli Head

MN

km 0   0.5   1
mi 0   0.5

59. Seaside Adjunct

◄- - -► 10.5 km (6.6 mi) return

⏱: 2+hrs

🏃: 2

Type of Trail: crushed stone, natural surface

Uses: walking, snowshoeing

⚠: Animals. Ticks. Exposed coastline.

🧭: Adequate throughout.

Facilities: benches, garbage cans, interpretive panels, outhouses, picnic tables, pop machine, water

Gov't Topo Map: 20P15 (Port Mouton)

Trailhead GPS: N 43° 50' 16.5" W 64° 51' 22.3"

Access: From the junction of Highway 8 and Highway 103 (Exit 19) at Liverpool, continue on Highway 103 west for 25.5 km (15.9 mi). Turn left onto St. Catherines River Road (see the park sign), and follow to its end in 6.5 km (4.1 mi).

Introduction: This must be one of the most popular, and busy, walking destinations in mainland Nova Scotia on a warm summer weekend. And why not? St. Catherines River Beach, composed of eye-achingly gleaming white sand ground from the granite shoreline, stretches for more than 2 km (1.25 mi), framing a magnificent turquoise bay.

Expect to see dozens of harbour seals lying on the rocks off St. Catherines River Beach. They appear to have become somewhat accustomed to human observation and frequently appear to be watching you just as intently as you are them!

This is a tremendous location for birdwatching, and signs of former settlement are also common: stone fences, rock foundations, old clearings, and cattle trails. My favourite time to visit is September through November, when there are fewer people and the ocean grey, rather than the blue, is more untamed.

Route Description: There is quite an elaborate entrance to the Seaside Adjunct, including a large parking lot and a number of buildings. In one of these structures there are some interpretive panels and a trail map; in another there are actual flush toilets and drinkable water.

From the parking area at St. Catherines River, the trail follows what was once the old cart track that connected the former homesteads on Port Joli Head with the rest of the community. This is quite wide and surfaced in crushed stone, at least at the start. Less than 100 m/yd from the start, on your right, is a large covered picnic area — it includes several tables — which contains more interpretive panels and has a view of the ocean in the direction of Port Joli.

Another map sign informs you that this section is part of the Harbour Rocks Trail, which we will follow. In 2011, the 5.5 km (3.4 mi) Port Joli Head loop was closed for refurbishment; I have not profiled it but can recommend it if it is open.

Starting out in a mixed forest thickly interwoven with oak and maple, by 700 m/yd the path emerges into barrens bordered by tall scrubs. Next to frequent wet areas, dense stands of alder provide hiding places for inquisitive common yellowthroats and other warblers.

As is common on the highly indented Atlantic coastline of the South Shore, the adjunct sits on a granite finger, carved and shaped by glacier action, thrusting into the ocean and surrounded on three sides by the water. Although undoubtedly scenic, with white sand beaches, lagoons, and waves breaking over granite headlands, weather conditions at the point are far more rugged than just a few miles inland. Fog, high winds, and salt-laden spray kill all but a few hardy plants, so the terrain takes on a tundra-like aspect.

The trail continues down the mid-dle of Port Joli Head. At 800 m/yd there is a bench, hiding inside a spruce thicket. Cranberry and bog rosemary become more common as you continue, and at a low spot 175 m/yd later pitcher plants line both sides of the path.

Climbing a little higher, where views of the approaching ocean goad your eagerness, you pass a rocky pinnacle at 1.2 km (0.75 mi). Informal footpaths suggest that the impatient climb it to obtain a better vista. You reach the junction with the Port Joli Head Trail 125 m/yd further on; a map should ensure that you continue straight.

You cross a boardwalk immediately afterwards, and you might by now even be able to hear the ocean's roar. However, the bordering scrubs grow so high that only the tallest can see above them. Fortunately, 350 m/yd past the junction there is a large viewing platform on the left, with three more interpretive panels. The view is excellent and tantalizing.

Continuing on, the path is now noticeably descending, and you are able to finally see the ocean ahead. About 350 m/yd from the lookoff there are outhouses, and 25 m/yd beyond that is the second junction with the Port Joli Head Trail — on the edge of tiny Isaacs Harbour, very close to the location of a former house site and now home to dozens of harbour seals.

Turning left, a distinct footpath leads along the rocky shore, occasionally dropping onto a stretch of sand. There is an oceanside lookoff 300 m/yd from the junction, where there is a bench and more interpretive panels. About 275 m/yd further there is a final interpretive site — appropriately, about the piping plover — next to a wooden railing fence.

Watch closely for "Area Closed" signs, and please respect them when present. Should you be able to continue past this fence beach, you will enjoy another 2.7 km (1.7 mi) of near effortless walking until you reach the narrow, deep outflow from Little Port Joli Basin. Along the way you will be walking on dazzling white sand, passing several rocky outcroppings.

There is no connecting bridge

Piping Plover

St. Catherines River Beach is a nesting site for the endangered piping plover. Perhaps fifty pairs visit Nova Scotia. Laying their eggs on flat beach areas just above the high-water line, they are at risk from beachcombers and sunbathers. Between May and August, any disturbance threatens their breeding success. The plover is so well camouflaged that their nests can rarely be detected before being destroyed.

Should you see park signs warning of nests, do not cross the beach yourself. Never take a dog onto the beach during these months; they will destroy both eggs and young.

or path, so you must return to the parking lot along the same route you walked in. Given the beautiful setting, I doubt this will be any cause for complaint.

60. West River

◄--- ► 14 km (8.75 mi) return

⏱: 4+hrs

🏃: 5 [navigation, remote location]

Type of Trail: natural surface

Uses: walking, snowshoeing, cross-country skiing

⚠: Animals. Ticks. Remote location.

📵: None from Liberty Lake Trail to the bridge at West River; adequate from there to campsite #22.

Facilities: firepit, outhouse, picnic table

Gov't Topo Map: 21A06 (Kejimkujik)

Trailhead GPS: N 44° 22′ 26.3″ W 65° 22′ 54.8″

Access: This trail can only be accessed as an add-on to the Liberty Lake Trail. Doing so will probably mean adding one extra day to that route. Day 2 will become campsite #42 to campsite #22; day 3 will become campsite #22 to campsite #37 (Mason's Cabin).

Introduction: This is a trail that very few people will ever hike. It can only be accessed two ways, either by entering from almost the midway point in the 61 km (38.1 mi) Liberty Lake Trail or by canoeing across Kejimkujik Lake and up the West River to campsite #22. Neither is likely to be undertaken by the casual walker.

However, for those who enjoy remote country, the West River Trail enables you to trek along a route followed by fewer than one hundred people a year. There are not many managed trails anywhere that can make such a claim. In fact, when I walked this route in the middle of the week in early November 2011, Parks Canada staff told me that I would be alone in the backcountry, an area of more than 300 km^2 (115 mi^2); in Nova Scotia, you cannot get much more alone than that.

Route Description: There is no formal announcement that you are starting the West River Trail, just an arrow pointing towards campsite #22, which it says is 9 km (5.6 mi) farther. (This differs from my own measurement, which was 7 km [4.4 mi].) As this is not a heavily used trail, I found it to not have a distinct treadway; in addition, when I hiked it in November 2011 it was often somewhat overgrown with brush. However, there were occasional — and I do mean infrequent — white metal markers attached to some trees.

From the junction you start with a beautiful 650 m/yd stretch along

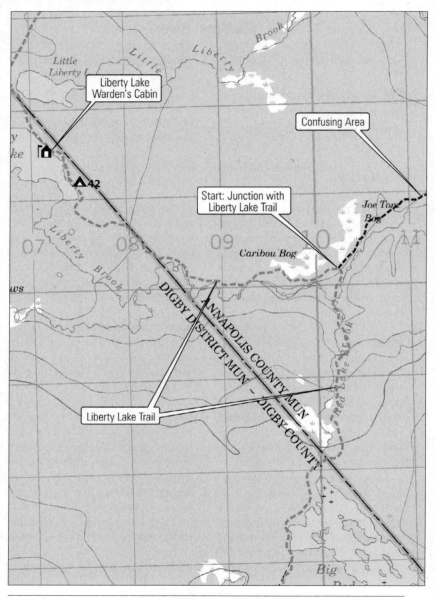

Little Liberty L

Liberty   Brook

Little   Liberty

Little Liberty Lake

Liberty Lake Warden's Cabin

Confusing Area

Joe Tom Bog

Start: Junction with Liberty Lake Trail

△ 42

07   08   09   10   11

Liberty Brook

Caribou Bog

ws

ANNAPOLIS COUNTY MUN
DIGBY DISTRICT MUN — DIGBY COUNTY

Red Lake Brook

Liberty Lake Trail

Big

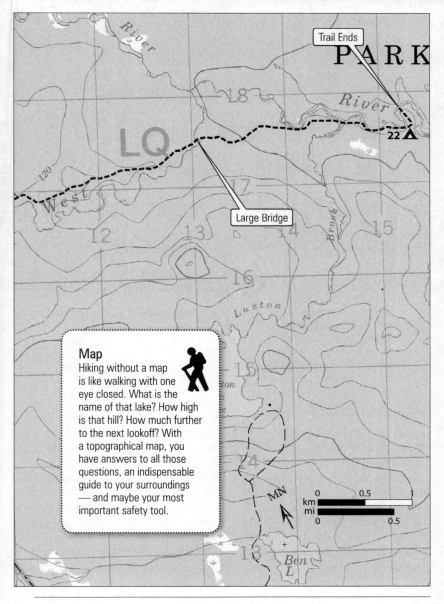

Trail Ends

PARK

River

18

LQ

West

120

12   13   14   15

17

Large Bridge

Brook

16

Luxton

15

Map
Hiking without a map
is like walking with one
eye closed. What is the
name of that lake? How high
is that hill? How much further
to the next lookoff? With
a topographical map, you
have answers to all those
questions, an indispensable
guide to your surroundings
— and maybe your most
important safety tool.

24

MN

13   Ben
          L

22

| km | 0 | 0.5 | 1 |
| mi | 0 | | 0.5 |

First Aid Kit

When you are out in the woods, even seemingly little problems can become very important. A small first aid kit with bandages, gauze, tape, moleskin, etc., can permit you to deal with the blisters, scratches, and bruises that require attention. Keep a kit in your pack, no matter what distance you are walking.

a pine-topped ridge (an esker) with the West River below to your right. To your left, you should be able to distinguish the open space of Joe Tom Bog. But too soon you lose sight of the river and come off that attractive ridge. Once you cross a small un-bridged brook 250 m/yd further, the path becomes quite difficult to follow, being severely overgrown with brush.

I actually walked off the route more than once through here.

This difficult section is about 700 m/yd long, after which you climb onto another pine-covered ridge. Without quite so much brush, the path is easier to follow. About 250 m/yd later there is a significant wet, mossy area that must be crossed. It looks as if it was once boardwalked, but now you can expect wet feet. Within another 500 m/yd you are back on another pine ridge, and after walking along it for 500 m/yd you sight the West River again on your right, 10-15 m (33-50 ft) below.

Ridge and river run together for only a short time before the trail moves away from the crest. It remains high, but the land is somewhat uneven so it meanders around somewhat. The trail joins the river again 650 m/yd from where you last saw it, at which time the path drops down to water level. You reach an open meadow 175 m/yd later, and as you cross it you sight the large bridge spanning the West River, which you cross 3.9 km (2.4 mi) from the junction with the Liberty Lake Trail.

The far bank is steep enough that a rope is provided to assist your climb. Fortunately it is not high, although when you are on top you have cell reception for the first time in the walk. The trail heads into the middle of the forest, mostly staying high as it cuts crosses across a bend in the West River and works over a substantial intervening ridge. You trek through waist-high ferns and thick brush for about 950 m/yd before you find yourself again on the bank of the West River, and this time at water level.

For the remainder of your trip, except for short intervals, the trail follows the West River, on your left, downstream. About 125 m/yd along there is a small, wet meadow (guaranteed wet feet) that must be crossed, but the reward comes shortly afterward, when you climb over a pine-covered hillside — my favourite spot on this route. More soggy meadows need to be negotiated,

then 800 m/yd after you rejoined the river a bridge assists you across small Luxton Brook.

For another 850 m/yd the path works downriver, alternating between small meadows and pine ridges. The West River appears slow moving and winding, with many large granite rocks dotting its banks.

When the trail makes a sharp left turn only 300 m/yd remains. As you walk along this low ridge, you might even notice, through the vegetation, that you can see the river both to left and to right. Shortly before arriving at campsite #22, you will see the largest glacial erratic boulder of the day sitting in the river. Beyond that, nestled beneath towering white pines in a bend in the West River, is campsite #22.

There is a picnic table, firepit, and outhouse located here, so even if you do not intend to camp it is a peaceful place for lunch. This is one of Nova Scotia's very remote sites; definitely do not be in a rush to return to the trailhead. But when you are, you retrace your route back to the Liberty Lake Trail.

7. North Granite Ridge Trail

Acknowledgements

The trail community has grown much larger in Nova Scotia in the past decade and is populated by knowledgeable, passionate hiking enthusiasts. It has been a rare pleasure, after so many years of feeling nearly alone in my interest in attracting more people into Nova Scotia outdoors, on foot, that I now see that I am only one member of a large and growing society of organized hikers and walkers.

These dedicated people are involved with the construction and maintenance of paths and the organization and promotion of activities on the province's pathways. So, when I publicly announced that I wanted to write the next edition of *Hiking Trails of Nova Scotia*, they quickly and unreservedly organized to provide me with information about new routes, make suggestions for which trails to include or delete, and provide answers to any questions I directed to them.

Many, many individuals contributed, and I am grateful for their assistance. Several groups, in particular the Cape to Cape Trail Association and Hike Nova Scotia, I consulted regularly — so often that they must be hoping that I will wait another ten years before undertaking the next rewrite. To all my colleagues, if I may so address you: my thanks.

On a personal note, I wish to especially thank the Lappin family — Joseph, Susan, and their children — who hosted me for seven months while I hiked more than 150 routes and 2,500 km (1,500 mi) while re-

13. Brier Island

searching *Hiking Trails of Mainland Nova Scotia* and *Hiking Trails of Cape Breton*. Considering how often I returned to their doorstep after a multi-day expedition, sodden, grubby, and extravagantly mosquito ravaged, they deserve my most sincere appreciation.

Finally, I must mention the work of my publisher, Goose Lane Editions. Together we have produced hiking guidebooks since 1995, works which I consider to be among the finest examples of their genre in North America. Goose Lane, unquestionably, deserves a great deal of the credit. We have collaborated eight times so far, and made improvements with each one. Hopefully, we will have the opportunity to continue to improve on many occasions in the future.

Michael Haynes
June 2012

Updates from
Hiking Trails of Nova Scotia, 8th edition

The following trails — detailed in *Hiking Trails of Nova Scotia, 8th edition* but NOT included in this volume — **remain essentially the same** as previously described and are still recommended:

Halifax – Marine Drive:
Black Duck Cove/Chapel Gully
BLT Trail
Guysborough Short Trails

Evangeline Scenic Travelway:
Mickeys Hill

Glooscap Scenic Travelway:
Partridge Island

Lighthouse Route Scenic Travelway:
Aspotogan Rail Trail
Centennial Trail
The Hawk
Port L'Hebert

Sunrise Scenic Travelway:
Fitzpatrick Mountain
Jitney/Samson/Albion Trails
Wallace Bridge

The following trails — outlined in *Hiking Trails of Nova Scotia, 8th edition* but NOT included in this edition — have been **replaced as noted, or altered slightly,** and are still recommended:

Halifax – Marine Drive:
McNabs Island: some changes from the profile included in the 8th edition.
White Lake Wilderness Trail: now known as South Granite Ridge Trail

Evangeline Scenic Travelway:
Balancing Rock/Sentier Piau: the farthest section of Sentier Piau has washed away

Lighthouse Route Scenic Travelway:
Wedgeport Tuna Museum: some changes from the profile included in the 8th edition

Sunrise Scenic Travelway:
Cape George: a different section of the trail system is outlined in this edition

56. Mersey River

The following trails — described in *Hiking Trails of Nova Scotia, 8th edition* but NOT included in this volume — have changed dramatically over the years. **These trails are NOT recommended:**

Halifax – Marine Drive:
Salmon River: replaced by Crowbar Lake Trail

Evangeline Scenic Travelway:
Moses Mountain

Glooscap Scenic Travelway:
Five Islands Provincial Park: Red Head Trail no longer usable

Select Bibliography

The following list includes some of the texts I used for research for my hikes, but it omits all of the brochures, management plans, and other similar documents that were, at times, invaluable to my studies. In addition to the written materials, there were many conversations that proved as helpful as any book. I acknowledge my debt to them all.

Billard, Allan. 2007. *Waterfalls: Nova Scotia's Masterpieces*. Nimbus Publishing, Halifax.

Claridge, E., and B.A. Milligan. 1992. *Animal Signatures*. Nimbus Publishing and The Nova Scotia Museum, Halifax.

Cunningham, Scott. 2000. *Sea Kayaking in Nova Scotia*. Nimbus Publishing, Halifax.

Davis, D.S., and S. Browne. 1996. *The Natural History of Nova Scotia*. Nimbus Publishing, The Nova Scotia Museum, and Communications Nova Scotia, Halifax. 2 vols.

Gesner, Abraham. 2010. *Remarks on the Geology and Mineralogy of Nova Scotia*. Nabu Press.

Haynes, M.C. 2002. *Hiking Trails of Nova Scotia, 8th edition*. Goose Lane Editions. Fredericton.

Moreira, W., N. Green, and T. Sheppard. 2005. *Keji: A Guide to Kejimkujik National Park and National Historic Site*. Nimbus Publishing, Halifax.

Roland, A.E., and Marion Zinck. 1998. *Flora of Nova Scotia*. Nimbus Publishing, Halifax. 2 vols.

Saunders, Gary. 2001. *Discover Nova Scotia: Ultimate Nature Guide*. Nimbus Publishing, Halifax.

Towers, Julie. 1995. *Nova Scotia Wildlife*. Nimbus Publishing and The Nova Scotia Museum, Halifax.

Tufts, Robie. 2007. *Birds of Nova Scotia*. 3rd ed. Nimbus Publishing, Halifax.

Web Pages

The URLs listed below were current as of July 2012. Regrettably, organizations often change their Web addresses, so if you find that a listed link does not work, I recommend that you copy the site's name and paste it into your preferred Internet Search Engine. This should direct you to the new link.

Updated links will be posted on the Hiking Trails of Nova Scotia blog at http://hikingnovascotia.blogspot.ca/ as they are discovered. You may also contact us on our Facebook page: www.facebook.com/HikingTrailsOfNovaScotia.

A. Outdoor Associations

Bicycle Nova Scotia: http://www.bicycle.ns.ca/
Canadian Volkssport Federation: www.walks.ca
Climb Nova Scotia: www.climbnovascotia.ca
Dartmouth Volksmarch Club: www.dartmouthvolksmarchclub.com
Explore Nova Scotia: www.explorenovascotia.com
Friends of Taylor Head Provincial Park: http://friendsoftaylorhead.com/
Hike Nova Scotia: www.hikenovascotia.ca
Musquodoboit Trailway Association: www.mta-ns.ca
Nature Nova Scotia: www.naturens.ca/
Nova Scotia Bird Society: http://nsbs.chebucto.org/
Nova Scotia Trails Federation: www.novascotiatrails.com
Orienteering Association of Nova Scotia: http://orienteeringns.ca
Trail Information Project: www.trails.gov.ns.ca
Trans Canada Trail: www.tctrail.ca

B. Park/Trail Web Sites

Beechville, Lakeside, Timberlea Rails to Trails Association: http://www.halifax.ca/trails/BeechvilleLakesideTimberleaRailstoTrailsAssociation.html
Blomidon Provincial Park Brochure: www.novascotiaparks.ca/brochures/Blomidon.pdf

Cape to Cape Trail: www.capetocapetrail.ca

Cape Chignecto Provincial Park Brochure: www.capechignecto.net/overview/
2007_colour_park_brochure.pdf

Cape Split Provincial Park Reserve Preliminary Management Plan: www.gov.
ns.ca/natr/parks/management/capesplit01.asp

Chain of Lakes Trail Map: www.halifax.ca/districts/dist17/documents/
Chain_Of_Lakes_Trail_revised_March17.pdf

Cobequid Eco-Trails Society: www.cobequidecotrails.ca

Crowbar Lake Trail Map: http://seacoasttrail.com/drupal/sites/default/files/
CrowbarLake_TrailHandout.pdf

Guysborough County Trails: www.gcrda.ns.ca/play/trails

Kejimkujik National Park: www.pc.gc.ca/eng/pn-np/ns/kejimkujik/index.aspx

Jerry Lawrence Provincial Park Brochure: http://www.novascotiaparks.ca/
brochures/JerryLawrence08.pdf

Municipality of Colchester Trails: www.colchester.ca/trails

Municipality of the District of Shelburne Trails Brochure: www.town.
shelburne.ns.ca/rails-to-trails-project.html

St. Margaret's Bay Rails to Trails Brochure: www.halifax.ca/rec/documents/
SMBRailsToTrails.pdf

Taylor Head Provincial Park Brochure: www.novascotiaparks.ca/brochures/
TaylorHeadTrail.pdf

The Bluff Wilderness Hiking Trail: http://wrweo.ca/BluffTrail

Thomas Raddall Provincial Park Brochure: www.novascotiaparks.ca/
brochures/thomasraddall.pdf

Tidnish Dock Provincial Park: www.novascotiaparks.ca/brochures/
TidnishDock04.pdf

Uniacke Estate Trail Brochure: http://museum.gov.ns.ca/site-museum/media/
UEMP/UEMPBrochure.pdf

Walking Trails in the Annapolis Valley: www.annapolis-valley-vacation.com/
walking-hiking.html

Victoria Park: www.truro.ca/vic-park.html

C. Animals

Bear Brochure, Parks Canada: www.pc.gc.ca/pn-np/inc/PM-MP/visit/
visit12a_e.pdf

Birds of Nova Scotia: http://museum.gov.ns.ca/mnh/nature/nsbirds/bons.htm

Coyote Information: www.gov.ns.ca/natr/wildlife/nuisance/coyotes-faq.asp

Moose Information: www.gov.ns.ca/natr/wildlife/large-mammals/mmoosefaq.
asp

Nova Scotia Department of Natural Resources Wildlife Article Index: www.
gov.ns.ca/natr/wildlife/CONSERVA/

D. General Interest

Atlantic Canada Geocaching Association: http://www.atlanticgeocaching.
com

Explore Nova Scotia: www.explorenovascotia.com

Heart & Stroke Walkabout: www.walkaboutns.ca

Keep It Wild Brochure: www.gov.ns.ca/nse/protectedareas/docs/KeepItWild_
recreation.pdf

Leave No Trace Canada: www.leavenotrace.ca

Natural History of Nova Scotia: http://museum.gov.ns.ca/mnh/nature/
umbrell2.htm

Nova Scotia Department of Natural Resources: www.gov.ns.ca/natr

Nova Scotia Museum of Natural History: http://museum.gov.ns.ca/mnh

Nova Scotia Provincial Park Events: www.novascotiaparks.ca/misc/park_
events.asp

Parks Canada: www.pc.gc.ca

Pet Friendly Travel: www.petfriendlytravel.com/dog_parks_canada

Province of Nova Scotia Wilderness Protected Areas: www.gov.ns.ca/nse/
protectedareas/wildernessareas.asp

Tick Information, Nova Scotia: http://www.gov.ns.ca/hpp/publications/
06037_LymeDisease_Pamphlet_En.pdf

Trees of Nova Scotia: http://www.gov.ns.ca/natr/forestry/treeid/

E. Weather

Weather Network: www.theweathernetwork.com/weather/cans0057

F. Cellphone Coverage

Bell: www.bell.ca/support/PrsCSrvWls_Cvg_Travel.page

Rogers: www.rogers.com/business/on/en/smallbusiness/rogers/coverage/

Telus: www.telusmobility.com/en/NS/Canada/3Gplus.shtml

Index of User Tips and Sidebars

Jack pine

23. Cape Chignecto Provincial Park

Index

349